The Best of
J.Vernon McGee

Other Books by the Author

Thru the Bible, Vols. I–V, with J. Vernon McGee

Ruth and Esther: Women of Faith

The Best of J. Vernon McGee

THOMAS NELSON PUBLISHERS
Nashville

Published in Nashville, Tennessee, by Thomas Nelson,
Inc., and distributed in Canada by Lawson Falle, Ltd.,
Cambridge, Ontario.

Printed in the United States of America.

*Unless otherwise noted, all Scripture quotations are taken from the King James Version
of the Bible.*

Scripture quotations noted ASV are from the American Standard Version.

McGee, J. Vernon (John Vernon), 1904–
   [Sermons. Selections]
  The best of J. Vernon McGee / by J. Vernon McGee.
     p.   cm.
    ISBN 0-8407-7442-7
    1. Sermons, American. I. Title.
  BV4253.M362 1988
  252—dc19   88-17485
                              CIP

1 2 3 4 5 6 — 92 91 90 89 88

CONTENTS

1

ON EAGLES' WINGS

Ye have seen what I did unto the Egyptians, and how I bore you on eagles' wings and brought you unto myself (EXODOUS 19:4).

"On eagles' wings" tells of the way Israel achieved freedom—all the way from slavery in Egypt to security in the land of promise, from death to life, from helplessness to the heart of God. It was not by fearless fighting and brilliant military maneuvering that they startled the nations of the world. Actually it was not by their own efforts at all. It was by what God did for them—God carried them on "eagles' wings."

Borne by wings is an apt symbol of God's gracious deliverance. But why eagles' wings? The eagle is one of the birds specifically labeled in Scripture as "unclean," that is, not to be used for food (see Leviticus 11:13). Also it is referred to as a bird of prey in the Word of God. Our Lord gave a verse that is in many ways the most difficult statement He ever uttered, *"For wherever the carcass is, there will the eagles be gathered together"* (Matthew 24:28). For this reason, and I think for this reason alone, the eagle is not used in Scripture as a symbol of God.

Yet the eagle is admired and applauded for its exploits. It is the jet plane of the bird family. It soars the highest, goes the fastest, and is superior to all other birds in this respect. These features are noted on the pages of the Word of God. David, in giving a eulogy of Saul and

---

*All Scripture references in this chapter are from the *New Scofield Reference Bible*.

Jonathan after they were slain, likens them to the eagle in his pane-
gyric of praise, *"Saul and Jonathan were lovely and pleasant in their
lives . . . they were swifter than eagles"* (2 Samuel 1:23). The eagle,
though in and of itself rejected as a symbol of God, is admired for its
ability to fly. Therefore its wings are given as a symbol of our God.
By the strength of its great wings it is able to soar to the heights and
perform unusual feats.

Another remarkable characteristic of the eagle is its tenderness
toward its young. No member of the bird family is more gentle and
attentive in watching over its young. It builds its nest high up on a
mountain crag. Both parents bring food to the little eaglets, and
when they teach them to fly, both parents are involved in the training
program. As the little one takes off from that dizzy height and attempts to follow its parent in flight, the eagle swoops beneath it and
bears the little fellow on its wings when he seems exhausted.

Thus the eagle is set before us as being a symbol of God's dealing
with His people, as He bore them "on eagles' wings."

EAGLE WINGS OF DELIVERANCE

They are set before us as the salvation which God, by grace,
wrought for us. This is given in the nineteenth chapter of Exodus,
verse four. You will recall that at this point God had brought Israel
out of Egyptian bondage to Mount Sinai. Now He is giving them an
opportunity to make a choice. As He does, He says this to them:

> *Ye have seen what I did unto the Egyptians, and how I bore you
> on eagles' wings and brought you unto myself* (Exodus 19:4).

In this verse God reviews their deliverance out of Egypt. He goes
back over their passage through the Red Sea and that which brought
them up to Mount Sinai. In doing this He says, I have brought you
this far; and the way I brought you—I bore you on eagles' wings.

It might be well to look at that statement for just a moment, my
beloved. This was a nation that was born in slavery and reared in the
brick yards of Egypt. No people, I suppose, were as helpless and
hopeless as were these people.

They had gone down to Egypt as one family of seventy souls

under their father Jacob. There they had become a great nation. But in the course of time there arose a Pharaoh who "knew not Joseph." Since it was so evident that God was blessing them, Pharaoh felt it was necessary for the welfare of Egypt to hold them down, and as a result he put them in slavery—hard slavery!

The Hebrews did slave labor in the brick yards of Egypt, but in spite of that they prospered. There they became a great nation— great in size and great in ability—yet they had no power to extricate themselves from that awful slavery. There was no way for them to throw off the shackles that were about them and go out free. There was no human possibility that they could get deliverance until the Pharaoh upon the throne was destroyed. Then the chances were that whoever came to that throne would not change their slave status but continue their awful plight. Such was the condition of these folk, and it was in that condition that God looked down upon them.

WHEN GOD REMEMBERS

The book of Exodus opens with God's looking down upon these people. As He looked down, He did not see their wonderful ability, because any ability they had was God-given. God never saw any goodness in them, because they had no goodness. And it is of no use to say that they were the only people on the top side of the earth at that time that had a knowledge of God, for they did not—they were in idolatry. They were just about as bad off as any people could be. God did not see anything in them that called forth any movement on His part because of meritorious acts or works or any character within them. The thing that He said when He called Moses to be their deliverer was this in effect: "I heard their cry; I have seen their awful condition; I have seen their plight down there. This has appealed to me. And I remember that I made a covenant with Abraham, Isaac, and Jacob; I am prepared to do what I promised to do. *I will deliver them.*"

Moses becomes the human agent. God chose this man from the back side of the Midian desert where God had trained him and schooled him. God gave him the only B.D. degree that I think is worthwhile—it is known as the Backside of the Desert degree. After forty years—it takes a long time to get a degree like that—God brings him back upon the scene in Egypt. God says, "Now I am ready to deliver my people," and Moses and Aaron go into the presence of Pharaoh.

Then a battle ensued, a battle literally of the gods. For God pitted Himself against the idolatry of Egypt and struck against that awful satanic system that shackled the minds and spirits of the people and was holding them (all of them, including the Egyptians) in spiritual darkness. Each plague was directed against a particular god of Egypt. The sacred Nile was turned to blood; frogs, lice, then flies swarmed over the land; the livestock sickened and died; boils broke out on both man and beast; hail and locusts devastated their crops; then darkness enveloped them for three days. When God finally came to the tenth plague, it was awesome in its severity, but it took this to release the trap that was holding His people in slavery. It turned the key in the lock and let them go free. The last plague was the death of the firstborn.

Now God is ready to show His people that He is redeeming them, not because of any merit within them, but by the sovereign grace of God.

AN UNFORGETTABLE NIGHT

God said it would be a night that they would never forget. Today if you go into the home of any orthodox Jew, you will find that on his calendar there is a Passover. After all these years it is still being remembered. It is the oldest holy day on any man's calendar on this earth. This is the day they remember; this is the day they shall not forget. This is the day that God wrought His deliverance for His own. These people were to select a lamb and slay it. The blood of that lamb was to be put outside on the doorposts and on the lintel that went across the top of the door. Someone has called attention to the fact that it was in the form of a cross. There the blood was sprinkled. And that night the death angel went over. He did not stop to enquire if the people on the inside of the house were saying their prayers. He did not stop to ask them if they had joined a church. He did not stop to ask what kind of lives they were living. He did not even stop to ask if they were Israelites. The only thing for which he looked was blood on the doorposts. When he saw the blood he passed over. When it was not there, then followed the death of the firstborn—both man and beast.

It was judgment from Almighty God upon a sinful nation and a sinful people. The firstborn who lived through that night knew that they were redeemed by blood. The only thing that wrought redemption was blood. That night these people ate the Passover, with loins girded and lights ablaze, then marched out a redeemed people, redeemed by blood.

That is what it means to travel on eagles' wings! *"Ye have seen what I did unto the Egyptians, and how I bore you on eagles' wings and brought you unto myself"* (Exodus 19:4).

TRAPPED

But this was only the beginning of their experience with the grace of God. These people came down to the Red Sea, and there they were trapped. I cannot imagine any people being more totally trapped in a military way than were they. They were down in a pocket; around them were the waters of the Red Sea, behind them were the advancing hosts of the Egyptians. These people had no weapons with which to protect themselves; they were easy prey for the Egyptians. They would have been slaughtered to a man at that time, but again God intervened.

Realizing their plight, these people were perfectly willing to go back to the brick yards of Egypt. In fact they begged to return.

And they said unto Moses, Because there were no graves in Egypt, hast thou taken us away to die in the wilderness? Wherefore hast thou dealt thus with us, to carry us forth out of Egypt? Is not this the word that we did tell thee in Egypt, saying, Let us alone, that we may serve the Egyptians? For it had been better for us to serve the Egyptians, than that we should die in the wilderness (Exodus 14:11, 12).

However, it was not God's intention to let them go back to Egyptian bondage. You see, when God redeems, He does a complete job of it. He never starts a work of redemption but that He finishes the work. And so God is prepared to deliver them again, but this time in an altogether different manner.

Moses goes down to the Red Sea and takes with him that rod that had been so potent when it was dedicated to God, the rod that had brought the plagues, the rod that had been used back in Egypt for the deliverance of Israel out of slavery. He takes that rod, he smites that water, and all night long those waters roll back. And the children of Israel go over on dry land.

The writer to the Hebrews said, *"By faith they passed through the Red Sea as by dry land, which the Egyptians, attempting to do, were drowned"* (Hebrews 11:29).

The same route that brought deliverance for them brought death to the Egyptians. Why? Because the Israelites happened to be people who were redeemed by blood, and redemption by blood leads to resurrection. Therefore they passed through those waters of death and came through on the other side.

Now do not tell me that they had great faith. I do not think they had any at all. When you read that passage in Hebrews, notice that it does not say, "By *their* faith they passed through the Red Sea." It just says, "by faith." Whose faith was it? It was Moses' faith. Who stretched out his hand over the Red Sea? Moses. Who said to go back to Egypt? *They* said to go back to Egypt. They had no faith, but because Moses did, that sea opened up and the people passed through it. They came through on the other side. And when they got on the opposite bank, they looked back and saw the Egyptians coming. They saw something else. The walls of water were breaking, and the Egyptians were being engulfed and destroyed.

SONG OF THE REDEEMED

Safely on the other side, they sang the song of Moses. They were now prepared to sing a song of redemption. They had been redeemed by blood, they had been redeemed by power, they had been redeemed by death, and they had been redeemed by resurrection.

My friend, that is what it means to travel on eagles' wings. *"Ye have seen what I did unto the Egyptians, and how I bore you on eagles' wings and brought you unto myself."* There is no travel quite like it. It speaks of our deliverance and our salvation.

"On eagles' wings" tells of what God did for the children of Israel all the way from slavery to freedom, from the brick yards to the

Promised Land, from Egypt to Sinai, from death to life, from Egyptian darkness to heaven's light, from helplessness to the heart of God, all the way from defeat to victory—they made the trip on eagles' wings. They did not come by their own effort, they did not come out by their own ability. They came out because God, by the mighty wings of deliverance and victory, brought them out of that awful place in which they were. And that became a symbol to them.

UNDER HIS WINGS

One day a little girl named Ruth left the land of Moab and came over into the land of Israel. She came there because she trusted God. This we find in the lovely words spoken to her by Boaz when he said,

The LORD recompense thy work, and a full reward be given thee by the LORD God of Israel, under whose wings thou art come to trust (Ruth 2:12).

Those eagle wings of salvation.

Then again, when the psalmist wanted to speak of our pilgrim journey through this earth and the salvation that God brings to pass, he speaks of being "under His feathers" and "under His wings we can trust." What a picture of God's method of salvation!

You see, God's method of transportation, as He leads lost sinners out of Egyptian darkness into heaven, is done by air. It is an air lift, it is by eagles' wings, it is by grace! But the tragedy of it is that when these people came to Mount Sinai, God reviewed their past and said in effect: "Now that you see what I have done, would you like to continue on eagles' wings, or are you prepared to receive my commandments and go in your own strength now?" And they replied in a very bold, audacious, and proud manner, *"All that the LORD hath spoken we will do"* (Exodus 19:8).

Yet they did not even receive the Ten Commandments until they had broken them. At the time the commandments were being written by the finger of God, they were making a golden calf.

The same tragedy is being re-enacted today. We are constantly in danger of making the same wrong decision. There is danger of our getting off or forsaking the eagle wings of the grace of God in salvation, and getting in the ox cart of law or good works or religion. Oh, it is so dangerous today! John opened his gospel by writing, *"For the law was given by Moses, but grace and truth came by Jesus Christ"* (John 1:17).

There are two utterly separate modes of travel through this life. They are just as different as an ox cart is from a jet plane. You cannot travel with one foot in an ox cart and the other foot in a jet plane—it is absolutely impossible. Yet today in the matter of religion, a great many folk are trying to go by law and grace. If you are trying to live by law, may I say to you that today it is all the way by grace. It is all the way "on eagles' wings."

Law demands—Grace gives.
Law extracts—Grace bestows.
Law says, "Do"—Grace says, "Believe."
Law say, "Work"—Grace says, "Rest."
Law threatens, pronouncing a curse—Grace entreats, announcing a blessing.
Law says, "Do and thou shalt live"—Grace says, "Live and thou shalt do."
Law condemns the best man—Grace will save the worst man.

Law reveals the character of God and also reveals the weakness of man. *"Now we know that whatever things the law saith, it saith to them who are under the law, that every mouth might be stopped, and all the world may become guilty before God"* (Romans 3:19).

BY THE LAW IS THE KNOWLEDGE OF SIN

The Law was given that you might know your sin. It was given that you might know that you have not attained to His standard. It was given that you might know that you will never get to heaven by that route. My friend, it will never take you there.

The Law will not get you to heaven any more than taking the blood pressure will cure a heart condition or making an X-ray will cure cancer. Taking the temperature is not the way to deal with leprosy today.

To change the figure of speech, sewing a patch on a pair of old trousers really never solved the problem. Of course so little is known about patches in this day of prosperity, but I know what it is to wear patched pants. I hope you do. There is something humbling in wearing patched pants. I remember as a boy that my mother used to sew a patch on a *patch*. Then one day my dad brought home for me a new pair of pants. What a joy it was to get rid of the old patched ones and wear new ones! May I say to you that the Lord Jesus Christ came, not to sew up the old pair of pants, but with a new pair! He came to put aside the Law—not to sew grace on it. At this moment the Savior by His grace can give you a garment that will enable you to stand before Almighty God.

There are only two kinds of religion in the world (southern California to the contrary). You can list every "ism," every cult, every religion in southern California under one category. They all say, "Do, do, do." Only Christianity says, "Done." Christ has done it all. Paul said to a young preacher, *"For the grace of God that bringeth salvation hath appeared to all men"* (Titus 2:11).

It is by His grace, it is by eagles' wings that He delivers us. That is His method today.

During a series on the Ten Commandments, several folk talked with me about the nature of the Law. One man said, "I'll be honest with you. I have always felt that somehow I would be able to work it out, and if I did the best I could, God would have to accept that. But I see now that when you put my best down by the white light of His standard, I cannot measure up even to that standard. I have no ability at all."

> Run, run and do, the Law commands,
> But gives me neither feet nor hands.
> Better news the Gospel brings,
> It bids me fly and gives me wings.

You have seen how I bore you on eagles' wings and brought you unto Myself.

DISCIPLINE

There is another thing I want you to notice about eagles' wings. They are set before us as discipline by grace, for God disciplines those whom He saves by grace.

As an eagle stirreth up her nest, fluttereth over her young, spreadeth abroad her wings, taketh them, beareth them on her wings, so the LORD alone did lead him, and there was no strange god with him (Deuteronomy 32:11, 12).

The eagle is known for its ferocity and cruelty. An eagle, as it is flying aloft, may see a lamb or some other animal down below, plunge out of the sky, leap upon the animal, and destroy it.

In sharp contrast is its tenderness toward its own young. The eagle builds its nest on a high mountain crag. After the eggs are laid and the little ones hatch out, both the male and female watch over the nest and bring food to the eaglets. Then comes the day when those little fellows are big enough to fly. But they do not want to fly, they are having it too easy up there in that nest. They are given breakfast each morning in bed! Why should they want to leave? The mother eagle knows that it is time for them to start flying. There they are on the dizzy heights of a mountain crag, and she tries to lead them out. She attempts to teach them by flying out herself and coming back, but they are reluctant to follow. They don't want her to know they are ready to fly, so they don't move.

Then she breaks up the nest and takes a little one to the edge of the cliff. It is a long way down, and she pushes him over! She does not push him over to destroy him. She watches that little fellow as he starts down and clumsily flaps his wings. If he doesn't take off as he should, she swoops underneath him, and her mighty wings hold up that little eaglet. He will never be dashed on the crags beneath. She brings him back up and tries again until eventually the little fellow flies as she has shown him. Each time she flies a little farther, and he follows her.

Davy, in one of his books, tells about an experience he had.

I once saw a very interesting sight above one of the crags of Ben Nevis as I was going in pursuit of big game. Two parent eagles were teaching their offspring, two young birds, the maneuvers of flight. They began by rising from the top of the mountain, right into the eye of the sun. They first made small circles, and the young birds imitated them. They paused on their wings, waiting until they made their first flight, holding them on their expanded wings when they seemed exhausted. And then they took a second and larger gyration, always enlarging their circle of flight, so as to make a gradually ascending spiral.

That is the eagle. And God made the eagle that way in order that He might give us a verse. Read it carefully:

As an eagle stirreth up her nest, fluttereth over her young, spreadeth abroad her wings, taketh them, beareth them on her wings, so the LORD alone did lead him, and there was no strange god with him (Deuteronomy 32:11, 12).

A HIGHER PLANE THAN THE LAW

My friend, if we have been saved by grace, we have been called to a higher plane of living than the Law ever called any man to experience. We are called to live above the valleys of this world, in fact, above the mountain peaks of the world. You see, the Law never raised man very high.

If you will recall when planes first started flying in a commercial way, they never flew above at six thousand feet in the air. Now and then they would bump into a mountain. But now with pressurized cabins, they are no longer limited to six thousand feet—they now go up to forty thousand feet. And when you say that a plane does not fly at six thousand feet, you do not mean that iit is on the ground, you mean it is higher.

When we say that a Christian is not to be under Law, what we mean is that he is to be on a higher plane. He is to leave the six thousand foot level and go up to where it is forty thousand feet because he is being borne on eagles' wings.

God has a way of training those whom He has saved by His grace. He now wants to teach them to use their wings. God does not want us to live on a low plane. He wants us above the mountain peaks of this world of human effort. He does not want us caged down here by some religious zoo of this world to be on display for spectators. We are to live for Him on a high plane. That is the thing Paul said to Titus. *"For the grace of God that bringeth salvation hath appeared to all men"* (Titus 2:11).

The eagle wings of God's grace have taken those who have trusted Christ and lifted them out of sin. But that does not end it. The same grace of God is *"Teaching us that, denying ungodliness and worldly lusts, we should live soberly, righteously, and godly, in this present age"* (Titus 2:12). And Paul wrote this, not in the language of Sinai, but in the language of love, the language of the mother eagle urging her young to come up higher: *"I beseech you therefore, brethren, by the mercies of God, that ye present your bodies a living sacrifice, holy, acceptable unto God, which is your reasonable service"* (Romans 12:1).

And again to the Ephesians he said, *"I therefore, the prisoner of the Lord, beseech you that ye walk worthy of the vocation wherewith ye are called, with all lowliness and meekness, with longsuffering, forebearing one another in love"* (Ephesians 4:1, 2). It is a high calling, but it demands walking in lowliness and meekness down here.

THEIR NESTS WERE BROKEN UP

Do you know the way He accomplishes this in our lives? He breaks up our nests. Oh, how comfortable we are, how comfortable we get in grace. And God has to come along and break up our nest. That has been His method.

Adam and Eve were put into the Garden of Eden—what a nest that was! Then they sinned, and God broke up the nest—it was for their good—and He drove them out of the Garden.

You follow the record of how He dealt with His own. Abraham was living in Ur of the Chaldees, which boasted a great civilization in his day. They had all sorts of comforts, and Abraham was a prosperous businessman. He was doing well, but one day God called him, broke up his nest, and moved him out. It was hard going from then on, but I can assure you that Abraham would never have exchanged that experience for a life of comfort in Ur of the Chaldees.

Moses, by what the world would call a trick of fate, got into the palace of Pharaoh and would have been the next Pharaoh on the throne. I have a notion that he could have given a very convincing argument for staying in that advantageous position. Certainly he could have said, "I can be of more help to my people here than if I attempted to step out." But he did not argue that way. In fact, Moses wanted to deliver them before God was ready. God broke up his nest and one day drove him out of that palace to the back side of the desert yonder at Midian. That was God's method.

Then there was David, a shepherd boy out yonder with his sheep. He described how peaceful it was by the cool, limpid water and the green pastures. It was so comfortable there. One day God broke up his nest, the anointing oil was poured upon him, and he became Israel's king, the like of which they never saw from that day on. But he went into hiding in the caves of the earth. He had to go underground for many years. Schooled and roughed up—my, how God put the sandpaper on that man! God disciplined him. He was God's man and, you see, his nest had to be broken up.

James and John were prosperous fishermen living in Capernaum on the Sea of Galilee. They were doing well until one day there came by a Man who called them. And they immediately left the ship and their father and followed Him. Their nest was broken up. They left the fishing business to become two of the twelve disciples of the Lord Jesus Christ. One of them died a martyr's death, and the other spent time yonder on an island in lonely exile. Way back there at Capernaum God had broken up their nest, you see.

WHAT IF GOD BREAKS UP YOUR NEST?

Since this is God's method, it is possible that He may break up your nest and he may break up my nest. Sometimes He not only breaks up the nest, but He pushes us off the cliff. Now I do not know about you, but I do not like being pushed off a cliff. However, God does this to his own. And generally He pushes them right into a peck of trouble, problems, and difficulties.

Remember that the Lord Jesus sent His disciples across the Sea of Galilee one evening definitely, directly, and deliberately into a storm. He did it purposely.

Some time ago I mentioned this incident at a Bible conference, and a lovely couple approached me after the service. They were highly incensed at what I had said.

"Now look here, you have no right to make such a statement about our lovely Savior. He would never send His disciples into a storm!"

I said to them, "Do you think He was God, or wasn't He God?"

"Oh," they said, "we believe He is God."

"Does God know everything?"

"Yes," they replied.

"Did He know that storm was coming?"

They said, "Yes."

"Well," I said, "He sent them into it."

Their honest comment was, "We hadn't thought of it like that."

My friend, He sent His own deliberately into a storm. This couple, who became wonderful friends of mine, now know what it is to be sent into a storm. It was their daughter in San Jose who was kidnapped and brutally slain. They knew what it was to sit night after night, waiting to see if the FBI had any word to give to them. They went into a storm.

Some through the fire, some through the flood—that is the way God leads His dear children along. That is His method. He will send His own into a storm.

But always remember that He will not let you fall.

There have been many times in my life when I have been pushed to the edge of the cliff and I was sure there would be a crash. But there wasn't.

In college I knew that God had called me to the ministry, but I had very little faith in Him. I had a notion that He would take me to a certain height and drop me off, let me go. When I graduated from college, I was the unhappiest person there. After having received my degree, I returned to my room in the dormitory, still in cap and gown, and sat dejectedly on the edge of my bed. My roommate came in and asked, "What in the world—did somebody die?" I said, "Just as well to. I thought God called me to the ministry. I'm through college, the depression has hit, and I do not even have a job this summer. I haven't a dime to go to seminary next year." Without going into details, let me just say that when I went to bed that night, I had checks that totalled $750 which had come from people whom I never dreamed would be interested in seeing me go to seminary. And $750 the year the depression hit, brother, was a whole lot of money! I thought He was going to drop me. He did, but He did not let me fall.

BE CONFIDENT

This verse was given to me at that time and it is my life verse: *"Being confident of this very thing, that he who hath begun a good work in you will perform it until the day of Jesus Christ"* (Philippians 1:6). You may think you are falling, my friend, but the wings will be there at the right moment. *"Underneath are the everlasting arms"* (Deuteronomy 33:27).

He will hold you on His wings, He will not let you fall. If, when you are reading this, you are at wit's end corner and do not know where to turn or what to do, let me give you this verse:

> *They that wait upon the LORD shall renew their strength; they shall mount up with wings like eagles; they shall run, and not be weary; and they shall walk, and not faint* (Isaiah 40:31).

In the eighteenth century this thought was put in a hymn that went like this:

> *Rise, my soul, and stretch thy wings,*
> *Thy better portion trace;*
> *Rise from transitory things*
> *T'ward heav'n, thy native place:*
> *Sun and moon and stars decay;*
> *Time shall soon this earth remove:*
> *Rise, my soul, and haste away*
> *To seats prepared above.*

"Ye have seen what I did unto the Egyptians, and how I bore you on eagles' wings and brought you unto myself."

2

THE LOVELINESS OF JESUS

Leviticus 2

Although the book of Leviticus may seem to be a musty record of empty ritual and meaningless ceremonies, may I say to you that Christ is in Leviticus!

He is, I believe, on every page of Scripture. It is due to our blindness that we cannot always see Him there. The Lord Jesus Christ Himself said, "Moses wrote of me." And then after His resurrection, there on the Emmaus road, He took His disciples through the prophecies. *"And beginning at Moses and all the prophets, he expounded unto them in all the scriptures the things concerning himself"* (Luke 24:27). Probably the oldest book in the Bible is the book of Job, out of which comes the heart-cry of humanity, "Oh, that I knew where I might find him." And then the answer comes down over the centuries when Philip, the quiet man, goes to the comedian, Nathanael, and declares, *"We have found him, of whom Moses in the law, and the prophets, did write, Jesus of Nazareth"* (John 1:45). Moses wrote of Him, and we find Him here in the book of Leviticus.

Actually, we have only four gospels in the New Testament, but we have five "gospels" in the book of Leviticus. There are five offerings in Leviticus, and each one of these offerings speaks of Christ and sets Him forth in a way found nowhere else in the Bible.

23

SWEET SAVOR OFFERINGS

These five offerings divide into what is known as sweet savor offerings and non-sweet (or bitter) offerings. The first three are sweet savor offerings, and they speak of the *person* of Christ—who He is. The last two (non-sweet) offerings speak of the *work* of Christ, what He did for us on the cross when He bore the sins of the world. The burnt offering, the meal offering, and the peace offering are all sweet savor offerings. Then the two non-sweet savor offerings are the trespass offering and the sin offering.

Now let me lift out the second of the sweet savor offerings, the *meal* offering. In the King James Version *meal* is translated *meat,* but when we read it carefully, we notice that there is no meat (as we understand the word) in it at all. If you have a Bible with good notes, you will see that *meat* offering is better translated *meal* offering. But even better than that, it is the *food* offering. And when you read the second chapter of Leviticus, it actually reads like a recipe of Betty Crocker. This is a recipe for bread, plain bread, unleavened bread— not very tasty, not like the hot biscuits you get down South. In fact, this kind of bread doesn't appeal to the natural taste whatsoever, but it pictures Christ in a remarkable way.

The meal offering speaks of the perfect humanity of Jesus. I hope I make that clear. It does not refer to His being perfect as God, for this offering does not set forth His deity. It sets forth His humanity, His perfect humanity and the fact that He was perfectly human. The man Christ Jesus is here. We're going to look at Him in probably a new way, not as Deity now (which we find in other offerings), but we see in this offering the thing that God had in mind for mankind.

God's goal for man was fulfilled in Jesus. That is the reason He is called the "last Adam"—the first Adam failed so miserably. The Lord Jesus is also called the "second man," not the last man. You see, God sent Him into the world to become a man, and He is the second one, because after Adam it says, "And Adam begot a son in his likeness." Poor Adam, he was a sinner; and ever since, Adams have been sinners. All of us are Adams. No matter what your name is now, it was Adam; and somewhere along the line it was changed. They say that the McGees in Scotland took that name to disguise their identity. That's the way most of us got our names, but it was Adam in the beginning. Although there have been many of them, there has been only the second man so far. But God has in mind a third and a fourth and a fifth—in fact there are going to be millions of them, millions of the redeemed. Adam and his family failed so miserably. But Christ is the last Adam because, my beloved, after Christ, God has no other arrangement to improve the human family. That's His final effort. If you miss Christ, God has no emergency measure worked out for you. Christ is the last Adam, but He is the second man. God has in mind a great improvement for the human race. And this meal offering pictures the perfect man.

WHAT IS MAN?

You may think I'm a pessimist when I say that man is the most colossal failure in God's universe. But have you considered this? Man is farther off the track than any creature God has. Scripture says this: *"They are all gone out of the way"* (Romans 3:12), and that means they're a wreck. All, not just some, but all of mankind is a wreck. You see a train that has been wrecked, cars derailed, lying there twisted and shattered. You think, *How tragic! It was made to run on those tracks. It would have been at its destination in the morning, but it didn't get there*. That's man. God created man and put him on the track. But he's gone out of the way. Man is wrecked.

God has more to say about man: *"All have sinned, and come short"* (Romans 3:23). *"There is none righteous, no, not one"* (Romans 3:10). All are *"dead in trespasses and sins"* (Ephesians 2:1). And notice this, *"And the way of peace have they not known"* (Romans 3:17). That's man.

Reports are seldom interesting to me, but here is one that is. It is the Rockefeller Report, put out by one of the biggest funds in America today. No expense was spared; experts in every field were employed to produce it. These are some of its findings:

The world is living through a period of swift and far-reaching upheavals. Standards and institutions which have remained unchanged for centuries are breaking down. Millions who have hitherto passively endured their place in life are clamoring for a new and more worthy existence. Western Europe, the fountainhead of our civilization, has lost its position of prominence in world affairs. Across the great land mass of Eurasia and on the continent of Africa new nations are rising in the place of colonial empires. Mankind is yearning to realize its aspirations in peace.

Well, why doesn't man have peace if he wants it? Notice—"But it is faced by two somber threats: the Communist thrust to achieve world domination which seeks to exploit all dissatisfactions and to magnify all tensions." That's one. Notice the second: "And the new weapons of technology capable of obliterating civilization." The way of peace, this report says, man does not know.

Although down deep in his heart man would love to have peace, he cannot have peace. And God's Word has been saying that all along. With feverish energy man is trying to perfect fiendish instruments of frightful destruction today. Why? Because mankind is the most colossal failure in God's universe.

But don't be discouraged, don't be disappointed. Look at Jesus today and take hope. His person and life down here among men is a revelation of God's goal for humanity.

Let us look at Him now, not as God, but as man—the beauty of Jesus, His winsome personality, the kingliness of His manner, the glory of His manhood, the loveliness of Jesus. His coming was a doxology; His presence was a blessing; His departure was a benediction. See Him now as He is depicted in this meal offering.

There are two important aspects of this offering: ingredients that were included and ingredients that were excluded. There were certain ingredients in this offering that were demanded; they had to be there. There were other ingredients that were forbidden and could never be there.

INGREDIENTS INCLUDED

First of all, let's look at what was in the offering.

And when any will offer a meal offering unto the LORD, his offering shall be of fine flour, and he shall pour oil upon it, and put frankincense thereon (Leviticus 2:1).

Fine Flour

The first ingredient is fine flour, and that illustrates the perfect humanity of Christ as probably nothing else does. The grain in

Moses' day was ground by hand, and it was often very coarse and uneven if the grinder was careless or in a hurry. The flour for the meal offering must be a special grind. It had to be ground very fine. You see, sin has made all of the race lumpy. You and I are lumpy—one part of our personality is overdeveloped at the expense of other areas. Psychology has come up with an expression that is saying in technical terms what God is saying in simple terms to the entire human race. We hear today a great deal about a well-integrated personality. However, we never see those folk. That's a species that the human race does not produce. But here is one who is perfect in thought, perfect in word, and perfect in deed. The fact of the matter is, He is the only perfect man who has ever been on this earth. The Lord Jesus Christ is the only perfect man.

A lecturer was once talking about man's imperfection. He wanted to enforce his point, so he asked rhetorically for anybody in his audience who ever had seen a perfect man to lift his hand. No hand went up. Encouraged by this fact, he asked the question the second time, "Has anyone here ever seen a perfect man?"

Still no hand was raised. After he had asked it a third time, way back in the rear a little timid fellow lifted his hand. Surprised, the lecturer asked, "Have you seen a perfect man?" "I haven't exactly seen him, but I've certainly heard about him," the little fellow replied.

"Who in the world is he?"

"He's my wife's first husband."

No doubt he had heard a great deal about him! But if he had met him, I think he would have found out that he was not perfect.

The only perfect man who ever lived on this earth is the Lord Jesus Christ. And Jesus was normal, the only normal person who ever walked this earth. You see, today psychologists arrive at what they call a normality by drawing a line where the majority is, and they call that normal. But who told them it was normal? If you are different, you are considered abnormal. And that is the reason both Peter and Paul said to Christians, "You are a peculiar people"—different from those who are in the world. But folk today are afraid of being different. Especially is this true among the dissenters who pride themselves in being different. If you take a second look at them, you will see that they all dress alike, act alike, talk alike, think alike. Not one dares to be different from his crowd which he considers normal. But when our Lord was here upon this earth, they said to Him, "Thou hast a demon." Do you know why they said that? Because He was different. Even those who were His loved ones came to take Him away, saying, "He is beside himself." Why? Because He was not like they were. He was different, my beloved. Oh, the smoothness and the evenness of His person. I do not know why more people are not attracted to Him. He was even, He was temperate, He was normal.

Mentally, physically, emotionally, volitionally there was equipoise. None of us holds those in balance at all. We today have no smoothness—we're lumpy. One attribute is overbalanced and out of proportion to other attributes. Jesus was not a religious genius, although at twelve years of age, when He stood yonder in the temple, "hearing them and asking them questions," the religious rulers marvelled at Him. Had He continued like that, I might agree with you that He was a religious genius, but He went back to Nazareth to the carpentry shop and became a carpenter. He was not out of proportion.

Notice what He was physically. He could go into the temple and drive out the money changers, and that crowd got out because they were afraid of Him. He was *man,* a physically powerful man. But this same one tenderly took the children into His arms. He was in balance.

See what He was mentally. They marvelled at His teaching. My, how wonderful He was! As they marvelled at His teachings, they said, "How is it that this man knows these things and He hasn't even been to our schools?" Yet He never appealed to His mind. You can't find anywhere in the gospels that the Lord Jesus said, "I've thought it through, and this is the best course of action." His mind was never the criterion. He did not appeal to His mentality as the basis for any judgment.

Emotionally He was in balance—and He had emotion. Yonder at the tomb of His friend Lazarus, He wept. But I tell you, when this fellow Simon Peter got emotional and said, "I will lay down my life for thy sake" (as we would say, "I want to put all on the altar for Jesus"), the Lord Jesus was not carried away by that kind of cheap emotion. He said, "Simon Peter, you're sincere but you don't know yourself. You'll deny me this night." Jesus was never swayed or guided by His emotions. He could get angry, angry against evil. When the scribes and Pharisees came to Him, He called them hypocrites. But when a woman taken in adultery was brought to Him, He forgave her. He was firm but tender; He was strong but not brutal; He was gentle but not weak. He was benevolent, saying to His disciples, "You give them to eat," but He was economical also for He said, "Gather up the fragments that remain, that nothing be lost."

He was not motivated by His volitional life. Although it is said of Him that He steadfastly set His face to go to Jerusalem, that His will was set, it was because He was responding to the Father's will. He said, "Not my will, but thine be done." His volitional nature was not the guideline for His action.

He was even; all of us are lumpy. Oh, the smoothness and evenness of His person.

With what humility He fell down before God yonder in the Garden of Gethsemane, but with what dignity He stood as they came to arrest Him. He was in perfect balance.

If you are at this time discouraged with yourself and you're disappointed in others, look at Jesus. He was a perfect person. There has been none like Him, *none* like him.

Oil

Then notice the second ingredient that went into the meal offering. It was oil—"he shall pour oil upon it." Oil is olive oil, and it speaks of the Holy Spirit. The flour was to be mixed with oil, and oil was to be poured upon it. The offering was drenched with oil. The prominence of the Holy Spirit in the human life of Jesus is very noticeable: He was born of the Spirit; baptized of the Spirit; led of the Spirit; He taught, performed miracles, and offered Himself in the power of the Spirit. If the Lord Jesus in His perfect humanity needed the Holy Spirit, surely you and I need Him to an even greater extent. May I say to you that the expression of the Christlike life is never in the flesh; it is only as the Spirit of God moves through us by our yielding ourselves to Him.

Frankincense

Now notice the third ingredient—"he shall . . . put frankincense thereon." The frankincense was made from a secret formula using probably a resinous gum taken from a tree. It could exude its fragrance only under pressure and fire. This is a beautiful picture of our Lord as He manifests the fragrance of His life under the fires of tension, pressures, and persecution. He is never more lovely than yonder upon the cross. His life has given out a fragrance that has filled this world so that even the enemies of Jesus have to stand in the presence of the cross, and though they reject all the redemptive value that is there, they have to say, "He was lovely in death as He was lovely in life." The fragrance of His person.

Salt

The final ingredient included in the meal offering was salt.

And every oblation of thy meal offering shalt thou season with salt (Leviticus 2:13).

Salt was required. Ordinarily salt is a preservative, but I think it has another value here. It is what Paul expressed to the Christians at Colosse, *"Let your speech be always with grace, seasoned with salt"* (Colossians 4:6). Some folk have misread that and think that they're to have a "salty" conversation. Unfortunately many Christians are very salty when you listen to them! But Paul had something entirely different in mind when he used the expression, "seasoned with salt." My, a believer's conversation ought to betray him. Just as Peter's tongue betrayed him, our tongue ought to betray the fact that we are Christ's.

A Chinese young lady, who had come to this country to study in one of our universities, was with a group of girls one Sunday afternoon as they were talking about this matter of salt—that we are said to be the salt of the earth. She contributed this, "One of the characteristics of salt is that it makes you thirsty." Do you ever make anyone thirsty for God? You're salt in the world. One of the loveliest compliments I have heard was about a woman who taught the mother's Bible class in a church I pastored. Long before I ever met her, I heard a lady say of her, "When I listen to her, it makes me want to know God." You can't say anything better about a teacher than that. Do you ever make anybody thirsty for God? What about the people with whom you work? Are they thirsty because you made them thirsty?

You're salt. The Lord Jesus was salt, and everywhere He went people got thirsty for God.

EXCLUDED INGREDIENTS

The ingredients excluded from this offering are as prominent as the ingredients included.

Leaven

The first one is leaven.

No meal offering, which ye shall bring unto the LORD, shall be made with leaven (Leviticus 2:11).

Leaven is to be excluded. Leaven throughout the Scriptures is used as a principle of evil and corruption. It is said of the Lord Jesus, relative to His humanity, that even in death His body did not see corruption. Certainly during His life there was no evil found within Him. He could say something that you and I could never say, *"the prince of this world cometh, and hath nothing in me"* (John 14:30). Also He challenged His critics with this, *"Which of you convicteth me of sin?"* (John 8:46). You and I wouldn't dare put out such a challenge because we are sinners. He was not. For over 1900 years they have looked at Him, and so far nobody has been able to point a finger and say that there was sin in His life. There was no evil in Him, no leaven. He was holy, harmless, undefiled, separate from sinners. It is said of us, "We are all as an unclean thing, and all our righteousnesses are as filthy rags" (Isaiah 64:6). But, my friend, this is not said of Him. He is different in His humanity. There was no sin in Him.

Honey

The second ingredient to be left out of the meal offering is, to me, almost amusing:

Nor any honey, in any offering of the LORD made by fire (Leviticus 2:11).

31

This offering was not to be sweet—it was not cake. Honey was excluded. Why was honey explicitly forbidden? Because honey speaks of natural sweetness, the sweetness of the natural man. Do you ever meet people like that—affected, having a pious facade? They wear a makeup that Revlon has nothing to do with, but the devil made it. They are trying to improve the natural man. As Paul said, "They desire to make a fair show in the flesh." You see them at church on Sunday, smiling with sweetness. They call everyone "dear" or "brother." You would think that their halo had been shined with silver polish, it is so bright on Sunday! But Monday morning when they get on the telephone, you have never heard such vicious slander, such malicious gossip! Hell never spewed forth so much venom as comes from their lips. They are more dangerous than any killer with a gun. They are spiritual delinquents. Their halo is now gone, and the horns appear (the devil doesn't have horns, but they do). A man said to me the other day, "McGee, it's getting so you don't know who to believe even in a church." Oh, I want to say this to you: You can believe Jesus. He has no natural sweetness; there was no "put-on" with Him. He never deceived anyone. Some gullible people today believe every religious charlatan that comes along. My friend, let me say it with all the strength I can muster: Jesus is the only one you can believe, the *only* one. Paul said to believers, "Let love be without dissimulation," which means let love be genuine. That's what Paul is saying. Don't back-slap if you don't mean it. Don't smile when it's not genuine. Don't pretend to be something that you're not. Our Lord was genuine. How wonderful He was!

Fire

Lastly the meal offering was put on fire. Seven times we read here that it was burned or put on fire. The fire is symbolic of the suffering that Christ endured at the hands of men. It is not the suffering He endured for sin but rather, because of sinful men. You see, the sufferings of the Lord Jesus can be divided into two categories: His suffering for our sin on the cross as our substitute, and also His suffering at the hands of men, which has nothing to do with our sins today. This meal offering being subjected to the fire speaks of that suffering which He endured all His life on earth—hunger, thirst, weariness, loneliness, misunderstandings, revilings, hatred, persecution, humiliation, ridicule, scorn. He was sensitive as no other person ever has been sensitive, and they broke His heart long before He went to the cross. Then yonder on the cross He hung there for six hours. The first three hours He suffered at the hands of men. At high noon God put a mantle of darkness down on the cross, and in the last three hours He went through hell as He paid for the sins of the human family.

But the meal offering represented the suffering that Jesus endured at the hands of men.

And he [son of Aaron] shall take of it his handful, of the flour of the meal offering, and of the oil thereof, and all the frankincense which is upon the meal offering, and shall burn it upon the altar for a sweet savour, even the memorial of it, unto the LORD (Leviticus 6:15).

My friend, are you discouraged with yourself? Are you disappointed in others? Are you weary and heartbroken? Then turn your eyes upon Jesus. He is wonderful. You're not, and I'm not, but He is wonderful.

He is altogether lovely.

3

GOLDEN BELLS AND POMEGRANATES

The first sermon that I preached on coming to California was "Golden Bells and Pomegranates." At that time I expressed my ignorance of just what a pomegranate was. I was confident that it was not what we called the pomegranate in Texas because there it grew on a vine. I was sure the pomegranate of Scripture grew on a tree. By four o'clock that afternoon I had five bushels of pomegranates on the back patio of the manse where I lived! Everyone contributed to my education of what a pomegranate really was. By the way, have you tried to eat five bushels of pomegranates?

THE WELL-DRESSED HIGH PRIEST

Now we are going to have a Scripture fashion show. We are going to see today what the well-dressed high priest wore in Moses' day. A male fashion show is comparatively new to us, but it is as old as the nation Israel. The matter of the dress of Christians has always been a controversial subject. You can go back to the days of the Puritans, and even move all the way back to the early church in the first century, and find that there has always been a great deal of disagreement on how a believer should dress. And that's been especially true of the female of the species. It's generally conceded today by spiritual and sensible believers that a Christian should dress in style but be modest in apparel so as not to attract attention to the physical. Following the injunction of Scripture in the matter of adornment, the ornament of the meek and quiet spirit is in the sight of God of great price. The Word of God puts a great deal of emphasis on the *inside* rather than on the *outside*. Candidly, the outer man is not too important if the inner man is not what it should be.

Now the garments of the priests in particular are given to us in Scripture with emphasis, and the dress of the high priest is given in great detail. His wardrobe was colorful and striking. Listen to this: *"And thou shalt make holy garments for Aaron thy brother for glory and for beauty"* (Exodus 28:2).

The garments of the high priest were glamorous; they were colorful and very beautiful. It is quite interesting that in nature the male is clothed more attractively than the female. That's especially true among the birds and fish. The male is much more colorful and ornate than the female. It's only among homo sapiens that the male is drab, dull, and subdued in his attire, while the female is the one who goes in for color and adornments. I'm not sure that we have it right, but, nevertheless, that's the way it is today.

In contrast, the high priest was magnificent in his clothing. No bird of paradise was ever dressed in a more colorful costume than he was, and certainly no peacock ever had more color.

THE GLORIOUS APPAREL

Now I want to briefly describe his garments, and then we will pay attention to just one minor detail of the garments of the high priest. He wore a basic garment that is called in Scripture "linen britches." Over that he wore a robe, the same kind of robe that was worn by all the priests. They all wore white robes made out of fine-twined Egyptian linen, the finest linen this world has produced—360,000 feet to the pound, while the best flax mills in Ireland have been able to make only 180,000 feet to the pound. This reveals how fine this linen was, very much like silk as we know silk today. That then was the linen robe, the basic robe that all the priests wore. Then over that the high priest, and he alone, began to put on color. He wore a sleeveless blue robe of the ephod. Then over the robe of the ephod was the ephod itself. I'm not sure just what it was. After reading at least a dozen descriptions of it, I'm confident that the writers are as much in the dark as I am about it. We are not quite clear just how it was made. In the middle of it was an opening for the head, and half of it would drop down over the back and half of it would drop down over the front. It also had straps on each shoulder, and on each shoulder was an onyx stone in a filigree setting of gold. On each one of these stones were engraved six names of the tribes of Israel, so that the high priest carried on his shoulders all twelve tribes of the nation Israel. Above that he wore a breastplate, very much like what we call a vest, with twelve costly gems on the front of it, each stone engraved with the name of one of the tribes of Israel.

The high priest wore on his head a "miter" or a "holy crown," apparently a high crown made of linen, but on the front engraved in solid gold were the words "Holiness unto the Lord."

This then gives us a picture of the high priest and the garments that he wore. You can imagine that when he functioned, first in the tabernacle and later in the temple, how beautiful he was in appearance.

Now I want us to look more carefully at the robe of the ephod, that robe that went on over the white garment. It was blue; it was not as long as the white linen, because particular instruction was given that it should never touch the ground. The thing that interests us about it is that on its hem there were golden bells and pomegranates, and that's where we get the subject of this message. There were actually golden bells attached there interspersed with pomegranates of blue and purple and scarlet. You can well imagine what a beautiful garment that was to see. First there would be a golden bell and then a pomegranate, a golden bell, a pomegranate, a golden bell, a pomegranate—and each pomegranate running the series of the three different colors around his garment.

THE MEANING OF THE GARMENTS

Now this colorful attire that the high priest wore had a spiritual emphasis. The high priest primarily pictures for you and me today our Savior, the Lord Jesus Christ, as our Great High Priest. When the high priest went into the holy place to function, the people could not see him; but because they could hear the bells, they knew he was busy ministering on their behalf. When was the last time you heard the bells of your Great High Priest? No wonder today many believers are confused; they haven't been listening to the bells. Our Lord is in yonder at the throne of the Father, busy for us today, and the bells are on His garment. Everything about the high priest speaks to us of Him. The white linen speaks of the righteousness of Christ, and the amazing thing is that He has made that garment over to us! The only way you and I could possibly stand in God's presence is to be clothed in the robe of Christ's righteousness which He gives to those who do no more nor less than simply trust Him as Savior!

As the high priest had the names of the twelve tribes on his shoulder, so our Great High Priest is yonder in heaven for us today.

> *But this man, because he continueth ever, hath an unchangeable priesthood. Wherefore he is able also to save them to the uttermost that come unto God by him, seeing he ever liveth to make intercession for them* (Hebrews 7:24, 25).

Even when a little lamb gets out of the fold and gets lost on the hillside, He goes out and finds the lamb. *"And when he hath found it, he layeth it on his shoulders, rejoicing"* (Luke 15:5). He brings it home on his shoulder. I love that because that's where our Shepherd carries us today.

And like the high priest, on His heart there are the individual names. Our Savior carries on His heart those who are His own. He says He knows all His sheep by name. He says some day He is to give us a new name.

> *He that hath an ear, let him hear what the Spirit saith unto the churches; To him that overcometh will I give to eat of the hidden manna, and will give him a white stone, and in the stone a new name written, which no man knoweth saving he that receiveth it* (Revelation 2:17).

The new name is His new name for each one of us, a very personal sort of thing. Today He carries those who are His own upon His heart.

Now the thing that interests me are those golden bells and pomegranates.

And beneath upon the hem of it thou shalt make pomegranates of blue, and of purple, and of scarlet, round about the hem thereof; and bells of gold between them round about: A golden bell and a pomegranate, a golden bell and a pomegranate, upon the hem of the robe round about (Exodus 28:33–34).

Pomegranates speak of fruit, if you please. We are told today that the blossom of the pomegranate is like a five-pointed star. We've all heard of the six-pointed star of David, but very few of us have heard of the five-pointed star of Solomon. May I say that it is quite interesting that the pomegranate blossom is like that. And then we are told concerning these golden bells:

And it shall be upon Aaron to minister: and his sound shall be heard when he goeth in unto the holy place before the LORD, *and when he cometh out, that he die not* (Exodus 28:35).

Now these two things, pomegranates and golden bells, speak of sweet sounds and fragrant fruit. There is something to hear and something to taste. May I say that the bells speak of profession; the pomegranates speak of practice. The bells speak of the calling of the believer; the pomegranates speak of the conduct of the believer. The bells speak of vocalization. Paul says, *"I therefore, the prisoner of the Lord, beseech you that ye walk worthy of the vocation wherewith ye are called"* (Ephesians 4:1).

We have a vocalization and then we have a vocation down here, and the calling and the vocation should correspond.

GOLDEN BELLS

Now we are going to look at golden bells first of all. May I say that everybody is ringing a bell. I don't care who you are, you are ringing a bell whether you like it or not. In fact everyone is really a preacher whether he likes it or not. You may recall the story I have told about an experience I had in Pasadena. There was a mother out there who had only one child, a grown son—in fact he was in his early forties at the time. He was a drunkard, an alcoholic—a real one. The mother asked me if I would talk with him, and I did talk with him on several occasions. He never liked to talk when he was sober, but when he was drunk, he would always stop by my study. One day when he came by the study, he was really drunk. I read the riot act to him. I told him that he was a bum. I told him that he was sorry, that he was a disgrace to his mother. He bowed his head and took it all. Then I said, "You're a preacher." Well, he got to his feet, doubled his fist, and said, "You can't call me a preacher!" He didn't mind being a bum, and he didn't mind being a no-good person, but he didn't want to be called a preacher! I had to go over and physically put him back down in the chair and almost sit on him while I talked to him about what I meant. I said, "Everybody is a preacher. You are preaching by your life some message. You're living your life into me and I'm living my life into you. It can't be helped. You never rub shoulders with anyone but what somehow or another you give a message to him, and he brings a message to you."

We are all preachers. We are preaching where we work, we're preaching where we go to school, we're preaching in our neighborhood. We're preaching all the time—it's like ringing a bell. We tell out to others all about ourselves.

You may remember how it was back on the farm when they used to bell the cow, especially if she was turned into a pasture where there was a lot of shrubbery or a lot of trees. You would have difficulty finding her in the afternoon when you'd go to bring her back to the barn for the night. You'd go down all along the branch of the creek and you'd look, but you wouldn't see her anywhere. So you'd stop and listen, and all of a sudden you'd hear her bell. She'd been grazing, and when she'd lift her head, you'd hear the bell. You would know where the cow was by the bell. My friend, you and I tell where we are by the bell that we are ringing.

Let me mention some of the bells that believers should ring and some of the bells that we do ring whether we like it or not. I'm going to mention only a few; you could add many to this list.

Tell Your Confidence in God's Word

The first bell that every believer rings is the bell concerning the Word of God. A real believer will ring a bell of the plenary inspiration of the Bible—that this Book that we hold is the Word of God. Now this Book has been under severe attack, and that bell is not clear today in the world, I can assure you. Someone has said concerning Dr. Julian Huxley that his chief purpose in life seemed to be to destroy faith in the Bible. He made the statement again and again that our present culture and the way the nations of the West are going today will not be after the Bible, but after Nietzsche, who said, "Christianity is the greatest of all conceivable corruptions, the one immoral blemish upon mankind." Again this man has said that Christianity is in competition with other truer and more embracing thought organizations, that the supernatural will soon be ruled out, and the Bible will soon disappear. And the commentator who quoted him made this statement, "Christians tremble for the West as they see unbelief ensconced in high places of influence in their supposedly Christian society. Given a mushrooming of this influence through educational institutions, who could question the divine indictment of plague on both your houses."

Again the commentator said, "The notion that much of the Bible is myth has long been held by some Protestant theologians, including the United States' Paul Tillich and Germany's Rudolf Bultmann." May I say that these two men are being studied even in some of our so-called evangelical seminaries. Instead of spending time studying the Word of God, they're putting an emphasis on men who deny the Word of God! I believe that this is the hour when we need to ring a clear bell regarding what we believe about the Bible. I think that every pulpit, every mission organization, every Christian school, and every other Christian organization needs to declare flatfootedly just what it does believe about the Word of God. We need to ring a bell; we need to let the world know today where we stand. My beloved, may I say that a weak view concerning the Word of God will not stand up in this hour in which we are living. You are either convinced the Bible is the Word of God or you have your doubts. If you have your doubts, you have no bell to ring today.

Declare the Deity of Christ

The second bell is concerning the person of Christ. It's a different bell, but it's a bell that needs to be heard today. Again may I say there's a great deal of confusion concerning who He is. Unfortunately, most of the denominational literature follows the teaching of one leading denomination which states, "Paul would never have understood the declaration of the Nicene Council in A.D. 325 that Jesus was very God of very God." It adds, "It was the church that exalted Jesus to the rank of deity." May I say that our Lord is being dishonored. The attempt is being made to pull Him down from His throne. If there ever was a time that we needed to ring a bell concerning our belief in the deity of Christ, this is the hour. We need to be very clear that we believe that Jesus is both God and man and that Paul did know the meaning of the statement that He was "God of very God." A careful reading of Paul's epistles reveals that Jesus Christ was God to the apostle Paul, the Lord of glory, God manifest in the flesh. Therefore, declaring the deity of Christ is a bell that every believer in this hour needs to ring.

Speak of the Redemptive Blood of Christ

Then, my beloved, the third bell I would mention is that the believer has been pardoned by the blood of Christ, that he has been saved because Christ shed His blood for his sins. This again is not quite clear today. Believe me, Paul was clear at this particular juncture. He said concerning Christ, *"In whom we have redemption through his blood, the forgiveness of sins, according to the riches of his grace"* (Ephesians 1:7).

Paul understood that the way he had been forgiven and the way he had been redeemed was not through the Mosaic law, not through ritual or through religious observance, but that he had been saved because Christ had shed His blood.

Personally I think testimonies have degenerated to the place where there is too much of personal experience—"I did this, I did that, and I did the other thing." My friend, if you've been saved, it's not because you did anything; it's because *Christ* did it all. And the thing He did was to shed His blood that you might have forgiveness of sins. I say to you, that's the bell that needs to be rung today. It needs to be sounded out among believers in a very definite way. You can't make too much of the blood.

When a new pastor went to the great Pennsylvania Avenue Church in Washington years ago, a dowager came down to him, holding a lorgnette (you know that a lorgnette is a sneer on the end of a stick), and said to this new preacher, "Oh, I hope you're not going to be like the last preacher we had who was everlastingly talking about the *blood*. I certainly hope that you're not going to make too much of the blood."

"Lady, I do not intend to make too much of the blood."

"I'm very happy to hear that!"

He looked at her and very seriously added, "It is *impossible* to make too much of the blood."

My friend, you can't make too much of the blood of our Savior. That is the bell that needs to be sounded in this hour. God can forgive sins only because Christ shed His blood upon the cross.

State Your Personal Convictions

The final bell I'll mention is the bell of personal conviction. It doesn't make much noise today. It ought to. Personal conviction is a bell that every believer should be ringing. *Conviction* is an interesting word. We get our word *convict* from it. Everyone in a penitentiary is a convict, and he is there because he has been convicted. Paul thought of himself like that. Paul said of himself, "I, the prisoner of the Lord." Today a great many people think that being a Christian means you stay out of jail. If that's the requirement, Paul could never qualify; he made the jail in nearly every town in which he preached. If you had met Paul in any of these jails and said, "Who put you here, Paul?" he would have told you, "I am the prisoner of Jesus Christ. I'm here because I have convictions."

We need today men and women with convictions. I'm of the opinion that in this hour in which we are living, Christians, as I have observed them, are able to rationalize their conduct regardless of what it is. They can explain it away somehow. I hear them say, "Well, after all, we've got to get along, you know. . . . We must cut our corners. . . . We want to make friends. . . . We want to have fellowship, and therefore we must keep silent at times." We encounter many Christians today who lack personal conviction.

Did you know that God's men have always been lonely men? Can you imagine Elijah giving a talk to Ahab on coexistence? Can you imagine John the Baptist talking to Herod on the subject of brotherhood? May I say to you that these men just didn't seem to have the art of making friends and influencing people, but they certainly had the art of standing for God. They were men of conviction.

Today we need men of conviction. It is well to hear an outsider evaluate us Americans, especially *Christian* Americans. A man whom I regard as being one of the best intellects of the present time, as well as being an outstanding Christian, was interviewed. He is Dr. Charles Malek from Lebanon. This man was for a time president of the United Nations General Assembly. He is a layman, a member of the Greek Orthodox Church, and a real believer. As he looks at us, he says this:

> I'm not sure your Western materialism is better than the Soviets'. If I were asked to choose between the dialectical materialism of the Soviets and the materialistic outlook on life and the practiced commercialism of the West, I'm not sure I would choose the Western brand of materialism at all. Every time I listen to an important radio broadcast which is repeatedly interrupted by an advertisement for some shoe polish or laxative or brand of marmalade, I have to say two or three prayers in order to remain human. Another sign of weakness, Christians are not speaking with conviction. Many Christians have become so worldly that one doubts whether their Christianity can resist the non-Christian and anti-Christian pressures. I could recite twenty or more signs of moral weakness in the Western world which are highly disturbing, weaknesses of people who ought to know better, people with a great tradition behind them, whose tradition alone can save them and the world ten times over if they understand it and live it and rise above their failures.

Now that is a fair and frank estimation from a man who is a great Christian statesman in this day. The thing that we need today is conviction. Oh, listen to the apostles: "Stand therefore, having your loins girt about with truth . . . Having done all, stand . . . Be steadfast, unmoveable, always abounding in the work of the Lord." Someone has said that silence is golden, but sometimes it's yellow. Christians need to stand up and be counted. Believe me, friend, we are ringing a bell, but right now the bell on personal conviction is pretty weak throughout the world. Oh, how we need to take a stand for God in this hour!

POMEGRANATES

Now I want to leave the bells for a moment and turn to the pomegranates. The pomegranates speak of practice; they speak of the fruit of one's life. The Lord Jesus Christ said, *"By their fruits, ye shall know them"* (Matthew 7:20). Also, *"Herein is my Father glorified, that ye bear much fruit"* (John 15:8). That fruit, of course, is the fruit the Holy Spirit produces in us. Note again the beautiful garment of the high priest. Right next to each bell was a pomegranate. And right next to the profession should be the practice.

The Fruit of Knowing the Book

Will you follow me now for just a moment?

We say today in our fundamental circles, "We believe in the plenary, verbal inspiration of the Bible." Do you? Well, how about the pomegranates? What do you know about the Book? May I say it has almost become a hideous travesty to hear a fundamentalist say today, "I believe the Bible from cover to cover," when he doesn't even know what is between the covers! If you are going to ring the bell that says, "I believe the Book," then, my friend, why not know it? Why not have a pomegranate along with it? Why not make the Word of God real and living in your own life? Paul wrote to a young preacher: *"Study to show thyself approved unto God, a workman that needeth not to be ashamed, rightly dividing the word of truth"* (2 Timothy 2:15).

We who are dispensational and those who are opposed to us have spent a great deal of time arguing about "rightly dividing the word of truth," but that does not happen to be the important phrase in this verse. In the Greek language the important word is always put first in a sentence. They could shift any word into first place, and that would make it the important word. The word that is leading the parade here is *study,* not "rightly dividing the word of truth." I'm getting a little impatient as I keep listening to people constantly talking about rightly dividing. What I'd like to know is how much time do you spend studying the Book? It's one thing to say, "I believe it's the Word of God." It's another thing to know the Book. And believe

45

me, in this hour even fundamentalists are woefully ignorant of the Bible. At one time a dozen preachers conferred together about going through the entire Bible in their churches, and their concern was: "Will I be able to keep ahead of the folk? Will I be able to present the entire Bible? After all, I've never been through it myself!" May I say to you, in our circles today we are woefully ignorant of the Word of God. It is wonderful to believe in the plenary, verbal inspiration of Scripture—let's ring the bell! But it is nice to have a pomegranate to go along with it. On the high priest's robe there was always a bell and a pomegranate, a bell and pomegranate.

The Fruit of Love for Christ

Notice the next one: the person of Christ. We say we believe that Jesus was God manifest in the flesh. I have another question to ask. Do you know Him? Paul the Apostle said, *"That I may know him, and the power of his resurrection, and the fellowship of his sufferings, being made conformable unto his death"* (Philippians 3:10).

I'm convinced that, not only in this life but in eternity, you and I will not fully know Him; yet I believe that our chief occupation in eternity will be to become acquainted with Jesus Christ. I can't conceive of an occupation that is higher than to know Him. It's one thing to believe upon Christ Jesus as your Savior; it's another thing to know Him today as your Great High Priest up yonder, your Lord and your Master, to know Him as the one who is coming some day as the Bridegroom. It's important to ring the bell of the deity of Christ, but is knowing Him our ambition? Is that the direction we're moving today?

More than that, there is the question that Jesus himself asks. After His crucifixion and resurrection, but before His ascension, Jesus met often with His disciples. What did He ask of them? Did He say to Peter, "Simon Peter, will you promise now to be true and faithful to Me? If I can count on you now, I want you to feed my sheep." No, our Lord did not say that because He knew He couldn't count on Simon Peter any more than He can count on me. If it were not for the Holy Spirit, I'd deny Him in the next five minutes. The only question He is asking us is the one He asked Simon Peter:

He saith unto him the third time, Simon, son of Jonas, lovest thou me? Peter was grieved because he said unto him the third time, Lovest thou me? And he said unto him, Lord, thou knowest all things; thou knowest that I love thee. Jesus saith unto him, Feed my sheep (John 21:17).

Do you love Him today? Honestly, what is your relationship to Jesus Christ? When Allen Fleece and I were in seminary, we were walking over a red clay hill when that Georgia moon was coming up. Both of us had been talking, but we became silent as we stood and watched the moon rise. For no reason in the world tears filled our eyes. Allen said, "Mac, every night when I go to bed the last thing I do when I pull the cover up is to look up, and I say, 'Lord Jesus, I love you.'"

Do you love Him? It's wonderful to be able to ring the bell declaring your belief in the deity of Christ, but do you have a pomegranate right next to it that tells your love for Him?

The Fruit of a Worthy Walk

As we have seen, we need to speak of the redemptive blood of Christ. You may say, "I've been pardoned by the fact that He shed His blood for me." Fine, but when Paul wrote to a young preacher, he said this to him:

This is a faithful saying, and these things I will that thou affirm constantly, that they which have believed in God might be careful to maintain good works. These things are good and profitable unto men (Titus 3:8).

If you've been saved by the blood of Christ, what about your conduct? Is your conversion showing in your conduct? Are you different from your neighbor? Are you different from the people you go to school with and work with? Or are you telling me you've been washed in the blood of Christ, but you are not different? Paul said to the Ephesians, after having explained their exalted position with Christ, seated with Christ in the heavenlies:

I therefore, the prisoner of the Lord, beseech you that ye walk worthy of the vocation wherewith ye are called, with all lowliness and meekness, with long-suffering, forbearing one another in love; endeavoring to keep the unity of the Spirit in the bond of peace (Ephesians 4:1–3).

"Lowliness and meekness" doesn't mean that you're to be a Mr. Milquetoast. It was said of Moses that he was the meekest man on earth, yet Moses is the one who walked into Pharaoh's court and said, "Let my people go!" Is that meekness? Yes! He is the one who came down from the mountain, saw the people worshipping a golden calf, threw down the stone tablets on which were the Ten Commandments, and broke them. Is that meekness? Yes! That's meekness. But you say, "I thought meekness means that you just get off in a corner and let everybody hit you." No, that's not meekness, that's cowardice—and there is a lot of cowardice today among Christians. Meekness means that without putting yourself forward, you stand for God! Meekness means that you have no irons in the fire for yourself, but the stand you are taking is for God only. When Moses went into the presence of Pharaoh, he went there because God told him to. He did not do it on his own initiative, but he did what God told him to do.

The Fruit of Steadfastness

I come to the last: personal conviction. The little bell doesn't make much noise; but, my beloved, let's make sure that next to it is a pomegranate that presents evidence of our willingness to pay a price for our faith. I know that paying a price is not popular today. I find it increasingly popular in fundamental circles to join the multitudes who are compromising and cutting corners. Although I am concerned about them, I am much more concerned about Vernon McGee because I want to stand for God.

Thank God, there are some who are standing for Him today. I am thinking of a young couple in the nightclub circuit. They were at the top; they made all the big clubs. Then they were converted to Christ. I got very well acquainted with them and counseled them, but I wondered, *Oh, they are so attractive! Will they hold out?* Then he went away to a liberal seminary, and I said, "Oh boy, write him off, write him off, he'll never stand." A number of years went by. I learned that he had taken a pastorate, then one day I met them again. He had gone before his denominational hierarchy. He gave up his standing, he gave up his pension, he gave up everything. He demitted the ministry, declaring, "I cannot compromise!" Thank God for young men like that today! They're not all gone. His wife said, almost weeping, "Dr. McGee, we couldn't go on and compromise." Can you?

All believers are ringing a bell; some are muted and muzzled. Some of them are empty, some of them are vain, some of them are uncertain. What kind of a sound are you making today? A lot of folk are listening to you—your co-workers, your fellow students, your friends, your neighbors, your family. They don't tell you so, but they know the kind of bell you're ringing, and they also know if there is a pomegranate to go with it. May God help us to have both profession and practice in this dark hour in which we live.

4

WHAT IS THIS WORLD COMING TO?

Why do the heathen rage, and the people imagine a vain thing?
The kings of the earth set themselves, and the rulers take counsel to-
gether, against the Lord, and against his anointed, saying,
Let us break their bands asunder, and cast away their cords from us.
He that sitteth in the heavens shall laugh: the Lord shall have them in
derision.
Then shall he speak unto them in his wrath, and vex them in his sore
displeasure.
Yet have I set my king upon my holy hill of Zion.
I will declare the decree: the LORD hath said unto me, Thou art my Son;
this day have I begotten thee.
Ask of me, and I shall give thee the heathen for thine inheritance, and
the uttermost parts of the earth for thy possession.
Thou shalt break them with a rod of iron; thou shalt dash them in
pieces like a potter's vessel.
Be wise now therefore, O ye kings: be instructed, ye judges of the earth.
Serve the LORD with fear, and rejoice with trembling.
Kiss the Son, lest he be angry, and ye perish from the way, when his
wrath is kindled but a little. Blessed are all they that put their trust in
him   (PSALM 2).

I like to think of the second psalm as a television program.

Several years ago, in fact, when television was in its infancy, we had a program in southern California. Since we were inexperienced with this new medium of communication, we asked a couple of Christian friends who were professionals in the field to advise us. They met with us and gave us some valuable advice.

One of the things they recommended was to use not just one camera but two cameras, because we couldn't have a smooth program with only one. Well, television has come a long way since those days.

I notice some of the programs today have as many as five to seven cameras. But it was new then. We turned that over in our minds, especially after we found that the extra camera would cost $250 for thirty minutes each week. I'm Scottish, and I want to tell you, I thought that one over a long time before I decided to do it. But we found that it was very much worthwhile because you do need more than one camera.

When we come to the second psalm, we find that the Spirit of God used two cameras in a dramatic way beyond the imagination of man. One camera is in heaven, and the other camera is on earth. First the camera on earth comes on, and when it does, we hear the voices of the masses. We hear little man speaking his little piece and playing his part—as Shakespeare puts it, "A poor player that struts and frets his hour upon the stage" of life. Little man. Then the camera on earth goes off, the camera in heaven comes on, and we hear God the Father speak. After He speaks, the camera shifts to His right hand, and God the Son speaks and has His part. Then the camera in heaven goes off, the camera on earth comes on again, and God the Holy Spirit has the last word.

CAMERA FOCUS: MANKIND

Now let's watch this presentation. First the camera on earth comes on, and we see mankind. They are put before us here in the first verse with this question: *"Why do the heathen* [Gentiles] *rage, and the people* [Jews] *imagine a vain thing?"*

The word *vain* here means "empty." It means that this which has so enraged the Gentiles and which has brought together mankind in a great mass movement, a great protest movement, will never be fulfilled, will never be accomplished. It is an empty, futile thing that has brought mankind together.

Well, what is it? *"The kings of the earth set themselves* [these are the political rulers]*, and the rulers take counsel together* [these are the religious rulers]*."* Not only do you have the masses of mankind in this protest movement, but also the establishment has joined in with it. Here are the rulers, both religious and political, joining together.

Now what is it they are protesting? Whom are they against?

"Against the LORD, and against his anointed." The word *anointed* here means "Messiah." That is what it is in Hebrew. When the word is brought over in the Greek New Testament, it is *Christos,* and in English *Christ.* Here is a great worldwide movement that is against God and against Christ.

Now when did this movement begin? Scripture lets us know about this. Over in the fourth chapter of the book of Acts, when the first persecution broke out against the church, we're told that the apostles Peter and John, after they had been threatened, returned to the church to give their report. *"And when they* [the church] *heard that, they lifted up their voice to God with one accord, and said, Lord, thou art God"* (v. 24).

We need to pause here just a moment because this is one of the things the church is not sure about today: "Lord, thou art God." Many people are not sure He is God. They wonder. The early church here in the book of Acts had no misgivings or questions. Listen to them pray:

> *Lord, thou art God, which hast made heaven, and earth, and the sea, and all that in them is: who by the mouth of thy servant David hast said, Why did the heathen rage, and the people imagine vain things?* (Acts 4:24–25).

As you can see, they are quoting Psalm 2. *"The kings of the earth stood up, and the rulers were gathered together against the Lord, and against his Christ."* Now this is the Holy Spirit's interpretation: *"For of a truth against thy holy child Jesus, whom thou hast anointed, both Herod, and Pontius Pilate, with the Gentiles, and the people of Israel, were gathered together"* (Acts 4:24–27).

Here is this movement beginning, we are told by the Holy Spirit, back yonder when Pilate joined with the religious rulers and Herod in order to put Jesus to death. This is a movement against God and Christ that has been snowballing as it has come down through the centuries, and it will break out finally in a worldwide revolution against God and against Christ.

Now somebody says to me, "You really don't think the world is moving in that direction, do you?" May I say to you, I think it is. Someone comes to me and asks, "Dr. McGee, do you think the world is getting better?" I say, "Yes, I do." Somebody else comes and says, "Dr. McGee, don't you think the world is getting worse?" I say, "Yes, I do." "Well," you may say, "what in the world are you trying to do? Go with both crowds?" No. Both are true. That is the same thing the Lord Jesus said in His parable of the tares (see Matthew 13:24–39). The Lord Jesus said that He Himself is the sower and that He is sowing seed in the world. Then He said an enemy came in and sowed tares. The servants wanted to go in and pull up the tares.

When I entered the ministry that is what I wanted to do. I was the best puller-upper of tares you've ever seen. But I soon found out that we're not called to pull up tares (I sure found that out the hard way!). That is the reason I don't try to straighten out anybody else. I'm having enough trouble with Vernon McGee, so I don't worry about the others. That is God's business. But what He said was that the wheat is growing, the tares are growing, they are both growing together; and He will do the separating. He will take care of that.

Today the good is growing. Did you know that there is more Bible teaching going out today than in any period in the history of the world? We brag about the radio stations that carry our Bible study, but others have been giving out the Word lots longer than we have. Across the world are many radio stations that are dedicated to the ministry of broadcasting the Word of God. The Word is going out today through many more avenues than it has ever gone out before.

The wheat is growing. But I want to tell you, brother, the tares are growing also. Evil is growing. There is an opposition against God and Christ today that is unbelievable. I could give you many incidents of the enmity that I've encountered. For example, I spoke at the funeral service of Audie Murphy. His wife, Pam, is a marvelous, wonderful Christian. She sent word to me before the funeral service to encourage me. She said, "You will be in enemy territory today." Believe me, I was. That Hollywood crowd resisted. Oh, how they hated it. They did not want to hear it. There is an enmity against the Word of God today.

Somebody says, "I just can't quite buy that. I believe that over there on the other side of the Iron Curtain atheism is growing, but not on this side." Well, it is growing on the other side, and it is rather amazing. Did you know that you and I have seen in our lifetime (those of you who are as old as I am) a nation appear whose basic philosophy, basic political economy, is atheism? There has been nothing like that in the past. No nation of the ancient world, that great pagan world of the past, was atheistic. Not one.

Somebody says, "I thought they were." No, they were the opposite. They were polytheistic. They worshipped many gods. None was atheistic. You see, they were too close to the mooring mast of revelation. Noah knew a man who knew Adam. When you are that close to it, you do not deny God. In Noah's day the world was filled with violence, but there wasn't an atheist in the crowd. When God gave the Ten Commandments He didn't give any one of them against atheism. He gave two against polytheism:

Thou shalt have no other gods before me. Thou shalt not make unto thee any graven image, or any likeness of any thing that is in heaven above, or that is in the earth beneath, or that is in the water under the earth (Exodus 20:3, 4).

He gave these two commandments against polytheism, none against atheism. Why? There were no atheists.

Now when you get to the time of David, you meet atheists, and there were a great many atheists by that time. David labels them, though. He says, "The fool hath said in his heart, There is no God" (Psalm 14:1). The word *fool* in the Hebrew means "insane." The insane, the nutty individual, is the one who is the atheist. Of course, he may be a Ph.D. in a university, but he's a nutty individual. The Bible says he is insane. It is insane for a man to say there is no God. A friend of mine had a marvelous ministry with atheists. He was in a crowd one day where a big-mouthed fellow was saying, "I do not believe there is a God. I think that when man dies, he's just like a dog. He dies and that's it." This friend of mine, a very courteous man, said, "Did I understand you to say that you don't believe there is a God?"

"Yes."

"Are you an atheist?"

"Yes."

"Well, I have a question to ask you. The Bible says that the fool, the insane, is the one who says there is no God. Now either you were insincere when you made the statement; you didn't really mean it, or else you're insane. Would you tell me which way it is?"

It has to be one way or the other when a man says there is no God. But, you see, we've come a long way since David's day!

There is, I believe, as much opposition to Jesus Christ on this side of the Iron Curtain as there is on the other side of the Iron Curtain today. I believe that with all my heart. There is opposition against Jesus Christ. Somebody says, "Wait a minute. I hear many talk about Jesus, and how wonderful Jesus is." Have you ever stopped to think that the Jesus of liberalism, the Jesus the world thinks of, actually never lived? The Jesus of the Bible and the Jesus of liberalism are two different individuals. And the Jesus of liberalism never lived at all.

Let me give you an example of what I mean. For many years when I was a pastor in downtown Los Angeles the leading liberal in this country pastored a church nearby. Actually I had great respect for him because he was one liberal who was honest. For instance, he would just come out flatfooted and say he did not believe in the virgin birth. And if you don't believe it, I'd like for you to say it and not beat around the bush. He had a question and answer program on radio; I had a question and answer program on radio. And listeners would feed questions to both of us to set us in opposition. Every year we went through that same little ritual during the Christmas season. I always enjoyed it. So one time we both were invited to a banquet, and (I think it was done purposely) we were seated together. I got there first and sat down. I saw his name there. In a minute he came in. I felt somebody put his arm around me and say, "You know, Brother McGee, you and I ought to be much closer together. We preach the same Jesus," and he sat down. I said to him, "Are you sure we preach the same Jesus?"

"Oh, don't we?"

"I don't think so. Let me ask you some questions. Was the Jesus you preach virgin born?"

"Of course not."

"Well, the one I preach is virgin born. The Jesus you preach—did He perform miracles?"

"I do not believe in miracles."

"Well, the Jesus I preach performed miracles. The Jesus you preach—did He die on a cross for the sins of the world?"

"Of course He died on a cross, but not for the sins of the world."

"The Jesus I preach died a substitutionary, vicarious death for the sins of man. Do you believe that Jesus rose bodily?"

"Oh, no, of course not."

"Obviously then, you and I are not preaching about the same Jesus. Now I want to ask you a question." You see, these liberal men have called some of us fundamentalists "intellectual obscurantists." (Now whatever that is, it's terrible!) So I said to him, "Look, what are the documents or where are the documents for the Jesus you preach?" He laughed, just laughed and passed it off.

"Of course we don't have any."

"Now isn't that interesting. We have documents for the Jesus we preach, and you don't—yet you call *us* intellectual obscurantists. I'd like to know who *is* an intellectual obscurantist!"

May I say to you, my friend, the Jesus that the world believes in today doesn't even exist. He never lived. The Jesus we preach is the Jesus of the Bible, and that is the one against whom there is opposition in the world. There is a tremendous build-up, a mighty crescendo of opposition against God and against Christ in this day in which we live.

Now how does it manifest itself? Exactly as He said it would. Notice again the second psalm. Hear what the heathen are saying: *"Let us break their bands asunder, and cast away their cords from us"*. What are some of the bands God has put on the human family? Marriage is one. God has made marriage for the welfare of mankind. Whether you are a Christian or not, God has given marriage to mankind. Today they not only *want* to get rid of it, they *are* getting rid of it.

I was rather shocked several years ago. I'm a square. I'm not really keeping up with it today, so I don't follow along in the way they are going in this modern thinking relative to God, relative to man, and relative to the Word of God. So I was startled at a young people's conference when the sweetest little girl got up in our question and answer period and said, "Dr. McGee, why does a young couple have to get married if they love each other? Why can't they just start living together?" God gave marriage, and God intends for it to be followed. But they say, "Let's break their bands asunder."

Also, "Let's cast away their cords from us." The Ten Commandments are cords. When somebody accuses me of saying that we don't need the Ten Commandments, they are wrong. We are not saved by keeping them—I tried it, and it won't work—but I'll say this: God gave them, and He gave them to protect mankind. They are thrown out the door today, and right now we are experiencing lawlessness in this country because of the fact that crime is not being punished.

There has been a terrible toll of lives that would not have been sacrificed had laws been enforced. You see, we are living in a day when the prevailing philosophy is, "Let us break their bands asunder, let's cast away their cords from us. We want to be free and do as we please." God says we can't make it that way. It won't work. We've got old evil natures that need to be restrained. But mankind is moving toward getting rid of all restraints today.

It is disturbing as we look at this world in which we are living. In the political world there is confusion. In the moral realm there is corruption. In the spiritual sphere there is compromise and indifference. And in the social sphere there is comfort. This affluent society never had it so easy, and the goal is to make it more easy. We are living in that kind of a day. It is disturbing, and I'll be honest with you, I do worry about it a little.

CAMERA FOCUS: GOD THE FATHER

The question arises, how does God feel about this? Do you suppose that God as He looks down at this little earth has moved over to the edge of His throne, is biting His fingernails, and saying, "Oh, my, look down there. They've slipped away from me completely"? Is there that kind of disturbance today in heaven? Of course not. May I say to you, there is perfect calm around the throne of God. God is not disturbed today. God is not biting His fingernails. He has not developed an ulcer. God is going on with His plan and program.

Notice now the fourth verse of the second psalm. The camera on earth goes off; the camera in heaven comes on: *"He that sitteth in the heavens shall laugh: the Lord shall have them in derision."* What kind of laughter is this? Let me say at the outset that it is not the laughter of humor. He is not being funny.

Do not misunderstand me—there is humor in the Bible. The devil has really hit a home run by making people think that going to church is quite an ordeal. We are living in a day when folk think you can't have fun in church. I think the Bible is full of humor. Those of you who study with us through the Bible know we find a lot of it. There used to be a dear maiden lady at a church I served who never found any humor in the Bible. When I gave a message which cited some humorous incident, she used to come down, shake a bony finger under my nose, and say, "Dr. McGee, you are being irreverent to find humor in the Bible." I said to her, "Don't you wish you could?" She's gone now to be with the Lord, and I certainly hope she's had a good laugh since she has been there, because she has gone to the place where she can have a good time. She needs to have a good time—she never had one down here. There are too many Christians like that today. My friend, it is going to be thrilling to be with Him some day. We're going to have a wonderful time with Him. It's going to be fun, and I'm looking forward to that. God has a sense of humor, and there is humor in His Word.

By the way, have you ever gone to a zoo with the thought of God's humor in mind? Look at the amimals He has made. He had to have a sense of humor to make some of them as He's made them. God has a sense of humor. And if you still doubt me, stand on a busy street corner and watch the folk go by. My friend, God has a sense of humor! Then if you still have doubts, close the door to your room and look in the mirror, and you'll see what I mean. God has a sense of humor. He made the lot of us, my friend.

However, God's laughter in the second psalm is not that of humor. *"He that sitteth in the heavens shall laugh."* What is it? Well, look at it from God's viewpoint—little man down there parading up and down, shaking his midget first in heaven's face and saying, "Come on out and fight me! I'm against you." God looks down at the puny little creature. It's utterly preposterous. It is so ridiculous! He looks down and laughs. *"He that sitteth in the heavens shall laugh: the Lord shall have them in derision."*

My friend, it is insane to oppose the living and true God! A man must be mad who would do a thing like that. *"Then shall he speak unto them in his wrath, and vex them in his sore displeasure"* (v. 5). This is the judgment that is coming upon this earth.

God is going forward to the accomplishment of His purpose. What little man does down here won't deter Him, detour Him, or defer Him at all. God did not read something in the morning paper that He didn't already know about. There is nothing that has surprised Him at all. He is moving according to His purpose. He has, I believe, a twofold purpose in this world. I think He has a heavenly purpose; I think He has an earthly purpose. Right now He is working on His heavenly purpose. The writer to the Hebrews (in 2:10) expresses this: He is *"bringing many sons home to glory."* God today is calling out of this world a people to His name. That is His present purpose.

However, God has another purpose, and it is stated here: *"Yet have I set my king upon my holy hill of Zion"* (v. 6). God is moving forward today undeviatingly, unhesitatingly, uncompromisingly to the establishment of that throne on which Jesus Christ will sit on this earth. When I hear folk say, "If the Lord delay His coming." Where in the world did that get in? He is not delaying anything. He is going to come on schedule, His schedule, not mine, because I don't know when He is coming. He is running on schedule and nothing will stop Him; nothing can cause Him to change His plan.

CAMERA FOCUS: GOD THE SON

Now the camera in heaven shifts to God the Son on His right hand. *"I will declare the decree . . ."* Those of you who have studied theology know that the Lord Jesus executes all the decrees of God. *"I will declare the decree: the LORD hath said unto me, Thou art my Son; this day have I begotten thee"* (v. 7).

This is a verse that the Jehovah Witnesses use a great deal. I wish they would listen long enough to find out what it means. It would help them to find it has no reference to the birth of the Lord Jesus Christ, which they would see if only they would turn to the New Testament and let the Spirit of God interpret. This verse was quoted by the apostle Paul when he preached in Antioch of Pisidia. This is, I believe, one of his greatest sermons, and he is talking about the resurrection of Jesus Christ:

God hath fulfilled the same unto us their children, in that he hath raised up Jesus again; as it is also written in the second psalm, Thou art my Son, this day have I begotten thee (Acts 13:33).

The reference in the second psalm is not to the birth of Jesus. He never was begotten in the sense of having a beginning. He is the eternal Son of God, and God the Father is the eternal Father. They had no beginning; they were this throughout eternity. This is their position in the Trinity. It hasn't anything to do with someone being born, but it does have something to do with someone being begotten from the dead. It has to do with resurrection. I'm afraid the Jehovah Witnesses have not heard this, but they could find with a little honest searching that the New Testament makes it very clear Jesus Christ is not a creature. He is the theanthropic person. He is the God-man. Psalm 2:7 sustains this doctrine.

God the Father continues: *"Ask of me, and I shall give thee the heathen for thine inheritance, and the uttermost parts of the earth for thy possession"* (v. 8). The scepter of this universe will be held by a man with nail-pierced hands. He is the one who is yet to rule.

This verse is often used in missionary conferences. I suppose I have heard a dozen sermons on missions using this verse of Scripture— and probably you have too. But it ought never to go to a missionary conference. It hasn't anything to do with missions. I remember listening to a graduate of Union Theological Seminary in New York City bring a missionary message using this verse. I was then a student in seminary. As a student I did something that was very impolite, very rude. I think I've got more sense than to do it today. I went up to him after he had preached the message, and I asked, "Doctor, why didn't you use the next verse?" He acted as if he didn't hear me, although I am sure he did, and began talking with somebody there. I said to him the second time, "Doctor, why didn't you use the next verse?" This time he turned his back on me, and just ignored me. Well, I should have left, but I didn't. I walked around in front, and I said to him, "Doctor, why didn't you use the next verse?" He looked me right straight in the eye and said, "Because it would have ruined a missionary sermon." And it sure would have!

Notice the next verse, the verse that follows it: *"Thou shalt break them with a rod of iron; thou shalt dash them in pieces like a potter's vessel"* (v. 9). Do you think this is the gospel of the grace of God we are to preach today? It is not. This passage hasn't any reference to Christ's first coming. This speaks of His second coming, when He comes to this earth to judge.

This is the way He will come the second time—to judge the earth. He has not asked me to apologize for Him, so I won't apologize. He says that He intends to come to this little planet and put down the rebellion that has broken out—and He will break them with the rod of iron. Maybe you don't like that. Well, you take it up with Him. He said it, and He is going to do it just that way.

Now I have a question to ask you, if you think He ought to do it the way some of our political leaders are suggesting. Suppose Jesus came back to this earth tomorrow like He came over 1900 years ago, the man of Galilee, the carpenter of Nazareth, the gentle Jesus. Suppose He were here. Suppose He went to the Kremlin and knocked at the door. Whoever keeps the store over there would come and say, "Yes?" He would say, "I'm Jesus. I'm here to take over." Do you think they would say, "My, we have been waiting for you"? No, they'd put Him before a firing squad in the morning. My friend, how do you think He could take over if He came to Russia today? He would have to break them with a rod of iron, would He not? Apparently that is what He is going to do.

Now suppose He goes to France. DeGaulle is not there anymore, but some ambitious men are there. They don't want Him. Suppose He went down to Rome. I was there just a few weeks ago. I went over the Tiber and listened to a man speak. Although I could not understand what he was saying, I was told that he was telling the world how it ought to act. He would like to take over. Suppose our Lord would go and knock on the door of the Vatican. The man with the long garment would come to the door, and the Lord Jesus would say, "I'm here to take over." What do you think he would say? I think he would say, "Now look, You've come a little too soon. I'm having trouble with some of my priests; they want to get married, but I'm going to work that out. I don't need You." I don't think he would want Him.

Suppose He came to this country. Suppose He went to the Democratic headquarters or the Republican headquarters and said, "I'm here to take over." They would say, "We're getting ready for a presidential campaign; we've already got our candidates; we don't need You." Now maybe you think their reaction would be different. Maybe you are saying, "Oh, they would take Him." Then why don't they take Him? They do not because they won't have Him! Suppose He went to the World Council of Churches today, and He said to Protestantism, "I'm here." Would they receive Him? Then why don't they receive Him today?

My friend, when He comes the second time, He will come exactly as God said, *"Thou shalt break them with a rod of iron; thou shalt dash them in pieces like a potter's vessel."* He intends to put down the rebellion when He comes to this earth the next time. Oh, my friend, this namby-pamby way of thinking that our God is not going to judge! You and I are living in a world that is moving to judgment day, and God is going to judge.

CAMERA FOCUS: GOD THE HOLY SPIRIT

The camera in heaven goes off. The camera on earth comes on. Now God the Holy Spirit speaks: *"Be wise now therefore, O ye kings: be instructed, ye judges of the earth. Serve the LORD with fear, and rejoice with trembling"* (vv. 10, 11).

One of the most startling things I have encountered in studying the Bible the past few years is a little thing like this: God in the history of this world has always gotten a message to the rulers of this world. Always. No exception. Down yonder in the land of Egypt, ancient Egypt, there was a Pharaoh on the throne; there was a boy in prison. God kept him in prison so that at the right moment He could bring him out to make him the prime minister of Pharaoh at one of the most crucial periods in the history of the world. That is the way God does it.

Down yonder when the first great world power came into existence, Babylon, God put at the side of Nebuchadnezzar the man Daniel. He not only became his prime minister, but he also brought him to a saving knowledge of the living God. And God kept him there until Cyrus, the Persian, came to the throne. And Cyrus even made his decree in the name of the living God. Napoleon said that he was a man of destiny, that he was told God had raised him up. It is interesting how God has gotten His Word to the rulers of this earth.

In passing let me just mention a more contemporary example of this. I had heard that before the late John F. Kennedy went to Texas he'd had an interview with Billy Graham for about three hours. I had not been with Billy nor seen any member of the team for two or three years until I was in Florida at a banquet where I was seated next to Grady Wilson. I said, "Grady, I've been waiting to ask some of you who know about this. Is it true that Billy had an interview with Jack Kennedy for three hours?" He said, "It is true that he had an interview, but the time is wrong. He was with him for eight hours." Some of the questions they discussed were these: What is the difference between my church and your church? What is this that you preach about Jesus coming back again? God has a way of getting the message in to the rulers of the world, those who are in high places.

God the Holy Spirit says to the rulers: *"Serve the LORD with fear, and rejoice with trembling."* Also He says: *"Kiss the Son, lest he be angry, and ye perish from the way, when his wrath is kindled but a little. Blessed are all they that put their trust in him"* (v. 12). The late Dr. George Gill used to tell us in class, "'Kiss the Son' is the Old Testament way of saying, 'Believe on the Lord Jesus Christ, and thou shalt be saved' (Acts 16:31)."

Do you remember who kissed Him? Have you ever noted what our Lord said to Judas after he kissed Him? The theologians today argue about predestination, election, predetermination, and foreknowledge, and that this man Judas could not help what he did since it had been prophesied he would do it. Now I'm going to let the theologians handle that. I'm just a poor preacher who doesn't know very much, so I stay away from those problems and let the theologians solve them. However, after I listen to them a while, I have a sneaking feeling they haven't solved them.

Notice what the Bible says, and it is well to listen to the Bible rather than to the theologians. Remember at Jesus' betrayal when Judas led the mob out to apprehend Jesus in the garden, he said, "I'll identify him for you by kissing Him." So he came to Jesus and kissed Him. Have you noted what Jesus said to him? *"And Jesus said unto him, Friend, wherefore art thou come?"* (Matthew 26:50). Why did He say that? Didn't He know why Judas had kissed Him? Of course

He did. Then why did He call him *friend?* What does He mean? Let me suggest this: "Judas, you have just kissed Me which has fulfilled prophecy and has satisfied all the theologians who are going to come along. Now you are free to turn and accept Me, free to turn that kiss of betrayal into a kiss of acceptance. You can do that, Judas. You are a free moral agent." And the Spirit of God says, "Kiss the Son. Believe on the Lord Jesus Christ, and thou shalt be saved."

My friend, the Spirit of God today is in the world saying to mankind, "Kiss the Son before it is too late. Believe on the Lord Jesus Christ before it is too late. He is coming some day, and He is going to establish His kingdom here upon this earth. He is going to rule, and He is going to put down all rebellion. He will bring peace and harmony to this little earth."

AN ILLUSTRATION FROM LIFE

When I first went to Nashville, Tennessee, as a pastor, some friends, thinking they were doing me a favor, called me and said, "We have tickets for the Philadelphia Symphony Orchestra (I think it was) that's coming to town, and we want to take you as our guest." Well, I love music, but I know nothing about it, and I can't sing it—I always help congregational singing by keeping quiet. Frankly, I can't think of anything more boring than a whole evening of symphony! But I had to go because they were polite and I wanted to be polite, so I accepted graciously and went along.

I had never been to a thing like that before, and I was impressed by what I saw. We went in, took our seats, and in a few moments there began to drift out from the sides the musicians. They were in shirt sleeves for the most part, and each man went up to his instrument and started tuning it. The fellows with the fiddles too big to put under their chins sawed back and forth—oh, it sounded terrible. The fellows with the little ones they put under their chins squeaked up and down with those. The ones with the horns—oh my, nothing was in harmony. It was a medley of discordant, confused noise. Then after they got through with that kind of a disturbance, they all disappeared again, went out through the wings.

Another five minutes went by when all of a sudden the lights in the auditorium went off, the lights on the platform came on, and the musicians walked out. This time they had on their coats. My, they looked so nice. Each one came out and stood or sat at his instrument. Then there was a hush in the auditorium, a spotlight was focused on the wings, and the conductor stepped out. When he did, there was thunderous applause for him. He bowed. Then he came up to the podium and picked up a thin little stick. He turned around again to the audience and bowed, then turned his back to the audience, lifted that little stick—total silence came over that auditorium, you could have heard a pin drop—then he brought that little stick down. And, my friend, there were goose pimples all over me. I never heard such music in all my life. Oh, what harmony, what wonderful harmony there was!

Today I live in a world where every man is tooting his own little horn. Every little group wants to be heard. Everybody wants to tell you what he thinks. Everybody is playing his own little fiddle; and I want to tell you, it's a medley of discord. Everything is out of tune. But one of these days the spotlight is going on, and the Lord Jesus Christ will come. When He comes to this universe, He is going to lift His scepter, and everything that is out of tune with Him is going to be removed. Then when He comes down with that scepter—oh, the harmony that will be in this universe! I'm thankful today that I do live in a universe where I can bow to Him; I can bring this little instrument of my body, my life, into tune with Him. I can bow to Him; I can acknowledge Him; I can make Him my Savior and Lord.

I said to a young fellow one summer at Mount Hermon, a hippie type, but a very sweet boy, "Why in the world do you dress like that?"

"I want you to know I'm in rebellion, and I'm living my own life and doing as I please," he said.

"I want to ask you something. If you took off that garb and dressed like a straight fellow would dress, would your crowd accept you?"

"No."

"Then you're not free, are you? You can't dress like you want to. You have to dress like they want you to. Look at me. I can dress like you or dress as I do. I'm free! You say you are free. I'm free. I have bowed to Jesus Christ. That is freedom."

I live in a world where He is rejected. I live in a world where the majority is not going with Him. I'm going with Him, and I'm going to bow to Him. He is my Savior and He is my Lord.

How about you?

5

WHAT IS WORSHIP?

Psalms 96; 150

On next Lord's day morning, if the ministers over this land of ours were to ask this question: "How many of you have ever worshiped God?" no doubt virtually every hand would be lifted. Therefore, it would be presumptuous, would it not, for me to say that very few people have actually worshiped God? But there are some Christians who have never really worshiped Him. We feel that is revealed today in the lack of vitality and vigor in our worship. It is a fact that public worship is anemic and aimless for the most part. It is further reflected in a lack of meaning and an abysmal ignorance of worship. It has been reduced to an empty shell and a hollow sham of ritual and cold liturgy—no warmth of life, just cold form! This, in a day when folk are saying, "We want reality in our Christian faith, we want reality in experience."

There is a rather amusing story that comes out of the days when oil was first found in East Texas. Several dirt farmers who had been on the very margin of starvation found themselves overwhelmed with untold riches. One such family that had been extremely poor became virtual millionaires overnight. As usual, they wanted to go the limit and make up for all the things they had been missing in life, so the wife in the family went to the beauty parlor. She wanted the "whole works." And when the beauty operator asked, "Do you want a shampoo?" she arose indignantly and said, "I do not want a shampoo; I want a genuine poo."

69

And so in the matter of worship, people are tired of the sham, the substitute; they want reality. We have probably examined a bin of books on the subject of worship, most of which have not actually dealt with the heart of the subject at all. They have to do with the accessories, the adjuncts, the accouterments that go with it. Generally there is a chapter on "Preaching" and one on "Music," perhaps one on "Lighting and Ventilation"; and then one on "Prayer" and one on "Reading the Scripture." But, in the strict sense, that is not worship. It may contribute to worship, but it is not worship.

Again there comes to us the story of the "flying field" which we have used with reference to prayer. The "flying field," known today as "the airport," no more flies than the "horseflies." Nevertheless, they were originally called "flying fields." It was tragic when a plane attempted to fly on the field, for it was only a taking-off place, and the flying was to be done up yonder in the air. The church is called a place of worship; actually it is the house of worship. But worship is not really done there; it is the place from which we take off. Worship is done up yonder.

Sometimes we just go out to the field and warm up the motor, race down to the end of the runway, and come home and say we have been to church and have worshiped God. We have not worshiped Him at all. But do not misunderstand this statement. I believe that we should go to the house of God where people are to worship Him because it is the "taking-off" place, and we are more apt to worship God in church than in nature. We are more apt to worship God in the singing of the hymn "There Is a Green Hill Far Away" than on the third green of the golf course. We are more apt to worship God in John 6, the feeding of the five thousand, than at a picnic lunch on a mountainside some Lord's Day morning. We are more apt to worship God by Lake Gennesaret than at Lake Arrowhead. We are more apt to worship God by the Sea of Galilee than down at Redondo Beach. We are more apt to worship God on the road to Emmaus than on Highway 66. We are more apt to worship God in the Gospel of Matthew than in our city's evening paper. But remember, it is possible for us to go to God's house and not worship Him at all.

THE OBJECT OF WORSHIP

We want to note several of the major aspects involved in worship, the first of which is the *object* of worship. This will require that we answer, in a general sort of way, the question, "What is worship?" To do this we shall deal with one statement found in Psalm 150:1: "Praise ye the Lord." We find in this first aspect that the emphasis is on "Praise ye the LORD." He is to be the object of worship. If He is the object of worship, we would do well to define worship at this point. We realize that in giving a definition we are using a crutch, and crutches are for cripples. But how else can we understand worship unless we begin with a definition?

Attempting to define worship is, for us, much the same problem as that of the soldier stationed on the West Coast when his mother, a native of Kansas, wrote saying: "When you come home, please bring a souvenir that will tell me something of the Pacific Ocean about which I have heard so much." And he took her a bottle of sea water.

Now that bottle of sea water may have said something about the ocean, but it told nothing of its vastness, of the breakers along the shore, nothing of the beauty of the sunlight on the whitecaps. It told nothing of the things of the deep, of the breeze that gently hovers. But such are the limits of a definition.

However, we know that the root of the word *worship* goes back to an Anglo-Saxon word meaning "worth." Webster defined worship as "courtesy or reverence that is paid to worth." We can see the carry-over of this Anglo-Saxon word in our courts today in the manner in which the attorneys address the judge on the bench. They call him, "Your worship." The intent is to show courtesy to someone who represents the law—courtesy or reverence that is paid to that of worth.

That is what worship is. It is courtesy or reverence that is paid to worth. Listen to the psalmist as he does this very thing in Psalm 96, the great singing psalm that shall be used in the eternal ages which lie before us. It reads:

For the LORD is great, and greatly to be praised: he is to be feared above all gods. For all the gods of the nations are idols: but the LORD made the heavens. Honour and majesty are be-

71

fore him: strength and beauty are in his sanctuary. Give unto the
LORD, O ye kindreds of the people, give unto the LORD glory
and strength. Give unto the LORD the glory due unto his name:
bring an offering, and come into his courts (Psalm 96:4–8).

We have here this great psalm which David composed when the
ark was brought into the sanctuary in Zion. And it is one of those
great psalms of praise and adoration of God. Someone has said that
an apple a day will keep the doctor away, but a psalm a day will keep
worry away. And here is one of those psalms that will keep worry
away. This psalm removes, as do the first two commandments, all
competitors from the field of worship. God said to man, "Thou shalt
have no other gods before me." There is no competitor. God has
none in this matter of worship. He recognizes none. He has a monopoly on this matter of worship. He alone is to be praised, He
alone is to receive adoration from man, and He says, "Thou shalt not
make unto thee any graven image, or any likeness," or anything that
represents deity at all. God stands alone in the field and alone is
worthy of worship. He is worthy of all your adoration and praise.

The Psalms put the emphasis upon two things: the fact that He is
the *Creator* and the fact that He is the *Redeemer*. God made this
earth on which we live, as well as the universe. This lovely sunshine
that you are enjoying is His. He is the Creator. There is not a thing at
your finger tips that He did not make. He is worthy today of our
worship because He is the Creator. He is also worthy of our worship
because He is the Redeemer. He is the *only* Creator and He is the
only Redeemer. You see, God works in a field where He has no competition at all. He has a monopoly on the field of creation and on the
field of redemption, and because of that He claims from all of His
creatures their worship, their adoration, their praise.

The Scriptures say that God is a jealous God. I can't find where He
asks us to apologize for Him for this. He has created us for Himself.
He has redeemed us for Himself. On the human level marriage is
used to illustrate the believers' relationship to Christ. A husband, if
he loves his wife, does not share her with other men. He is jealous of
her. Her love is to be for him alone. So believers, called in Scripture
the bride of Christ, are created solely for Him. He doesn't like for us
to give our hearts to anyone else except to Him. He alone is to have

our adoration, and He alone is to have our praise today. And you will recall that John, on the Isle of Patmos, felt constrained to fall down and worship the angel who had been so helpful in bringing all of the visions before him, but the angel rebuked him and said, "See thou do it not; worship God." He does not even want His angels worshiped; He does not want Mary worshiped! He wants none worshiped but Himself. He alone is *worthy* of worship, and He says there is coming a day when, "Let everything that hath breath praise the Lord." He has created everything that it might praise Him.

WHO IS TO WORSHIP?

And here we come to the second aspect, objections to worship. God is the *object* of worship. There are, however, *objections* to worship. And in this we must answer the question Who can worship? Will you notice our verse again? It is very brief: "Praise YE the Lord." The emphasis now is upon *ye*. He is saying to mankind, "Praise YE the Lord." God apparently created man for one purpose, to have fellowship with and to praise Him. There is no other reason for man's existence. What is the chief end of man? Man's chief end is to glorify God and enjoy Him forever.

God created the universe that it might glorify Him. It was not brought into existence for you and me. Job says in chapter 38, verse 7 that "When the morning stars sang together they were praising God." And the psalmist says in Psalm 96:5, *"But the LORD made the heavens."* He made the heavens that they might be a musical instrument to sing forth His praises throughout the eternal ages of the future. You know man was created for that high purpose, but he got out of harmony and out of tune with God; he got out of fellowship with God. Perhaps Shakespeare expressed it when he wrote in *The Merchant of Venice:*

> There's not the smallest orb which thou behold'st
> But in his motion like an angel sings,
> Still quiring to the young-eyed cherubims.
> Such harmony is in immortal souls;
> But, whilst this muddy vesture of decay
> Doth grossly close it in, we cannot hear it.

Today you and I are living in a created universe that is actually singing praises to God. But man is out of tune. Man is in discord, and God's great purpose is to bring man back into the harmony of heaven.

I want to move into the realm of music about which I know nothing but have made careful inquiry. And I am reliably informed that on every good organ there are four principal stops. There is the main stop known as "diapason," then there is the "flute" stop, the "string" stop, and then the "vox humana," the human voice. I am told that that stop is very seldom in tune. If you put it in tune while the auditorium is cold, it would be out of tune when the auditorium is heated. And if you put it in tune when the auditorium is heated, it would be out of tune when the auditorium got cold. My beloved, it is hard to keep "vox humana" in tune.

This great universe of God is a mighty instrument, and one day Jesus Christ went to the console of God's great organ—His creation—and He pulled out the stop known as "diapason." And when He pulled that stop out, the solar and stellar spaces broke into mighty song. Then He reached down and pulled out the "flute" stop, and these little feathered friends, the birds, began to sing. Then He reached in and pulled the "string" stop, and light went humming across God's universe and the angels lifted their voices in praise. Then He reached down and pulled out "vox humana," but it was out of tune.

Now the great Organist was not only a musician, but He knew how to repair the organ. So He left the console of the organ yonder in heaven and came down to this earth, that through redemption— the giving of His own life—He might bring man back into harmony with God's tremendous creation. And, my beloved, the redeemed are the ones today who are to lift their voices in praise. They are the only ones that can. The psalmist says again, *"Oh, give thanks unto the LORD, for he is good; for his mercy endureth forever"* (Psalm 106:1). *"Let the redeemed of the LORD say so"* (Psalm 107:2). And, brother, if they don't say so, no one will! Oh, to be in tune with heaven! Today sin has intruded into this world and has taken man out of God's choir, but he can come back in—and many have—through Jesus Christ, the Son of David, his Creator and Redeemer. The Lord Jesus has brought man back into a redemptive and right relationship with God that he might lift his voice in praise to Him.

WHY WORSHIP?

There is the object of worship: God. There are objections of worship: man. And there are *objectives* of worship, and we want to answer the question now: Why worship? Here we move our emphasis in this verse from "Praise YE the Lord" to "PRAISE ye the Lord." Move it over to the verb—to that which is active. "PRAISE ye the Lord." Perhaps you are beginning to see why we said at the beginning that very few people actually worship God. There really is no such thing as public worship. It was the great Chrysostom who put it like this: "The angels glorify, men scrutinize; angels raise their voices in praise, man in disputation; they conceal their faces with their wings, but man with a presumptuous gaze would look into Thine unspeakable glory." Today how many actually go to the church to worship? Some person, in a very facetious manner, said that some people go to church to eye the clothes, and others to close their eyes. How many go to church in order that they might worship God? Worship is a divine intoxication, and if you don't believe that, there is a fine illustration of it. On the day of Pentecost Simon Peter got up and preached a sermon. We talk a great deal about that sermon, but actually it was an explanation to the people that these Spirit-filled men were not drunk at all. Drunkenness was not the explanation. How many people today would get the impression that *we* are intoxicated with God? We need an ecclesiastical ecstasy. We need a theological thrill in this day in which we live.

There are three words that we must associate with worship, and these three words denote an experience of the human heart and the human soul as it comes into God's presence to worship.

Prostration

The first is *prostration*. In the Orient people are accustomed to getting down on their faces. In the West we talk a great deal about having a dignified service. Now don't misunderstand me; we are not contending for a posture of the body. Victor Hugo once said that the soul is on its knees many times regardless of the position of the body. We are not trying to insist on a posture of the body, but we need to have our *souls* prostrated before God.

Two Bible words are used. The Hebrew word *hishtahaweh* actually means to "bow the neck." The Greek word *proskuneo* means to "bow the knee" to God. And today we need to get down on our faces before God in heaven. In the book of Revelation there are some things we don't understand about heaven, but there is one thing we are sure about—that every time we read of those in heaven, they are either getting down on their faces or getting up off their faces from worshiping God. And, friend, if you don't like to worship God, you wouldn't like heaven anyway, because that is the thing with which they are occupied; most of the time they are worshiping God, prostrating themselves before Him on their faces. Beloved, we need that today.

When my spiritual life gets frayed and fuzzy at the edges and begins to tear at the seams, I like to get alone, to get down on my face before Him and pour out my heart to Him. Friend, when was the last time you got down on your face before God? When was the last time that you prostrated yourself before Him? Oh, it would do us good; it would deliver us from deep freeze; it would deliver us from the shell in which we live; it would create within our hearts a different attitude if we would learn to prostrate our souls before God.

Adoration

There is a second word that goes with worship. It is the word *adoration*. It is a term of endearment. There is passion in that word. *"Oh, worship the LORD in the beauty of holiness."* That is what this 96th psalm says. Worship is a love affair; it is making love to God. You know Michal, the first wife of David and the one who witnessed the day he brought the ark into Jerusalem and composed this 96th psalm. It is said in the historical book of 2 Samuel 6:16 that she despised him. Sure she did; she discovered that David loved God more than he loved her and that he was making love to God. Worship without love is like a flame without heat; it is like a rainbow without color; it is like a flower without perfume. Worship should have spontaneity. It should not be ersatz bread; it should not be synthetic. It should have an expectancy, a tenderness, and an eagerness in it. My friends, some types of worship today compare to going downtown and sitting in a department store window and holding the hand of a manikin down there. It has no more life in it, it has no more vitality in it than that. Oh, today to have a heart that goes out to God in adoration and in love to Him.

A young fellow wrote to his girl and said to her in very elaborate language, given to much hyperbole: "I would climb the highest mountain for you, I would swim the widest river for you, I would crawl across the burning sands of the desert for you." Then he put a P.S. to the letter: "If it doesn't rain Wednesday night I will be over to see you." There is a whole lot of worship that is like that today. It will not take very much to keep us away from God. In the marriage ceremony there is something I occasionally use. I think how sacred it is. I have the two being joined in marriage say, "With my body I thee worship." Leander swam the Hellespont every evening to be with Hero, the girl he loved. One evening he did not come. She knew something had happened, and the next day she found his lifeless body washed ashore. Oh, my friend, to have a heart that goes out to God in adoration. Gregory Nazianzen said, "I love God because I know Him; I adore Him because I cannot understand Him; bow before Him in awe and in worship and adoration." Oh, have you found that adoration in your worship?

Exaltation

And then, last of all, there is *exaltation* in worship. And I do not mean the exaltation of God; we put God in His rightful place when we worship Him. When you and I are down on our faces before Him, we are taking the place that the creature should take before the Creator. But I am not speaking now of the exaltation of God at all; rather, I am speaking now of the exaltation of man. Humanism, with its deadening philosophy, has been leading man back to the jungle for about half a century, and we are not very far from the jungle. It is degrading to become a lackey, a menial. And think of the millions of people who got their tongues black by licking the boots of Hitler! Humanism did that. They turned their backs on God, and when you turn your back on God, you will worship a man. No atheist, no agnostic has ever turned his back on God who did not get his tongue black by licking somebody's boots. There is nothing that will exalt man, there is nothing that will give dignity to man like worshiping God.

Dr. Fosdick wrote a sermon way back in the 1920s. The title of it was "The Peril of Worshiping Jesus," and in that sermon he commented that men have tried two ways to get rid of Jesus, one by crucifying Him and the other by worshiping Him. The liberal doesn't like you to worship Jesus. My friend, *I* worship Him; He is my Lord, He is my God. I do not find it humiliating to fall down before Him. There is nothing as exalting and as intoxicating as to get down on your face before Jesus Christ. Paul fell off that little donkey into the dust on the Damascus road, and the Lord Jesus dealt with him. Then do you notice that He said to him, "But rise and stand on thy feet." Only the Christian faith has ever lifted a man out of the dust and put him on his feet. John, on the Isle of Patmos, saw the glorified Christ and said, "I fell at His feet as dead." Then he continued, "He laid His right hand on me, saying, Fear not." The creature now can come to the Creator. Man, who has been lost in sin and in the gutter, can come up and worship God. It was during the seventeenth century when Muretus, a great scholar of that day, was going through Lombardy. He suddenly took ill and was picked up on the street. Thinking he was a bum, a passerby took him to the hospital of that day, and when he came to, he heard the doctors talking in Latin. They had no notion he could understand it, and they were saying something like this, "Let's try an experiment on this worthless creature." And Muretus answered them in Latin and said, "Will you call one worthless for whom Jesus Christ did not disdain to die?"

My friend, only Jesus Christ and the worship of Him has lifted man up. Man is yet to be restored to his rightful place some day and brought back into harmony with heaven. In that great 150th psalm you start out with His pulling the stop "diapason." And as you read that tremendous psalm—*"Praise God in his sanctuary; praise him in the firmament of his power"*—then listen, the "flute" stop is pulled out: *"Praise him with the sound of the trumpet; praise him with the psaltery and the harp."* Then the "string" stop is pulled out: *"Praise him with the timbrel and dance; praise him with stringed instruments and organs."* Then listen, my beloved, *"Let everything that hath breath praise the LORD!"* And God breathed into man a life, soul, and spirit, and man departed from God. Now there is coming a day when everything that has life, everything that has breath shall praise the Lord. But in this day in which you and I are living, we can lift our hearts and lives to Him in adoration and praise.

As I look about me in this world today, there is nothing but bedlam. Every man playing his own little tune. One of these days out from the wings will step the Conductor—the Lord Jesus Christ. And when He lifts His baton, from the ends of God's universe those galactic systems will join in, and every bird, every angel, and then man will join the heavenly chorus. In the meantime, you can bow before Him and bring your own little soul and your own heart into the harmony of heaven.

6

THE POWER OF
NEGATIVE THINKING

Trust in the LORD with all thine heart, and lean not unto thine own understanding. In all thy ways acknowledge him, and he shall direct thy paths. Be not wise in thine own eyes; fear the LORD, and depart from evil (PROVERBS 3:5–7).

"Accentuate the Positive" was not only a popular song many years ago, but it has been the popular philosophy for America for many years. A prominent preacher in the East has incorporated it into religion with the catchy phrase, "the power of positive thinking." It has become a fad today and a form of fanaticism with multitudes of people. There are dedicated disciples to this cult that make it a sin to say no to anything. You have to be positive. You are not to use the word *no*. In fact the word *not* has all but disappeared from the English language in the thinking of many people today. *Negative* is a bad word, and you don't use it in polite society. The chamber of commerce has adopted the positive approach and developed it. Politicians and automobile dealers are always in a positive frame of mind. Radio and television announcers are splendid examples of the positive cult that is in our midst. In fact our nation has had difficulty saying no to any nation that wanted to borrow money. Today many parents just don't say no to a child. They think they must not say no to any of their whims or any of their wishes. Someone asked a modern father the other day, "Do you strike your children?" He said, "Only in self-defense." America today has become the land of the positive and the home of yes-men.

MEN LIKE MOSES

We need today men and women who can do some old-fashioned negative thinking like Moses, who turned his back on the pleasures of sin, said no to the throne of Egypt, and walked out to take a stand for God. We need young people today who can say no to temptation, as Joseph said no to Potiphar's wife. We need to put an emphasis on the negative as well as on the positive.

The Bible is filled, it is true, with positive thinking. It is likewise true that the Bible is filled with negative thinking. We need to be well-balanced; we shouldn't go overboard on either side.

You see, God actually began with a negative in the Garden of Eden with man. God wrote in neon lights over that garden the word *no*.

And the LORD God commanded the man, saying, Of every tree of the garden thou mayest freely eat; but of the tree of the knowledge of good and evil, thou shalt not eat of it (Genesis 2:16–17).

God put a *not* over the Garden of Eden, and He asked man to do a little negative thinking.

It was Satan who came along and suggested that man emphasize the positive. He said to him, "I don't think you ought to put the emphasis on the negative. I think it would be very nice if you did eat of the tree because you would then have the knowledge of good and evil. Then you would become as gods."

It is interesting to see as you move through the Bible that the Ten Commandments major on the negative. Eight out of the Ten Commandments contain the negative (Exodus 20:1–17):

Thou shalt have no other gods before me.
Thou shalt not make unto thee any carved image.
Thou shalt not take the name of the LORD thy God in vain.
Thou shalt not murder.
Thou shalt not commit adultery.
Thou shalt not steal.

Thou shalt not bear false witness.
Thou shalt not covet.

It looks as if God puts the emphasis on the negative in the Ten Commandments.

Then when you come to the first beatitude given in the Bible, which is in the first psalm, you find that it really majors in the negative. There are three negatives in one verse:

Blessed is the man who walketh not in the counsel of the ungodly, nor standeth in the way of sinners, nor sitteth in the seat of the scornful (Psalm 1:1).

OTHER NEGATIVE EXAMPLES

Then when you come to the Sermon on the Mount, to which the liberals like to run, you will find many dead-end streets that are blocked with the negative. You will find our Lord saying, *"Think not that I am come to destroy the law"* (Matthew 5:17). *Think not* is negative thinking. Then He says, *"Lay not up for yourselves treasures upon earth"* (6:19). Also He said, *"Judge not"* (7:1). Our Lord put the emphasis on the negative.

Then as you come to the epistles you find there also an emphasis on the negative. Paul has a little expression that occurs in many of his epistles, and it is "Know ye not?" (e.g., Romans 6:3, 16; 1 Corinthians 3:16; 5:6; 6:19). Paul suggests to believers that they try the negative approach. Also Paul says, *"Happy is he that condemneth not himself in that thing which he alloweth"* (Romans 14:22). Then when we come to the marvelous love chapter of the Bible, 1 Corinthians 13, we find that, although love is the subject of the chapter, there is an emphasis on the negative. It tells us that love "rejoiceth *not* in iniquity" (v. 6) and that "love *never* faileth" (v. 8). That is a good, hearty negative.

Then when you come to the final message which our Lord Jesus Christ gives to the church, the Laodicean church, the lukewarm church that was torn between yes and no, you will see He did not mind giving a negative message. He said, *"Thou . . . knowest not that thou art wretched, and miserable, and poor, and blind, and naked"* (Revelation 3:17). You will find all through the Word of God an emphasis on the negative.

Now this does not always mean negation; nor does it mean that you are being contrary. It does not mean that you are being disagreeable if you emphasize the negative. You see, the negative sometimes is the most positive approach you can make. For instance, I see signs which read Do Not Touch in many places of industry, especially around certain materials. That is one of the most positive statements you can find, and the emphasis is upon the negative.

The church has come to the place where it is attempting to take a position that reveals it has no conviction whatsoever. As a result, compromise is the motto of the present-day church.

We do need people who will say *no* at the proper time, who will say *no* in a lovely way, who will say *no* without being controversial, who will say *no* to that which is wrong, and say *yes* to that which is right.

The book of Proverbs reveals the power of negative thinking; in fact, that is the approach made in this book. The book contains short sentences. Cervantes defined proverbs as "Short sentences drawn from long experience." Evidently proverbs originated in the East, but many countries have proverbs. Let me cite just a few that have interested me a great deal. One comes out of the Far East. Laotse, the co-founder of Taoism, said, "Doing nothing is better than being busy doing nothing." There is a Danish proverb that says, "Give to a pig when it grunts, and to a child when it cries. You will have a fine pig and a bad child." Then there is a good old American proverb that goes like this: "Nobody don't never get somethin' for nothin' nowhere, no time, nohow." That is probably the best American proverb that we have. There are interesting proverbs that come from a variety of backgrounds.

WHAT PROVERBS SAYS

But the book of Proverbs is comprised of gems of wisdom that God has given to us. They are written in a form of poetry. Hebrew poetry is not achieved by rhyming or using dactylic hexameter. It is attained by what is known as parallelism in the form of couplets of two related clauses. There are different kinds of parallelism. There is synonymous parallelism, which states a truth, then restates it. There is antithetic parallelism, which states a truth, then states the negative. This is what we have before us: antithetic or contrast in parallelism. The positive is given, then the negative is given, and we need both.

"Trust in the LORD with all thine heart" (Proverbs 3:5). This is the positive side. The word *trust* is one that occurs over one hundred times in the Old Testament. Actually it is the Old Testament word for the New Testament word *believe*. Bringing it up into New Testament terminology makes it the same as what Paul said to the Philippian jailor, *"Believe on the Lord Jesus Christ, and thou shalt be saved"* (Acts 16:31). It is the Old Testament way of saying the same thing.

To trust means to lean upon. A wonderful picture of this is given in the book of Genesis where it says that Abraham *"believed in the LORD; and he counted it to him for righteousness"* (Genesis 15:6). He trusted God. The picture is of a man who had exhausted all of his resources. Abraham had gone down every avenue and had found them dead-end streets. He reached the place in life when he was a century old—one hundred years old. Yet he considered not his own deadness nor the deadness of Sarah's womb, and he believed God when He said He would give them a son. He had nothing else to hold onto or look to in this world. He just believed God. It simply means that he leaned on God. He could do nothing else but lock his arms around God and hold on.

"Trust in the LORD with all thine heart" means your total personality. When you come to Jesus Christ, you do not bring just your emotions, although I do not think you ought to leave out your emotions. It is too bad today when emotion is revealed in the church, and the critics say, "That is too emotional"; yet these same people will go to a movie and dampen two or three handkerchiefs. After all, a block of ice is weepy! They are not really moved. But we need to bring our emotions when we come to Christ. We also need to bring our intellects when we come to Christ. We need to bring our wills when we come to Christ. And we need to bring our bodies when we come to Christ. Trust in the LORD with all thine heart—your total personality and every fiber of your being. That is what He is saying.

Now we have the negative side of Proverbs 3:5: *"And lean not unto thine own understanding.*" The positive is stated, then the parallelism is negative. It comes at it from the other side. "Trust in the LORD with all thine heart"; then the negative is "lean not unto thine own understanding."

Apparently God has made man the most helpless creature in His universe. There is no angel as helpless as man; no creature beneath in the animal world is as helpless as he is. Even the dumbest of animals have an instinct that guides them. Man is helpless from the moment he is born, and even for the first few years he is perfectly helpless. There are some creatures that from the moment of their birth can take care of themselves.

Man is also born ignorant. Most animals know at the time they are born all they need to know on the physical side. Man, a human being, higher than the animals, is ignorant. I don't know about you, but I didn't know *a* from *b* when I was born. I had to go to school. Man has to be educated and trained to cope with his environment.

Then when man learns and begins to use the front lobe of his brain, there is a danger of his thinking he is smart. He learns to depend on his intellect. There are a great many who think they are smart enough to get along without God, and they are living without God today. With biting irony, Isaiah in his day reminded his people how foolish it was to try to live without God. He said: *"The ox knoweth his owner, and the ass, his master's crib, but Israel doth not know, my people doth not consider"* (Isaiah 1:3).

Look at the animals he uses for an illustration. The ox is noted for being dumb; we still have the expression "dumb as an ox." But the ox has sense enough to know his owner. And the ass, the little long-eared animal, doesn't have a reputation for brains. Those little animals do not have Ph.D. degrees. And the ass is not known for his brilliance. Yet when his master comes and puts hay in the crib, he has sense enough to know who is feeding him. But man doesn't know. Man thinks he is smart and leans on his own understanding.

The writer of the Proverbs, Solomon, wanted to enforce this. Solomon was a man who was wiser than any man on this earth, and he still holds that reputation. He said, "Lean not on your own understanding." He went on to say, *"Be not wise in thine own eyes"* (3:7). Then following through Proverbs to chapter 28, he added, *"He that trusteth in his own heart is a fool"* (v. 26). What strong language! He that trusts in his own heart is a *fool*.

I believe that there is a proverb to fit every person on this earth. They characterize many men in the Word of God. You can go back into the Old Testament and find those who were trusting in the Lord with all their hearts. You can find those who were wise in their own eyes and were going their own way.

For an illustration let's take the servant of Abraham. This man was sent to the land of Haran to get a bride for Abraham's son. You would think that this man, a man of the world, so experienced and capable that he had charge of all Abraham had, would be smart enough to make a choice and select a bride for Isaac. But he wasn't. And he knew he wasn't. When he reached the land of Haran, he paused. Listen to him:

And he said, O LORD God of my master, Abraham, I pray thee, send me good speed this day, and show kindness unto my master Abraham. Behold, I stand here by the well of water; and the daughters of the men of the city come out to draw water (Genesis 24:12–13).

He did not know which one to choose. So he asked the Lord to give him an indication and show him which girl he was to select. "Trust in the LORD with all thine heart." That means in all the relationships of life. This man depended upon God. What a wonderful thing it is to watch him as God leads him!

Turn over a few pages and you will come to another man whose name is Jacob. He comes to that same land, and he comes on the same kind of a mission, a bride for himself. At the same time he is running away from his brother who certainly is planning to kill him. As he comes to the same place, you would think that he would depend upon God. He is in a foreign country and doesn't know where to turn, but look at him: *"And he said, Lo, it is yet high day, neither is it time that the cattle should be gathered together: water ye the sheep, and go and feed them"* (Genesis 29:7). He hasn't been in that land fifteen minutes, standing there at that well with the other shepherds, but Jacob is telling them how to raise their sheep; he's telling them how to feed them and where to take them.

What a smart one he was! He was not depending upon God at all. He was not looking to God. In fact he was in the position of giving advice to anybody that wanted it, and in this instance he was giving it unasked. Here is a clever boy all the way through this account depending on his own ability. Before long it brings tragedy into his life. He is the example of the one who was "leaning on his own understanding." He is the example of the one who was "wise in his own conceit." He was the one who thought he could handle his own life.

Two other men in the Scriptures illustrate this proverb. First, there is David the shepherd boy. Even when he went out against the giant, he could say: *"The LORD who delivered me out of the paw of the lion, and out of the paw of the bear, he will deliver me out of the hand of this Philistine"* (1 Samuel 17:37). David is a man who throughout his life depended upon God and could say in the conclusion of his life, *"The LORD is my shepherd"* (Psalm 23:1). He had depended upon Him to lead him through life.

Another man with whom David was associated was King Saul, a big man in his own estimation. On more than one occasion he took matters in his own hands; and when Samuel, God's prophet, challenged him, he said in substance, "Well, after thinking it over, I came to the conclusion that God's commandment was a very foolish one, and I have acted on my own decision in the matter."

> *And Samuel said, Hath the LORD as great delight in burnt offerings and sacrifices, as in obeying the voice of the LORD? Behold, to obey is better than sacrifice, and to hearken than the fat of rams. For rebellion is as the sin of witchcraft, and stubbornness is as iniquity and idolatry. Because thou hast rejected the word of the LORD, he hath also rejected thee from being king* (1 Samuel 15:22–23).

"Be not wise in thine own eyes." Trust not in your own heart or your own understanding.

There are other men who fit this proverb whose stories are recorded in the Old Testament. There was a man whose name was Jeremiah, a prophet of God who wanted to quit because the message he was relaying to his people was breaking his own heart. In fact he went to the Lord and said he wanted to quit.

Then I said, I will not make mention of him, nor speak any more in his name. But his word was in mine heart like a burning fire shut up in my bones, and I was weary with forbearing, and I could not refrain (Jeremiah 20:9).

He found that he couldn't quit because God's Word was like fire in his bones. Then he sent God's message to the king whose name was Jehoiakim. Now Jehoiakim was a young man who was wise in his own eyes, trusting in his own strength and ability. When the written message from Jeremiah was read to him, he got a penknife, cut it to shreds, and pitched it into the fire. That's what he thought of God's Word. The history of these two men reveals the foolishness of Jehoiakim and the wisdom of Jeremiah.

EXAMPLES FROM THE NEW TESTAMENT

Also I think of men in the New Testament who fit this proverb. I think of Simon Peter and Judas, both disciples of our Lord and both denied Him. One sold Him and the other denied Him. But Simon Peter was never wise in his own conceits; he was not a man who trusted his own ability. When he fell down, he always got up and came back to the Lord. After Peter failed so miserably, our Lord appeared to him privately. We are not given any of the details because it was a private matter. But I have a notion that Simon Peter wept out his soul and said, "Lord, I've failed You again! Why don't You turn me out? Why don't You get somebody else?" Our Lord didn't turn him out because here was a man who was trusting in the Lord with all his heart. But Judas—what went on in that crooked mind I do not know. There is a mystery about that man, as there is always a mystery about crookedness and iniquity. But deep down within this man was confidence in his own wisdom and ability. Even at the last moment when he admitted he had betrayed innocent blood and could have gone to Christ in repentance, he was still leaning on his own understanding.

Paul was no different when he was Saul of Tarsus. Giving his own testimony, Paul said, *"I verily thought within myself, that I ought to do many things contrary to the name of Jesus of Nazareth, which thing I also did"* (Acts 26:9–10). He was following his own wisdom.

89

He was a smart boy, the most brilliant of the Pharisees. He was going his own way until that day on the Damascus road when Jesus Christ appeared to him. Then he said, *"I was not disobedient unto the heavenly vision"* (26:19). That day he yielded himself to Christ and learned to trust Him with all his heart. No more did he lean on his own understanding. In all his ways he acknowledged Him, and God did direct his paths.

In conclusion let me turn to a statement that our Lord gave which I think is the greatest negative statement that has ever been given. It has three negatives in it:

> *He that believeth on him is not condemned; but he that believeth not is condemned already, because he hath not believed in the name of the only begotten Son of God* (John 3:18).

There are three *nots* in that verse; you could hardly get more than that in one sentence. We think that a double negative is bad, but in the Greek language the double negative is for emphasis, and the triple negative increases the emphasis. Here it is triple. "He that believeth on him," that is, on the Lord Jesus Christ, that He is the Son of God who was lifted up on a cross, the one whom God gave that men might not perish but have everlasting life. "He that believeth on Him is not condemned." But if you do not believe, you are condemned already. You and I are born lost sinners. We are born in a world of sinners. We have a sinful nature. "He that believeth not is condemned already." Why? "Because he hath not believed on the name of the only begotten Son of God."

Our Lord put up three great signs at dead-end streets. He says if you believe in Him you are not condemned. On the other hand, He says if you do not believe, you are condemned. And you are condemned because you believe not. You see, that *not* takes us down the road of leaning on our own understanding.

John Locke was the English philosopher who introduced empiricism into philosophy. He is the man who is responsible, some think today, for dialectical materialism, which is the basis of Communism. It is thought that Karl Marx got his philosophy from John Locke. He was a materialist until the last fourteen years of his life. Up to that point John Locke had trusted in his own wisdom. He was a brilliant fellow. Until then this man had gone in his own strength, and he was clever. Then one day he was brought face to face with Jesus Christ, and he made his decision. He made it for Him. Before he died he said, "The Scriptures have God for their author; eternity for their object; truth without any mixture of error; and doctrine of fact for their subject matter." He came to the place of trusting the Lord with all his heart.

Michael Faraday's biography was one of the most thrilling biographies I read while in college. He is the man who introduced what is known as theoretical science, and today millions of dollars are being expended on experimentation. He was known as the greatest scientific experimenter the world has ever seen. This man came to the Lord Jesus Christ. He no longer trusted in his own understanding but learned to trust the Lord with all his heart. Then he wrote, "But why will people go astray when they have this blessed Book of God to guide them?"

Earlier I said there was a proverb for every person. There is a proverb for you. Which is it? Can it be said of you that you are trusting the Lord with all your heart? Or are you given to the positive way of thinking and leaning on your own understanding? Which proverb fits you?

7

THE SECRET
OF POWER

And the angel that talked with me came again, and waked me, as a man that is wakened out of his sleep, and said unto me, What seest thou? And I said, I have looked and, behold, a lampstand all of gold, with a bowl upon the top of it, and its seven lamps on it, and seven pipes to the seven lamps, which are upon the top of it, and two olive trees by it, one upon the right side of the bowl, and the other upon the left side of it. So I answered and spoke to the angel who talked with me, saying What are these, my lord? Then the angel who talked with me answered and said unto me, Knowest thou not what these are? And I said, No, my lord. Then he answered and spoke unto me, saying, This is the word of the LORD unto Zerubbabel, saying, Not by might, nor by power, but by my Spirit, saith the LORD of hosts (ZECHARIAH 4:1–6, *The New Scofield Reference Bible*).

This is a day of the display of physical power. It is revealed in the tremendous engines and machines which reshape the face of our earth and launch us into the adventure of space travel. It is seen in the release of atomic energy in the fantastic detonation of atom bombs and the enormous potential of energy from nuclear fission. Research is going on in thousands of laboratories for new sources and avenues of power.

THE CONDITIONS OF TODAY

Likewise this is a day of the display of spiritual weakness and impotency, or moral feebleness and flabbiness. The church has lost its influence. Christians have lost their voice. We are no longer an influence in halls of legislation, in the schoolroom, in the business world, or in the social life of our nation. Spiritual power is in inverse ratio to physical power. As physical power increases, spiritual power is ebbing. It is going down and down and down. Christians today are walking like little Lilliputians among the giants of this world system. Believers today are no longer the salt in the earth. They are not even a cup of weak tea—no tang is there at all. Believers today are no longer positive light in the world, but are merely a pale reflection of the times, casting doubts into dark corners. We have lost the optimistic song of victory, and we are playing the funeral dirge of pessimism for a dying age. Someone has described a pessimist as the one who blows out the light so we can see the darkness. It does seem that certain religious leaders are doing just that in our day. No longer are we singing "Onward, Christian Soldiers," but a cry of alarm has gone up, "Stop the retreat!" What has happened? What is it that is taking place? You will find that question being asked everywhere. It was asked by the editor of a Christian periodical:

> Why are we so helpless? Why do we allow our wonderful free countries to be overrun by unsavory libertines who prey upon and pervert the normal desires of ordinary people? Why do we submit to the cultural and social combination of filth-vendors, pimps, addicts, hoodlums, gamblers, barflies, homosexuals, sex maniacs, and power-crazed lawbreakers?

And the church today remains silent and impotent in the presence of all that is taking place. What has happened?

Simply stated, it can be put like this: *We have lost our power.*

THE LESSON OF ZECHARIAH

We need to learn the secret of power. Let us turn to the little book of Zechariah. It is an unexpected place to look for the answer to our question, but I think we can find it there.

Zechariah was a young man, a young man with a vision. In fact, he had ten visions! God raised him up, raised him up in a day of discouragement and defeat. A small remnant of Israel had returned from the Babylonian captivity, fewer than 50,000. Jerusalem lay in rubble and ruin. The enemy was pressing them from the outside. And they were discouraged by failure.

To get a picture of that day, we can go back to Nehemiah, who was contemporary with Zechariah. Nehemiah gives us a bird's-eye view. When he came to Jerusalem he made a survey of the city; he was a very practical businessman. He saw the tremendous work required to clear the debris of the city and rebuild it. Then he called the people together and gave them his report:

Then said I unto them, Ye see the distress that we are in, how Jerusalem lieth waste, and its gates are burned with fire; come, and let us build up the wall of Jerusalem, that we be no more a reproach (Nehemiah 2:17).*

Also we get another picture over in the fourth chapter:

And Judah said, The strength of the bearers of burdens is decayed, and there is much rubbish, so that we are not able to build the wall. And our adversaries said, They shall not know, neither see, till we come among them, and slay them, and cause the work to cease (vv. 10, 11).

This was part of the handicap and the almost insurmountable difficulties that these people had to overcome. So God raised up, among others, this young man Zechariah. He encouraged the people to rebuild. He gave them a vision, showed them there was a purpose behind all of this and that what they were doing was fitting in with God's overall purpose for His people.

Now let us look at one of the visions. It has a message for us also.

And the angel who talked with me came again, and waked me, as a man that is wakened out of his sleep, and said unto me. What seest thou? And I said, I have looked and, behold, a lampstand all of gold, with a bowl upon the top of it, and its seven lamps on it, and seven pipes to the seven lamps, which are upon the top of it (Zechariah 4:1, 2).

This vision is very simple as you can see. It is identified with the lampstand in the Holy Place of the tabernacle.

---

*All Scripture references in this chapter are from *The New Scofield Reference Bible*.

It is my personal judgment that the lampstand in the tabernacle is the most beautiful picture of the Lord Jesus Christ that we have in the Old Testament. It was a work of indescribable beauty. It was beaten out of a piece of solid gold. There was one main branch and three branches going out on each side. It was a work of art done by Bezaleel, the gifted head craftsman. Each branch was fashioned like an almond bough with a great open blossom at the tip in which was placed the olive oil lamp. It pictures Christ in His deity. Because it was of beaten work, it symbolized the fact that Christ was crucified on the cross. This beautiful thing just supported the seven lamps. The lamps in turn revealed the beauty of the lampstand. This is the same thing our Lord said concerning the Holy Spirit (for those lamps symbolize the Holy Spirit as the lampstand itself speaks of Christ): *"He shall glorify me; for he shall receive of mine, and shall show it unto you"* (John 6:14). And these lamps revealed the beauty of the golden lampstand.

Now when Zechariah saw it in his vision, it was the same with the exception of two added accessories which were not on the actual lampstand. He sees something here that is unusual. There was a bowl on top, a bowl that was like a great reservoir.

The lamps, as God instructed Moses to make them, each had a wick in them, and they would draw up the oil through the wick. In my generation we had lamps like that. But here in Zechariah's vision, the oil was supplied to the lamps by gravitation. The oil flows down out of the bowl and is fed to each one of the lamps.

Notice there are pipes that lead from the bowl to each lamp—and not just one pipe, but seven pipes to each one of the seven lamps. It looked like an oil refinery with all the oil pipes around it. And all of this has a message. It symbolizes the plenitude of power that was available. It is that which speaks of the Holy Spirit. This is the picture that is before us in the lampstand itself.

Something else has been added which we find in the next verse: *"And two olive trees by it, one upon the right side of the bowl, and the other upon the left side of it"* (v. 3). Again this all augments the abundance of power that is available. The bowl which supplies the lampstand of seven lamps, each one fed by seven pipes coming out of the bowl, is in turn connected to two olive trees. The oil comes directly from its source right to the consumer; the middleman has been eliminated here. No one has to go to the filling station to get the oil. It comes to the lamps directly.

I have often thought it would be wonderful to own an oil well and to have a very elastic rubber hose that would stretch as far as I wanted to go, one that I could just stick in the gas tank and it would stretch anywhere I took a trip and keep my gas tank filled up. That would be a marvelous thing! And that is exactly the kind of supply this vision indicates. The lampstand doesn't move, but there is a direct connection with the source of power.

"So I answered and spoke to the angel who talked with me, saying, What are these, my lord?" (v. 4). Zechariah has no inhibitions about asking questions. There was no reluctance on his part, if he didn't understand something, to say so. You will find that the other men who had great visions, like Ezekiel, Daniel, and John on the Isle of Patmos, all stood back reverently and waited. But not Zechariah—if he saw something he didn't understand, he'd say, "I'd like to know what that is." And he is always questioning somebody. He had a vision of a man who came by with a measuring rod, and he said, "Wait a minute! Where are you going, and what are you going to do?" He had a big curiosity bump (and the right kind of one, by the way).

Now exactly what is he asking? He said, "What are these?" Yet he was familiar with the lampstand. He knew what it was and knew the meaning of it. His question is, "What does this total vision mean— this lampstand with all these additions—what is the purpose behind it?" And further, "What is the application for us today as we are attempting to rebuild the temple? What does it mean to *us?*"

Notice how the angel draws him out: *"Then the angel who talked with me answered and said unto me, Knowest thou not what these are? And I said, No, my lord"* (v. 5).

In other words, the angel said, "You mean to tell me you don't know what this means?" This man Zechariah is as honest as the day is long, and he says, "Well, I don't know, and I'd like for you to tell me." And I am of the opinion that a great many of us, if we didn't have an explanation, would still be in the dark as Zechariah was until the explanation was given to him.

Here is the explanation: *"Then he answered and spoke unto me, saying, This is the word of the LORD unto Zerubbabel, saying, Not*

by might, nor by power, but by my Spirit, saith the LORD of hosts"
(v. 6).

Notice that this is God's message to Zerubbabel. Now who is
Zerubbabel? He was the head of the tribe of Judah at the time of
their return to Jerusalem after the seventy-year Babylonian captivity.
He is the one who led the first group of his people back to their
homeland, as described in the book of Ezra. Zerubbabel's great
work was that of rebuilding the temple, but the work was dogged by
danger from the outside and discouragement from within. God is
giving this vision to strengthen the faith of Zerubbabel.

Note also that the answer is an abridged and abbreviated sentence. In fact it is no sentence at all. If you want to talk about the
grammar the angel is using, he is not using good grammar. This
statement has neither subject nor predicate. It is not a sentence. This
reveals to me one of the wonders of the Word of God. He did not
finish the sentence because he is going to let us supply the remainder.

Let me give it all to you now as it applied to Zerubbabel: "Not by
might, nor by power, but by my Spirit, saith the LORD of hosts, will
the temple be rebuilt." This is the meaning to Zechariah and to those
of his day. If you want to bring it up to date, you can fill in the
sentence. Not by might, nor by power, but by my Spirit, saith the
Lord, will anything today be accomplished for the glory of God.

Also this verse is eschatological, that is, it is for a future day. It has
an application for the future that has not yet been fulfilled. But it was
also for Zechariah's day in the past and for our day in the present.

That leads me to make this statement: There is always a great danger in studying prophecy. The danger is that you feel it is so far out, it
has no application for you. My beloved, let me assure you that prophetic teaching is not to tickle the curiosity of the saints. It is not to
provide an intellectual titillation where we can get a little excitement.
It is not to satisfy our ego in knowing something which someone else
may not know. Prophetic teaching is given to us in order that you and
I might have a hope. And we are told that the one who has this hope
purifies himself (see 1 John 3:3). My friend, if prophetic study does
not affect your life, it is not worth even the snap of the finger. Prophecy is to be geared into our lives. That is the great meaning here.

Therefore there is a threefold application that we want to note.
First, it is directed to the people in Zechariah's day. Second, it is

destined and deferred to a future day for its final fulfillment. Third, it is delivered and defined for any day, including our day. Now let us notice these three.

DIRECTED TO PEOPLE IN ZECHARIAH'S DAY

The two olive trees were identified in Zechariah's day. Zerubbabel, who was the king in the line of David, is one of the olive trees. The other olive tree was Joshua the high priest. They would be the two instruments God would use to bring light back into the nation Israel and to make it a light to the world.

The olive oil as I have already indicated (the word in the Hebrew is beautiful: *golden oil*) represents the Holy Spirit. Hengstenberg, one of the greatest scholars of the past, said, "Oil is one of the most clearly defined symbols in the Bible. It is a type of the Holy Spirit." That is exactly what it pictures here. The Lord says, "Not by might, nor by power, but by my Spirit." The word for *might* illustrates physical strength. The word for *power* is human strength—either mental or material. Let me give you my translation: "It's not by brawn nor by brain, but by my Spirit, says the Lord." That's the picture.

God would see to it that the temple would be rebuilt by His Spirit, totally apart from all human resources. I find it is very comforting to know that God says in effect, "I'll do it. I will not have to depend on your weakness. I will not have to depend on your ignorance. I'll not have to depend on *you*. *I* will do it. It is not by brawn. It is not by brain. But it's by my Spirit."

DESTINED AND DEFERRED TO A FUTURE DAY

Now this prophecy is also destined and deferred to a future day for its final fulfillment. The final fulfillment will be during the Great Tribulation period. This is clearly identified for us in the book of Revelation:

And I will give power unto my two witnesses, and they shall prophesy a thousand two hundred and threescore days in sackcloth. These are the two olive trees, and the two lampstands standing before the God of the earth (11:3, 4).

Out yonder in the Great Tribulation period there will be no witness on the earth because the Antichrist, with the power of Satan (since God withdraws His hand for that brief moment), will have stopped the mouth of every witness on topside of the earth—with the exception of two. God says that always in the mouth of two witnesses a thing is established. Also God says He will never leave Himself without a witness. During that period there will be these two men who will witness for Him. Who they are is speculation. I think Elijah may be one of them, but whether the other is Enoch, whether he is Moses, whether he is John the Baptist, or somebody else, I do not know. But their identity is not the important thing. God will have two witnesses, and they will speak in the power of the Holy Spirit in that day. They will be God's witnesses. That is His promise for the future just as He used Zerubbabel and Joshua in Zechariah's day.

There are other related matters here concerning the future which we will pass over at this time, but let me lift out just one of them. In the future God will pour out His Spirit upon all flesh, according to Joel. This is pictured here in Zechariah's vision of the lampstand, the abundant, unlimited power of the Holy Spirit in constant supply. God says, "I will pour out my Spirit upon *all* flesh." This has never yet been fulfilled. It will be in a future day.

DELIVERED AND DEFINED FOR ANY DAY

Now let us move on to that which is for us today. Since prophecy is to be practical, the application is for any day, including our day. The nation Israel was the olive tree, but God has set Israel aside temporarily. Paul says this in his epistle to the Romans:

For if thou wert cut out of the olive tree which is wild by nature, and wert grafted contrary to nature into a good olive tree, how much more shall these, who are the natural branches, be grafted into their own olive tree? (11:24).

Now God has set Israel aside and raised up the church (by which I mean the body of believers in Christ) as the second olive tree which is today to exhibit God's power in the world.

Now the whole operation reveals a great principle, and this is the secret of power. God's will and God's work is instigated, promoted, and carried through to a successful accomplishment by the Holy Spirit (apart from man's ability and help). Oh, if we only recognized that we can do nothing in our own strength for God! It would cause us to cast ourselves upon Him and get connected with the real powerhouse, the Holy Spirit. God utterly and entirely repudiates the work of the flesh of man. He will have nothing of it. Let's look at this again: God says it is not by brawn, not by the display of the physical. The day in which we live is impressed by brawn, that which reveals muscle. Well, my friend, the dinosaurs were big, but they are not here today. But the little lowly flea is still with us! Powerful nations flex their muscles. So what? The time will come when God will put them down, my beloved.

It is man who made the din of the city with its nerve-shattering noises. It is man who made the horn and the siren, the gaudy and garish lights that illuminate the brick and cement canyons of our cities. In contrast, God made the silent depths of the forest with its pleasant shadows.

It is the spring of the year as I write this, traveling through Illinois—oh, what a carpet of green has been laid down! And in Missouri the trees are beginning to leaf out. In Kansas the grain is coming up. Then out on the desert the flowers are unfolding. It is beautiful. Today, my friend, the nitrogen is silently crawling up the stalks and up the limbs, making leaves and flowers. There is enough power being released to blow this little earth to smithereens! God is doing it without any show, without any display. It is not by might; it is not by brawn. "It is by my Spirit," saith the Lord.

You could characterize the greatest national force the world has ever seen, which was Rome, with one word: power! It was the greatest power machine the world has ever seen. The legions of Rome marched on every frontier. They were invincible and victorious. But one day they took into custody a Man who seemed to be very weak. Pilate said to Him, "Knowest thou not that I have power to crucify thee, and power to release thee?" The Lord Jesus answered, "Thou couldest have no power at all against me, except it were given thee from above."

My beloved, today we have a perspective of that. The legions of Rome have marched into oblivion. As Kipling said, "The tumult and the shouting die, the captains and the kings depart." They are all gone. But the gospel of that Man who died on the cross is still being carried by weak men to the ends of the earth—by men who are as weak as you and I. His death was a victory, my beloved. God is not impressed by brawn and a display of muscle.

God's purposes are not being accomplished by brain. This is a day when we attempt to do God's work by committees. Someone has said that committees are made up of the incompetent, appointed by the indifferent, to do the unnecessary. That characterizes the work of the church today! We have complex organizations, new methods, boards, committees, programs, plans, drives, contests, budgets, sponsors, rallies, pep talks, psychological approaches, and high-powered advertising. The church has it all today and it is going nowhere. The machine is out of gas. The church goes forward today like a little Samson shorn of its locks of power. It parades up and down, boasting of its accomplishments, and, like Samson, it knows not that the Spirit of God has departed from it. The thing that makes this so tragic is that the church could go forward like a little David with a simple slingshot of the Holy Spirit to meet the enemy with all of his stratagems and come off with a victory! Oh, how we need the power of the Holy Spirit! God's work in the world is not done by brawn; it is not done by brain. It is accomplished only by His Spirit.

Now let's bring this down to the life of the individual. We need the power of the Holy Spirit to even become a Christian. Do you know that none of us can make ourselves Christian? We cannot do it. God says, "That which is born of the flesh is flesh; and that which is born of the Spirit is spirit," and we can't reverse it.

Do not misunderstand me, you can improve the flesh. You can educate it. You can teach it culture and refinement—it needs that. But after you have given it an education, after you have given it culture and refinement, and made it polite (and, believe me, the flesh in our nation could stand a little of that!), after you have done all this, it is still flesh.

Therefore one dark night our Lord said to an outstanding ruler of the Jews, a man religious to his fingertips, *"Except a man be born again, he cannot see the kingdom of God"* (John 3:3). God could not save him by his own righteousness or his own efforts. The Holy Spirit regenerates. You see, God justifies the sinner when he confesses his sin and receives Christ into his life, but that does not change him inside. The minute that sinner trusts Christ, he stands justified before God, where no one can condemn him. But he is changed on the inside when the Holy Spirit comes in and regenerates. By this he is born again. "Not by brawn, nor by brain, but by my Spirit," says the Lord.

HOW GOD SAVES

God does not save us by our own efforts. Nothing man can do can atone for his sin. That which is born of the flesh is flesh. It is ugly, it is sinful. In the beginning of the human family, He put down that principle:

And God looked upon the earth, and, behold, it was corrupt; for all flesh had corrupted his way upon the earth. And God said unto Noah, The end of all flesh is come before me; for the earth is filled with violence through them; and, behold, I will destroy them with the earth (Genesis 6:12, 13).

If God looked down at the time of the Flood and saw the violence in the earth, what must He think as He looks down at our earth today? Did you ever hear so much talk about peace? Yet there is violence and bloodshed on every continent. Fighting is going on everywhere. Many parks in this country are so dangerous no person, man or woman, will walk through them at night. The streets of our great cities are more dangerous than the jungles of Africa today. Flesh is flesh. As God looks down on it, He must ultimately judge it.

Let me give you another definition of a Christian: A Christian is one who has no confidence in himself, and his entire confidence is in Christ. *"For we are the circumcision, who worship God in the spirit, and rejoice in Christ Jesus, and have no confidence in the flesh"* (Philippians 3:3). Where is your confidence today? Are you trusting yourself? Or have you seen yourself without brawn or brain, helpless before Almighty God? And have you turned to Christ for salvation?

My beloved, listen to our Lord: *"It is the spirit that giveth life, the flesh profiteth nothing. The words that I speak unto you, they are spirit, and they are life"* (John 6:63). The flesh profits nothing. God

103

is not accepting anything from you when He saves you. He will do it all, if you will let Him. The trouble with us is we think we can do something to merit salvation. God says we cannot.

God saves those who will believe in Christ.

For the Jews require a sign [they want to see the brawn], *and the Greeks seek after wisdom* [they want to know about the brain power]; *but we preach Christ crucified, unto the Jews a stumbling block, and unto the Gentiles foolishness; but unto them who are called, both Jews and Greeks, Christ the power of God, and the wisdom of God* (1 Corinthians 1:22–24).

If a Jew will come to the place where he is no longer looking for a sign, and if that Gentile is no longer looking to wisdom, but both of them are looking to Christ, God by His Spirit will make them His children through faith in Jesus Christ.

You cannot be a Christian in your own strength or your own wisdom. Only the Holy Spirit can make you a child of God.

We need the power of the Holy Spirit to live the Christian life. Listen to Paul speaking to the Galatian believers: *"Are ye so foolish? Having begun in the Spirit, are ye now made perfect by the flesh?"* (Galatians 3:3).

A great many people today think, *Yes, God can save me only through faith in Christ, but after He has saved me, He expects me to live for Him. So I'll grit my teeth, I'll pull myself up by my bootstraps, and I'll keep the Ten Commandments.* My friend, you never kept them before you were saved, and you will never keep them afterward in your own strength. If you began in the Spirit, and God saved you by the power of the Holy Spirit revealing Christ to you, then by the power of the Holy Spirit you are to live for God.

You cannot live the Christian life. You cannot show me a verse of Scripture where God asks you to live the Christian life! And we have a lot of "fundamental" believers who are super pious, and they think they are living the Christian life. Yet they are carrying animosity, bitterness, and hatred in their hearts. My friend, that is all hypocrisy. Yet God has made a way for us to live the Christian life. Again, it is so simple that most of us miss it, and we keep stumbling along trying to live like Christians by our own efforts.

God's plan and program is by yielding: *"Neither yield ye your members as instruments of unrighteousness unto sin, but yield yourselves unto God, as those that are alive from the dead, and your members as instruments of righteousness unto God"* (Romans 6:13).

This concept has been developed into the so-called "surrendered life." Surrender is sort of a "giving up" process, but to yield to God is an act of the will where you definitely yield yourself to Him. It is not something that is done when you are out of gear—you know, this flabby, emotional sort of thing. It is when you actively, objectively, definitely, and positively go to Him and yield yourself to Him. That is necessary not only to live the Christian life, it is the only way to truly serve God. *"I beseech you therefore, brethren, by the mercies of God, that ye present your bodies a living sacrifice, holy, acceptable unto God, which is your reasonable service"* (Romans 12:1). The word *present* is *yield*. It is the same word in the original language.

My beloved, it is only as you and I yield and our will moves out of the way that the Spirit of God can move in and bring God's will to bear in our lives.

> *Impatient, like a little child, I find myself to be;*
> *Not waiting for the Lord to work His perfect will in me.*
>
> *I try with my poor skill to push the hands of time ahead,*
> *And reap far less than if I were at all times Spirit led.*
>
> *Oh Lord, to whom a thousand years are sometimes as a day,*
> *Give me the patience that I need to walk in wisdom's way.*
>
> *Teach me to rest in Thee, and wait, so that Thy best may be*
> *My portion throughout all my days, and for eternity.*
> *(Author unknown)*

How comforting to know that all I need to do is yield to Him.

May I be personal? It has been my privilege to preach the Word of God for over forty years. Before I stand behind a pulpit I do two things. First of all I tell the Lord, "I can't do it." If that were the end of it, I'd never come to a pulpit; I'd go out the back door. But He has told me, "I don't ask *you* to do it. In fact, if *you* do it, *I don't want it!* You let *me* do it through you." The second thing I do is yield myself to Him. That is all He asks.

105

A young boy by the name of Dwight L. Moody sat in the balcony. He heard an unknown preacher by the name of Henry Varley make this statement, "The world has yet to see what God can do with a man who is fully yielded to Him." That boy sitting in the balcony by the name of Dwight Moody said, "By the grace of God, I'll be that man." In my opinion he was that man, but when Moody was dying, he said to his family around him, "When I was a boy, I heard Henry Varley say, 'The world has yet to see what God can do with a man who is fully yielded to Him,' and I said, 'By the grace of God, I'll be that man.' But I can say now that the world has yet to see what God can do with a man that is fully yielded to Him."

Not by might, nor by power, but by my Spirit, saith the LORD of hosts.

Not by brawn, nor by brain, but by the Holy Spirit, will anything be done for God.

8

'TWAS THE PRAYER BEFORE CHRISTMAS

There was, in the days of Herod, the king of Judaea, a certain priest named Zacharias, of the course of Abijah; and his wife was of the daughters of Aaron, and her name was Elisabeth. And they were both righteous before God, walking in all the commandments and ordinances of the Lord, blameless. And they had no child, because Elisabeth was barren, and they both were now well stricken in years. And it came to pass that, while he executed the priest's office before God in the order of his course, according to the custom of the priest's office his lot was to burn incense when he went into the temple of the Lord.

And the whole multitude of the people were praying outside at the time of incense. And there appeared unto him an angel of the Lord, standing on the right side of the altar of incense. And when Zacharias saw him, he was troubled, and fear fell upon him. But the angel said unto him, Fear not, Zacharias; for thy prayer is heard; and thy wife, Elisabeth, shall bear thee a son, and thou shalt call his name John. And thou shalt have joy and gladness; and many shall rejoice at his birth. For he shall be great in the sight of the Lord, and shall drink neither wine nor strong drink; and he shall be filled with the Holy Spirit, even from his mother's womb. And many of the children of Israel shall he turn to the Lord, their God. And he shall go before him in the spirit and power of Elijah, to turn the hearts of the fathers to the children, and the disobedient to the wisdom of the just, to make ready a people prepared for the Lord (LUKE 1:5–17).

There is a question which is often asked, "Where does the New Testament properly begin?" May we say to you that there are several answers to that question, and it will be necessary for us to move back in our study in order to gather up those answers.

Malachi delivered the final message from God in the Old Testament. Then there was a strange silence of four centuries. Malachi was the last loudspeaker that God used to broadcast; he was the last

107

one to bring a message from God to man. Then God "went off the air" for four centuries. It was a very solemn word that Malachi had given at the conclusion of his message, in fact, a very strange word. It was this: "Lest I come and smite the earth with a curse." It was such a strange expression that ever after that when Israel read Malachi they did not end with those words. They went back and read over the verse again until they came to that expression, and then they stopped. They had included all the Scripture, but they had not ended with that strange expression.

REVELATION SILENT

But after God had spoken those words, the heavens were as brass—God no longer communicated with man. All communication lines were severed and down, the ear of God seemed heavy, and the cry of man went unheeded. No radio on earth was able to pick up any word from God at all. If there was a word, it was obscured by interference or jammed because it did not get through. And yet, during that period there was a desperate desire to have a word from heaven. The literature of that era reveals that.

The Apocrypha is made up of several books with which we are not acquainted. These are books that come out of that period. They do not belong to the inspired Word of God for they are not a communication from Him at all.

So for four hundred years there was no recorded message from God, yet the human heart, not only in Israel but throughout the world, was crying out. It was during that time of silence that the great culture and civilization of the Greeks thrived. There was a cry that came out of that nation—it was expressed by their chief spokesman, Socrates, when he said, "We will wait for one, either God or a God-inspired man, to teach us our religious duties and to take away the darkness from our eyes."

And there was that restlessness throughout the Orient of that day which was expressed with a great question mark when wise men came out of that mysterious land saying, "Where is He that is born King of the Jews?" They had a question, the whole world had a question, and God had not spoken.

This four-hundred-year period that we know as the intertestamental period was, in many respects, the most tragic that Israel ever endured. Yet on the other hand, it was the most heroic they ever had. The greatest deeds were accomplished during that period. And you have to turn, of course, to secular history to be filled in with what took place. A great wave of anti-Semitism rolled over the world. It sounds almost up-to-date, for it was sparked by Syria of that day. Out of Syria there came a king by the name of Antiochus Epiphanes. He came against these people; he destroyed their city; he slaughtered them as if they were animals; he desecrated the Temple—in fact, he finally destroyed it. He remains today the symbol of the Antichrist that is yet to come.

Now this does not mean that God had ignored this period, for God had not. It was through prophecy that God had spoken of this period and this man. Antiochus Epiphanes is clearly set before us in Daniel 8 as the "little horn" that is the figure of the Antichrist that is finally to appear in this world.

We want to state again that for the nation Israel this was a period that was rich as far as heroic deeds were concerned. This was the time when the Maccabees were raised up. As you know, the Maccabees were Jewish patriots who headed a religious revolt against Antiochus Epiphanes. Their courage and bravery paint one of the glowing episodes on the pages of their history.

There were men in this period who were equally as great as Elijah or Jeremiah, but none of these men had a message from God. There was no revelation at all from God during this long night of suffering. God did not speak. He had no word!

Finally Palestine and these people fell under the iron heel of Rome, a Western power. Pious and godly people who belonged to the remnant of Israel began to ask the question, "Has God forgotten?" With a puzzled look, they scanned the heavens and said, "Has He withdrawn?" The silent night was punctuated with question mark after question mark—"Has He deserted us?"

It is Dr. Wilford Funk who says that in the English language, or in any language, the most bitter word that can be spoken is the word *alone*. For four hundred years God left these people alone—they were alone. And yet, He was overruling all; He was directing from the background during all that time.

THE MESSAGE BEGINS

Finally we arrive at the New Testament, and where does it begin? Well, chronologically the New Testament begins way over near the end, at the epistle of James, for that is the first document that was written. That is the first document that comes out of our Christian literature; that is the first inspired word. But by that time we have had the death, burial, resurrection, and ascension of Jesus Christ, and the day of Pentecost has come. All of those things have taken place, and surely we would not want to begin there with the epistle of James.

Someone says, "Logically, the New Testament begins where it begins—at the gospel of Matthew." My reply is that this is one beginning, and it belongs there. I am not insisting that the arrangement of the books of the Bible is inspired, but I do believe the Holy Spirit had something to do with the arrangement of the books of the Bible. Therefore, I believe that there is a reason that Matthew is put first. But let us understand one thing, the story does not begin there! The first event that Matthew records is that the angel Gabriel appears to Joseph. And we have the story of the coming of the wise men. That did not happen until eighteen months to two years after the Lord Jesus was born.

Historically—and it is that with which we are concerned in this study—the New Testament opens with the gospel of Luke. Luke is the one who opens the New Testament. His narrative does not open with the birth of the Lord Jesus at all—it opens with the announcement of the birth of the forerunner, John the Baptist. And the very fact that the forerunner is announced is an indication that the One who is to come is a person of importance and significance as far as heaven is concerned. One is to go ahead of Him and make straight the highway of the Lord. There is to go before Him One as a voice crying in the wilderness, announcing that He is coming and will appear among men.

The New Testament, therefore, opens with Luke's account of the appearance of the angel Gabriel to the father of John the Baptist. After four hundred years of silence, God rent the iron curtain of man's sin. God broke the sound barrier of man's resistance and came through and intruded upon the history of this world—He broke in!

He broke in with the announcement of the birth of John the Baptist, and it was a tremendous announcement.

He is saying, also, that the Old Testament did not end His story. He did not write *finis* over the Old Testament. Actually it is true to say that the Old Testament is *expectation* and the New Testament is *realization*. God finished nothing back there, but now God has broken through and is going to speak again.

Man may defer God's plan, but he can never finally defeat God's plan. Today you may resist Him—you may, He permits that. You may "stiff arm" Him; you may turn your back upon Him; you may be in rebellion against Him. You may, for a moment, postpone His action, but you will not finally delay it. It will come. He will move; He will accomplish His purpose. God will ultimately prevail! You cannot permanently hold God from His plan and from His purpose.

GOD BREAKS THROUGH

To me it is a thrill to look at the place where God broke through. Let us examine the language in Luke 1, verse 5: *"There was, in the days of Herod, the king of Judaea, a certain priest named Zacharias, of the course of Abijah: and his wife was of the daughters of Aaron, and her name was Elisabeth."*

That is where God broke through. Now when you read that verse you immediately discover that what was true of that day was true of a later day of which Shakespeare spoke when he said, "The times are out of joint."

Will you notice several things here? First of all we read that Herod was the King of Judaea, and that tells an awful story. This Herod who was the king at this time is the one who was called "Herod the Great," which does not mean that he was a great man. He was not, although he was a man of great ability, I would say. He was great in the sense that he was the greatest of the Herods. This means that although all of them were rascals, he stands at the head of the list. He yields first place to no one; everybody else must line up after him—he is Herod "the Great."

Herod was also an Idumaean and was not of the stock of Israel. When you say he was an Idumaean, you mean that he belonged to Edom. When you say that he belonged to the nation Edom, you

111

mean he came from Esau. When you say he came from Esau, you need to go back to the record in Genesis and put Jacob and Esau together and find, even before they were born, that these twins struggled in the womb. They were struggling and they are struggling even to the present hour. And do you know that the trouble in the Middle East is between the Arab, the son of Esau, and Israel, the son of Jacob? It will always be a struggle until Christ comes!

And there is that spiritual struggle today, for Esau represents the flesh and Israel, the prince with God, represents the Spirit. The Spirit and the flesh are at war against each other. Here we find Herod, representative of the flesh, on the throne.

Now you may wonder about this because God said through Jacob, when he gave his blessing to Judah, *"The sceptre shall not depart from Judah . . . until Shiloh come"* (Genesis 49:10). And will you look—Herod holds the sceptre! May I say that he is only playing at king. The Roman senate made him king. He was the first one to bear the title over these people, and the Roman senate did it for a price. Herod paid for this title. He was only a figurehead. He was always accountable to Rome. He could never act upon his own volition or authority. He never was a true king, but he bore the title. When you read here that "Herod the king of Judaea" was reigning, all you can say is that the flesh had triumphed. The Spirit was down and the flesh was on top in the land. It is evident now that the throne is debased; the king is degenerated and debauched.

Herod on the throne is the first part of the picture. Will you notice the second thing that is here? It says, "a certain priest named Zacharias." At this particular time we are told there were about twenty thousand priests in that land. God did not come to the *high* priest. He couldn't for we know that the high priest at that time was utterly corrupt. But there was still one priest at least, a certain priest by the name of Zacharias, with whom God could make contact. But the very fact that He had to come down to a "certain" priest tells the story that the priesthood was decayed and defaulted.

That is not all. There stood the temple. This was not Solomon's temple, for it had long ago been destroyed. We are told here that the temple was being used; it was functioning. It was continuing the worship that God had ordained in the tabernacle. Solomon's temple continued it, as did the temple that was built during the times of

Haggai and Ezra (which was destroyed), and now this is Herod's temple in which they are serving. And Herod's temple at this particular time was only fifteen years old. The way we know this is that when our Lord began His ministry at about thirty-one years of age, He talked about "destroying this temple" (He was referring to His body). And they answered Him and said, "Forty and six years was this temple in building," which means that the angel's message to Zacharias took place when the temple was fifteen years old. Now it was not even completed at the time our Lord began His ministry. It was never completed; it was destroyed by Titus the Roman in A.D. 70 without having been completed. It was an ornate thing, it was elaborate, but it was desecrated and deteriorating. And all the way from the throne to the temple there was defection, but it is at this moment that God breaks through!

There is something here that is rather startling. God did not bypass His appointed means. We want you to note that. He came to the temple; He came to a priest. He did not detour around His own appointment. He is the One who had ordained the temple; He is the One who had ordained the priesthood, although both had become utterly corrupt. The temple was polluted. A little later on our Lord is going to say, "Your house is left unto you desolate," but now God will not bypass it. This ought to be a lesson for us today.

There are some that are saying in this hour, "The church is in apostasy; therefore, we want to move outside of the church"—and they have. And we have today many organizations that are attempting to function outside the framework of the church. They ignore the church, they give as their excuse that the church is in apostasy. Let me state that there are churches through which He can function; there are a few today that are still true. We find that as long as God had a priest in that temple upon whom He could put His hand, God came through at that particular place. He did not go around His appointed place or the appointed person. God used the means He had appointed.

THE PLACE

The place was the temple. *"And it came to pass that, while he [Zacharias] executed the priest's office before God in the order of his course."* Now David is the one who had organized the priests into courses. There were twenty-four courses, and this one is known as Abijah (there is no *j* or *h* in the Greek so it is translated in the Authorized Version "Abia," but it is Abijah). And we have here the eighth course where this man Zacharias served. He served only two sabbath days, and on only one of these days was he permitted to go into the Holy Place and serve. So then one priest one time a year was permitted to go into the Holy Place and serve. On that particular day when Zacharias went in, it was not by chance or by accident, but by the appointment of God that God broke through!

THE TIME

Now here is an interesting thing; we actually know the time. It may surprise you to have me state that it was three o'clock in the afternoon when Gabriel appeared from heaven. Naturally you will question why I think that. Well, we are told the time.

According to the custom of the priest's office his lot was to burn incense when he went into the temple of the Lord. And the whole multitude of the people were praying without at the time of incense (Luke 1:9, 10).

Therefore we know that it was at the time of the evening sacrifice. At that time the incense was put upon the altar, and that was at 3:00 o'clock in the afternoon after the sacrifice was made out on the brazen altar. It was the priest's one day out of the year. As the priest he went in the Holy Place on that day. He was the one who lifted the incense and put it upon the fire on the golden altar, and that incense ascended. As it ascended in that temple, that incense spoke of prayer. It was David who said, *"Let my prayer be set forth before thee as incense"* (Psalm 141:2).

We find in Revelation 8:4 the prayers of the saints are mingled with incense. *"And the smoke of the incense, which came with the prayers of the saints, ascended up before God out of the angel's hand."* And at this particular time the people were outside praying.

Now this I must impress upon you—God broke through at a prayer meeting. God came through at the particular time His people were praying.

THE PERSONS

The persons who are involved here are extremely important. We go back to verse 5 of the first chapter of Luke: *"There was, in the days of Herod, the king of Judaea, a certain priest named Zacharias, of the course of Abijah; and his wife was of the daughters of Aaron, and her name was Elisabeth."*

It is interesting to note what is said of this couple. God did not pick just anybody at random; He used those who were dedicated to Him. *"And they were both righteous before God, walking in all the commandments and ordinances of the Lord, blameless"* (Luke 1:6).

Now this does not mean that they were perfect; it does not mean that they kept all of the Ten Commandments and all of the law. It means this: they were righteous before God. Because the Mosaic system required for sin a sacrifice, and every one of those sacrifices for sin was pointing to the coming of the Lord Jesus Christ, "the Lamb of God that taketh away the sin of the world," they brought that sacrifice in obedience to God. And in the sight of God who saw them in Christ, if you please, they were made acceptable. That is the way in which they were righteous—they were obedient unto God.

Here are two of the small remnant who are still true to God, and because of that, God breaks through. Notice this: the name of the priest was Zacharias; the name of his wife was Elisabeth.

You must think very carefully at this point, for names in the Bible have meaning, and these Hebrew names mean something. *Zacharias* means "God remembers"; *Elisabeth* means "the oath of God." And herein lies the great significance: God broke through and spoke to Zacharias and Elisabeth—God remembers. What does God remember? God remembers His oath.

People were saying in that day, "Has God forgotten us? Has God forgotten?" Now heaven answers and says, "God remembers; God remembers His oath." What is His oath? Did God ever take an oath? Turn back to Psalm 89:

My covenant will I not break, nor alter the thing that is gone out of my lips. Once have I sworn by my holiness that I will not lie unto David. His seed shall endure forever, and his throne as

115

the sun before me. It shall be established forever like the moon, and as a faithful witness in heaven (Psalm 89:34–37).

Will you notice, my beloved, God said in effect, "I have made an oath to David. I promised him, and then I took an oath, that I would never, never, never, no never let that throne lapse; I would send One who is to sit on that throne."

Beloved, for about two thousand years there has been One sitting at God's right hand waiting until that day when He will come and sit on David's throne, because "God remembers His oath." And He broke through at this particular time.

The people were saying, "God has forgotten." God says, "I have remembered." And so He sends this angel forth: *"And there appeared unto him an angel of the Lord, standing on the right side of the altar of incense"* (Luke 1:11).

Now this angel, a heavenly messenger, the first one to appear in over four hundred years, is recorded here as naturally as the account of Zacharias is recorded. And the reason is that it is given from God's viewpoint. You are reading God's story, and when you read His story there is no fanfare of trumpets, there is no going into a trance. He will move naturally over to the supernatural realm—supernatural to us—and then record the appearance of an angel.

Now when this angel appears to this man, Zacharias, he tells him that his prayer has been answered.

And when Zacharias saw him, he was troubled, and fear fell upon him. But the angel said unto him, Fear not, Zacharias [every time heaven breaks through upon this earth, if you will notice, it is with a "fear not"]; *for thy prayer is heard; and thy wife, Elisabeth, shall bear thee a son, and thou shalt call his name John* (Luke 1:12, 13).

Now we know what this man Zacharias was praying about that day as he stood by the altar of incense. No doubt he had been waiting all year, and probably this was the first time in his life he had ever stood before that altar. He had doubtless said in his heart that if he ever got to that altar he knew what he was going to pray for; he was going to pray for the Messiah to come.

You see, the tragedy of his home was that they had no child. Elisabeth was barren and they both were old. You have no notion what a tragedy that was for Elisabeth—a barren Hebrew woman was in disgrace—and what a tragedy it was for this priest Zacharias.

He must have often wished, *If I could only get there to pray it would be for a son—that my son might be the Messiah.* And that was the dream of every Hebrew woman of that day: *Oh, if I could only bear the Messiah!*

So when he finally got to the altar there that day, we see him taking the incense, putting it on the altar, and with a great smoke it went up. There was the sweet smell of the incense. You see that godly priest bowing there before God and saying as it were, "Oh God, send the Messiah and, if it is Your will, let Elisabeth be the mother of the Messiah." That, in effect, was his prayer.

And now God sends word through Gabriel and says, "Zacharias, your prayer has been heard. I have heard your prayer and the thing that is going to take place is that your wife Elisabeth will bear the forerunner of the Messiah."

Let us now look at verses 16 and 17:

And many of the children of Israel shall he turn to the Lord, their God. And he shall go before him in the spirit and power of Elijah, to turn the hearts of the fathers to the children, and the disobedient to the wisdom of the just, to make ready a people prepared for the Lord.

And that, my friends, is a quotation from next to the last verse in the Old Testament. You see, it is as if God is saying, "I am now picking up the story where I left off. I promised you that I would send one, now I am sending the one whom I promised."

If you turn to Malachi and read the very last verses of the Old Testament, verses five and six, they read like this:

Behold, I will send you Elijah, the prophet, before the coming of the great and dreadful day of the LORD; and he shall turn the heart of the fathers to the children, and the heart of the children to their fathers, lest I come and smite the earth with a curse.

117

And then the Hebrew always went back and read: *"And he shall turn the heart of the fathers to the children, and the heart of the children to their fathers"* and ended the Old Testament right there.

Now God says that is where He is picking it up. This man, John the Baptist, is coming in the Spirit. He is not Elijah, but he is coming in the spirit of Elijah. He will do this thing God promised would be done. The Messiah is coming, a Savior is going to be born, prayer has been answered, a priest was on the job, and he was praying. And the people outside were praying—praying for what? They were praying for the Messiah. And God says, "I heard the prayer and I am sending Him."

THE FINAL WORD

We must go to the end of the New Testament now for the conclusion of this message. When we come to the end of the New Testament we find that it concludes with a prayer; it concludes with the same prayer that was being prayed at the beginning: "He who testifieth these things saith, Surely I come quickly."

And I never yet have found where that "Amen" belongs. I do not think it belongs to the prayer of our Lord Jesus at all; I think that "Amen" comes from the earth—"Amen, Even so, come, Lord Jesus."

The New Testament opens with a prayer for the Messiah; the New Testament closes with a prayer for the Messiah. The New Testament opens with a cry in a prayer meeting for God to break through and come. The New Testament closes with His promise that He is coming, and then the prayer, "Amen. Even so, come, Lord Jesus."

My friend, He came about two thousand years ago, intruded into history, became the Savior of the world. He was not born just to live, but born to die. He went to a cross for your sins and mine, was buried and raised again, and ascended back to heaven. When He went back to heaven, He sent witnesses to tell His own: *"Ye men of Galilee, why stand ye gazing up into heaven? This same Jesus, who is taken up from you into heaven, shall so come in like manner as ye have seen him go into heaven"* (Acts 1:11).

He will come just as He went!

After Christ's first coming, heaven has been silent again, and this time it has been a long time, and heaven is as brass today. Many of God's people are saying: "How long, how long?"

My friend, and I say this carefully, Herod is on the throne again—that is the flesh is predominant. Do not misunderstand me, you can either label it "Democratic" or "Republican"—it is the same. How tragic today. Herod is on the throne, and it does not make any difference on which side of the iron curtain you are. Herod is on the throne.

The temple today is desecrated. The church is in an awful apostasy, you do not have to tell me that.

The priesthood today, God's ministers, the preacher in the pulpit is no longer "a voice crying in the wilderness," but is a sounding board just telling out to people what they want to hear. A comfortable gospel is being preached today that would not disturb anyone. *"Where is the promise of his coming? For since the fathers fell asleep, all things continue as they were from the beginning of the creation"* (2 Peter 3:4).

I do not know about you, but I am not going to Bethlehem. I want to join in prayer with those who are saying, "Amen. Even so, come, Lord Jesus." For one of these days there will be a break in the blue again. One of these days—I do not know how long, I honestly do not believe it will be too long—He is coming through!

I think it is going to be embarrassing if you are not inviting Him back, friend. Have you prayed this prayer recently? "Amen. Even so, come, Lord Jesus." Honestly, it is so easy at the Christmas season to sing about a baby in Bethlehem. Just so easy to sing about "O Little Town of Bethlehem," but, my friend, do you really want to see Him?

He is, this very moment, at God's right hand. And my statement to you now is: God remembers His own, and He is coming through; He is coming through.

That is going to be Christmas when He comes through!

9

GLAD TIDINGS OF GREAT JOY

And the angel said unto them, Fear not: for, behold, I bring you good tidings of great joy, which shall be to all people (LUKE 2:10).

When the seventeen young missionaries arrived in the Hawaiian Islands in 1820, the first missionary who volunteered, Hiram Bingham, was the first one to preach a sermon in Honolulu, and his text was Luke 2:10: *"Behold, I bring you good tidings of great joy, which shall be to all people."* It was not Christmas, and it was not a Christmas sermon that he brought, but it was an appropriate and right message that can always be used to introduce the gospel.

This is the way the angel introduced Jesus to the shepherds: "Behold, I bring you good tidings of great joy!" Regardless of all the propaganda to the contrary, it is the gospel of the Lord Jesus Christ that has been the vanguard of joy and blessing in this world.

Let me use again the Hawaiian people as an illustration. These were a depressed people. They were chained to gross superstitions, filled with fears, frightened by every noise they heard. You cannot image how a lava flow terrified them in those dark days. They offered human sacrifices. They engaged in internecine warfare. And when the white traders came, especially to Lahaina, they brought venereal disease that decimated the population. The Hawaiians were by no means a happy people. Then the missionaries arrived and brought a message: Behold, I bring you glad tidings of great joy! The gospel was faithfully preached by these young missionaries. Finally a revival swept across the islands like the gentle trade winds. Joy came

121

to the hearts of multitudes. The *alohas* now spoke of love, and the leis were eloquent tokens of deep and abiding friendships. The ocean, the beaches, surf and sand, the mountains and the sky were no longer vengeful gods for them to fear. Now they recognized them as gifts to be received from the hands of a benevolent Creator who gave them all things richly to enjoy. This is what the gospel has done for multitudes of people in different climes and times, to all races, tribes, and tongues.

The preaching of Christ is always the harbinger of joy. For 1900 years the gospel has brought joy to people who have been sitting in darkness.

JOY IS ABSENT FROM THE AMERICAN SCENE

It is a very strange thing that great joy is absent from Christmas this year in this land of ours. You hear only children giving forth squeals of joy, and gales of laughter come only from young lips today. Our comedy shows cease to be funny, and we are looking for new comedians. The television comedian has had to resort to dirty stories in order to get laughs—and that, we've discovered, is usually canned laughter. We can rewrite now our Christmas poem: "'Twas the night before Christmas, when all through the land, not a laugh was heard except in a tin can." Even the laughter, we are told, was canned in the past. The smog of sadness has settled down over the church; there is a fear of the future. Today men are not satisfied with things as they once were.

The question, of course, arises: How can joy and satisfaction be restored to the human heart? Well, let's think back to what prompted the angel to make this startling announcement. He said that he was bringing to *all* people good tidings of great joy. Notice that it was not merely of joy, but of *great* joy. What prompted him to make such an amazing statement? Let us go back now to the Christmas story to see first of all the event, then second, the explanation of the event, and third, the experience that comes from the event.

THE EVENT

The event is well known to us. It is the familiar record of the Christmas story which you probably have heard several times already this season. However, let us look today at Luke's account. It is matchless, majestic, magnificent, mysterious, but very meaningful. It is a superb, sublime, yet simple story surpassing all others. Luke states this great event with poignancy, with pathos, and with pity. He begins by saying: *"And it came to pass in those days, that there went out a decree from Caesar Augustus, that all the world should be taxed"* (Luke 2:1).

The word *world* is the Greek *oikoumenē,* meaning "habitable earth," and here it really refers to the Roman Empire. If you had asked any Roman in that day what the word meant, he would have told you that when you moved beyond the boundaries of the Roman Empire you were no longer in the world. The Roman Empire was the world.

Caesar Augustus sent out a decree "that all the world should be taxed." Who was Caesar Augustus? Well, he was a very interesting individual. To begin with, he was not born a Caesar. He was the adopted son of Julius Caesar, and he took the Caesar name. *Augustus* is a title. When he came to power, he got rid of the republic and became the first emperor. As such, he wanted a title. He was not satisfied with the title of *emperor,* and he didn't like the title *king,* nor did he like the title *dictator,* by the way. He wanted something more grand that that. So they gave him the name *Augustus,* which carries a religious significance. In other words, this is the beginning of the worship of the Roman emperors as gods. So we see that behind the pomp and circumstance and the ritual of religion of that day stood Caesar Augustus, a man who was cold and callous, cruel and calculating, a man who engaged in brutality. He did not care for human lives; he was only interested in power. He made now a decree that all should be registered for the purpose of taxation. That decree went out through all the Roman Empire. He was raising money to keep the legions of Rome marching because he intended to extend the empire. He was a great ruler, no question about that, but we see him here in his proper perspective. We're told:

And she brought forth her firstborn son, and wrapped him in swaddling clothes, and laid him in a manger; because there was no room for them in the inn (Luke 2:7).

That just about tells the story. When that decree went out, there were two members of the family of David living in Nazareth who had to go back to their home town to be registered—and that was Bethlehem. So it was necessary for Joseph to take with him Mary who was great with child. She should not have been traveling, but that would not have made any difference to this brutal Roman emperor who was concerned, not with babies but with battles, and certainly could not be expected to be tender at a time like this. She must go along. They arrived in Bethlehem in time for Jesus to be born there. To get the full significance of this, we need to go back 700 years to a prophet in Israel who wrote:

But thou, Beth-lehem Ephratah, though thou be little among the thousands of Judah, yet out of thee shall he come forth unto me that is to be ruler in Israel; whose goings forth have been from of old, from everlasting (Micah 5:2).

According to the prophet, He was going to come out of Bethlehem, but in order for Him to be born in Bethlehem, it was necessary to get Mary down there. If we had been looking over the shoulder of Caesar Augustus when he signed that tax bill, we would have heaved a sigh of relief and said to him, "We've been wondering how Mary was going to get down to Bethlehem, but that bill you have just signed will get her down there. God is using you to fulfill a prophecy He made over 700 years ago." Caesar Augustus would have brushed us off, "What are you talking about? I don't even recognize any god but myself." Yet this man was merely a pawn on the chessboard of life, and he was being moved of God to accomplish His purpose.

Actually the Christmas story is one of pathos. Notice that here: *"And she brought forth her firstborn son, and wrapped him in swaddling clothes, and laid him in a manger; because there was no room for them in the inn"* (Luke 2:7).

This word *inn* interested me. This past week I have had a lot of time to do things that I ordinarily would not do, so I began to trace down this word *inn*. I had thought it occurred many times in the Bible, but I found it occurs only twice in the New Testament, and both times are in Luke's gospel. I was very interested to see that though it occurs twice, it is not the same Greek word. The other place where it occurs is in the tenth chapter of Luke.

You will recall one of the parables our Lord gave about a man who went down from Jerusalem and fell among thieves. A good Samaritan came along, *"bound up his wounds, pouring in oil and wine, and set him on his own beast, and brought him to an inn, and took care of him"* (10:34). The word *inn* in this instance is a *pandocheion,* which is the word for a better inn. Associated with it is the thought of a host, which means there were private rooms. The inn of the parable would correspond to a Holiday Inn or a Hilton today. But back in Luke 2:7 where it says *"there was no room for them in the inn,"* he is talking about something altogether different. The Greek word is *kataluma.* All that a *kataluma* was in that day was a shelter with four walls. It didn't even have a roof. It was actually an enclosure for animals, and people could sleep there also. There was no room for Him in that place.

In thinking of this, I remember the wagon yards of the Middle West, especially in Texas and Oklahoma, in the old days when that country was being settled. When I was a boy, after the cotton was picked and ginned, everybody made a trip to the little town that was nearby. My father would hitch up a horse to the buggy, and we would drive into Ardmore. In Ardmore there was a wagon yard. I never shall forget it. As a boy I thought it was a great place, a place of real luxury. We would drive in—there were quite a few other buggies and wagons there—and during the day I could come back to where our buggy was and lie down for a nap. There was no roof on the wagon yard, there were no rooms, nothing was furnished but water. It was just a place to stay. I think my dad paid twenty-five cents to stay in there, and they furnished the hay. If we didn't use hay and feed for the horse, it was ten cents—very expensive accommodations, let me tell you! I am of the opinion that Bethlehem's inn would correspond to a wagon yard. It was a place for animals primarily, but people could sleep there as well.

This reveals something that is just a little different from the conception that we are given at this time of year. Luke describes an emergency situation; Mary is going to give birth to a child! She can't get to the hospital because there is no hospital. She cannot get into the inn, a place where animals are, because there is no room. They have to look about, and they find an outbuilding. That is what it was, a cave or an outbuilding that housed animals. That is where Jesus was born. Nobody ever has been born in a place lower than that, my beloved. This is what Luke is trying to tell us. It is not a very pretty picture he is painting. Jesus went to the very depths when He came into this world.

Then Luke tells us there was a manger. By the way, today they are finding all over that land stone mangers that can be moved about. Mary found such a manger and put her baby in it. This simple expediency has immortalized mangers.

To clothe Him there was no baby layette, just swaddling clothes, just rags. This is a little different from the nativity scenes that are presented today. I heard on a television newscast of a nativity scene being destroyed some place here in southern California and how distressed folk were because it was such a beautiful nativity scene. My friend, if it was beautiful, it did not depict the place Jesus was born. He could not have been born in a place more crude and unlovely than where He was born.

Now notice that Joseph and Mary did not complain about their lot. They did not protest. They did not demand of God something better. They didn't say, "Look, if You are going to send this little one to us, You've got to provide for Him just a little bit better than You are." This story contradicts modern standards of living and human values. There is today, I would say, an insane notion that you can get rid of slums by tearing down old buildings.

My friend, if luxury and comforts and gadgets are essential to the development of character, I think we can reasonably assume God would have provided them for His Son, but He did not. The things that are being discounted today are the spiritual and moral values of life. It is obvious now that our young people are being short-changed by a short-sighted policy that if they are given the right kind of environment and very fine school surroundings, they'll be educated. I think we are learning the hard way today that this is not the way to educate. Television has turned its spotlight on the schoolroom, and instead of developing character, it looks as if we are developing characters. We need to get back to the development of that which is spiritual and moral, or we're doomed, friend.

We have today everything to make life enjoyable, yet many of us are not happy at all. For instance, take just one room in our home, the kitchen. We have toasters, mixers, and blenders; we have electric knives and dishwashers, garbage disposals, and miracle washing powders. I saw an advertisement that read, "Take your wife out of the kitchen this Christmas, get her away from the drudgery, and take her out for Christmas dinner." Out of what drudgery, my friend, in this day in which we are living? We have everything today, but we have lost our sense of values and are not happy. The American scene is not a happy one, although we have everything.

THE EXPLANATION

We have seen the event, now look at the explanation of this event. The angel gave the explanation: *"For unto you is born this day in the city of David a Saviour, which is Christ the Lord"* (Luke 2:11). In order to make a good sentence, the translators inserted articles that are actually not in the Greek. We lose something of the tremendous force of this by not leaving it as the angel said it. There is no article at all to go with the three words that are used: Savior, Christ, Lord!

As Savior His person is presented to us. As Christ His program is presented to us. As Lord a personal relationship is presented. In the word *Savior* His office of priest comes to the forefront; with the title *Christ* the office of king comes to the forefront; and with the title *Lord* the office of prophet comes to the front.

Or looking at it another way, the word *Savior* takes us back to Psalm 22, where the Good Shepherd gives His life for His sheep; *Christ* reminds us of Psalm 24 which speaks of the door and the gates being opened and the King of Glory coming in; then *Lord* takes us to Psalm 23, where He is the Great Shepherd of the sheep, the One who even today watches over those who are His own.

What the angel said to the shepherds was, in effect, "Get down to Bethlehem. You'll find Him wrapped in swaddling clothes, just in rags there, but He is Savior, He is Christ, He is Lord."

The Only Savior

Now, the word *Savior* is primary. When Joseph had some questions in his mind about Mary, the angel that appeared to him said that she was to bring forth a boy, and that he was to call His name Jesus because He would save His people from their sins. That is His purpose in coming into the world: He is to save His people from their sins. He is a Savior, the only Savior, by the way. Then when He began His ministry, He revealed to Nicodemus the fact that He was to be lifted up on a cross. *"And as Moses lifted up the serpent in the wilderness, even so must the Son of man be lifted up: that whosoever believeth in him should not perish, but have eternal life"* (John 3:14, 15).

Now He had not revealed that to anyone, as far as the record is concerned, but to Nicodemus. But six months before He went to Jerusalem for the final time, while they were way up yonder in Caesarea Philippi, He called His disciples together and began to quiz them, "Whom do men say that I, the Son of man, am?" In other words, "After two and one half years of ministry, what is the judgment of men concerning me?" It differed, just as it does today. They told Him of the differences of opinion. Then He put the test to them, and they came up with the right answer through their spokesman Simon Peter, *"Thou art the Christ, the Son of the living God"* (Matthew 16:16). After this He revealed something new to them:

> *From that time forth began Jesus to show unto his disciples, how that he must go unto Jerusalem, and suffer many things of the elders and chief priests and scribes, and be killed, and be raised again the third day* (Matthew 16:21).

The apostles were not ready for that, which is obvious from Peter's immediate protest, *"Be it far from thee, Lord"* (v. 22). In other words, "Lord, you are the Messiah. You have not come to die, you have come to *reign.*" They were not ready for it at all. But, Dr. Luke says, Jesus steadfastly set His face to go Jerusalem to die, and on the way He called these men aside five times to explain to them why He was going to Jerusalem. The fourth time is found over in Matthew 20:18, 19:

> *Behold, we go up to Jerusalem; and the Son of man shall be betrayed unto the chief priests and unto the scribes, and they shall condemn him to death, and shall deliver him to the Gentiles to mock, and to scourge, and to crucify him: and the third day he shall rise again.*

He specifically outlined that which would take place step by step. He was going now to Jerusalem to die; He was going as the only Savior. His men, who for three years have followed Him, still didn't get it. Not until after His resurrection could they go back to His teaching at the beginning when He said, *"Destroy this temple, and in three days I will raise it up"* (John 2:19), and know He was talking about His body. How difficult it was to get over to these men why He had come into the world. Frankly, friend, it is just as difficult today. The average person, as we approach this Christmas season, thinks that Jesus Christ came into this world to do nothing but teach. Jesus himself said that He came *"to give His life a ransom for many"* (Matthew 20:28). Today He is the only Savior. He came to stand between our sin and God, and on that cross He bore it all. After all these years the world can present many things, but it does not have a Savior. Jesus is the only Savior.

Three men make a lonely trip to the moon. They have in their module an engine. That engine is their only hope of returning to earth. If that engine does not fire, they will be in orbit from now on. That engine is their savior, their only savior. Right now the world is in the orbit of sin, and, my friend, the only thing that can pull us out of that orbit of sin and draw us to God and to heaven is the Lord Jesus Christ. That is the reason the angel's tidings were of great joy—born in Bethlehem was that *Savior,* man's only Savior.

And the angel said unto them, Fear not: for, behold, I bring you good tidings of great joy, which shall be to all people. For unto you is born this day in the city of David, a Saviour, which is Christ the Lord (Luke 2:10, 11).

The Future King

The title *Christ* is the Greek form of *Messiah,* the Anointed One, which has to do with His kingship. It speaks of God's purpose with this earth. Notice in Psalm 2 that in spite of the rebellion and revolution of man down here, God's second great purpose will be accomplished.

Why do the heathen rage, and the people imagine a vain thing
[an empty thing that shall never be accomplished]? *The kings of*
the earth set themselves, and the rulers take counsel together,
against the LORD, and against his anointed, saying, Let us
break their bands asunder, and cast away their cords from us.
He that sitteth in the heavens shall laugh: the Lord shall have
them in derision (Psalm 2:1–4).

God's laughter is not that of humor, but of the utter futility of it all.
Who is little man? He is making a great deal of going to the moon,
but after he's been to the moon, where has he been? Compared to the
vastness of space, he's been out to the front gate to pick up the morning paper. Who is little man? He imagines a vain thing, and the One
sitting in the heavens will laugh at him. Imagine little man walking
out and shaking his midget fist in heaven's face and saying, "Come
on out and fight me!" God says that's preposterous. Man is a tiny,
fragile creature that won't be here but a little while. He will soon
disappear. What has happened to the great men of the past? I think
of Hamlet's evaluation:

> *"Imperious Caesar, dead and turn'd to clay,*
> *Might stop a hole to keep the wind away;*
> *O, that that earth, which kept the world in awe,*
> *Should patch a wall to expel the winter's flaw!"*

God makes the declaration: *"Yet have I set my king upon my holy hill*
of Zion" (Psalm 2:6). This is God's second great purpose. It is an
earthly purpose. His heavenly purpose today is to bring many sons
home to glory, but in this earthly purpose God is moving forward
today with His plan of putting His Son on the throne down here. He
is Christ, the Anointed One. He is the ruler. Nothing, *nothing* can
change or stay God's plan to bring that to pass. All of God's earthly
purposes are gathered together in that little baby wrapped in swaddling clothes in an outbuilding behind an inn, in a little out-of-the-
way place called Bethlehem, in a nation that is under the iron heel of
Rome. But this is the way God moves.

THE EXPERIENCE

Now we come to the last point: Experience. *"For unto you is born this day . . . Saviour . . . Christ . . . Lord!"*

Lord is a glorious title that He has. A great deal is being said right now about the lordship of Jesus, that He is to be made Lord of our lives. In fact it is being substituted for saviorship. But notice that the angel put them in the correct order. First of all, He is Savior, and you have to know Him as Savior. Also I think you have to know Him as Christ. God's earthly purposes are all to be consummated in Him. And then, third and last, He is Lord.

Our Lord

Lord speaks of a personal relationship with Christ, a very personal relationship with Him. Our concern is with the living Christ who is not in Bethlehem, who is no longer on a cross, no longer in a tomb, but at this moment is at God's right hand. The invitation of the Word of God is: *"Draw nigh to God, and he will draw nigh to you"* (James 4:8). This is a Christmas when we need to draw near to the person of Christ.

Paul reminded the Colossian believers of this: *"If ye then be risen with Christ, seek those things which are above, where Christ sitteth on the right hand of God. Set your affection on things above, not on things on the earth"* (3:1, 2).

If ever there was a time when men have fixed their minds on things on earth, this is the day. If you and I are to know anything about the peace and joy that Jesus brought to this earth, we are going to have to get our minds off the things of this world and get our minds on Him—off the thing, onto the Person. Is Christ a reality to you on blue Monday morning? Before we talk about lordship, let's talk about reality.

How much time do you spend with Him during the week? The psalmist says, *"Return unto thy rest, O my soul"* (Psalm 116:7), that sanctuary which is a place of power. It is forsaken today.

You remember that Paul spoke of it to the Philippians when he was talking to them about power. Paul never said that he could do all things through Christ until he had made some other statements.

131

Finally, brethren, whatsoever things are true, whatsoever things are honest, whatsoever things are just, whatsoever things are pure, whatsoever things are lovely [gracious], whatsoever things are of good report; if there be any virtue, and if there be any praise, think on these things (4:8).

Again, as Paul wrote to the Colossians, *"Set your affection on things above, not on things on earth."* Do you have your mind set on *things* this Christmas?

This week I have been reading John Bunyan's *Pilgrim's Progress* and *Grace Abounding,* which I consider his greatest work. He opens up his heart and his life, speaking out of a past century. In this century we think we are out of step with the past; we're going out in space, we're moving to new frontiers, but where are we going? And where is our joy? Where is the joy of the Lord today? Listen to John Bunyan:

> But the next day, at evening, being under many fears, I went to seek the Lord; and as I prayed, I cried and my soul cried to him in these words, with strong cries: O Lord, I beseech thee, show me that thou hast loved me with everlasting love (Jer. 31:3). I had no sooner said it but, with sweetness, this returned upon me, as an echo or sounding again, "I have loved thee with an everlasting love." Now I went to bed in quiet; also, when I awaked the next morning, it was fresh upon my soul—and I believed it.

How wonderful this is! Also one other excerpt:

> And now I found, as I thought, that I loved Christ dearly; oh! methought my soul cleaved unto him, my affections cleaved unto him. I felt love to him as hot as fire; and now as Job said, I thought I should die in my nest; but I did quickly find that my great love was but little, and that I, who had, as I thought, such burning love to Jesus Christ, could let him go again for a very trifle; God can tell how to abase us, and can hide pride from man.

John Bunyan opens up his heart and lets us know that he had a personal relationship with Jesus Christ. He was just a poor mortal, just a hunk of humanity as you and I are today—filled with fears, weaknesses, and yet enjoying that wonderful communion and fellowship with the person of Christ. This is joy, friend; this is what the angel meant when he said: "Behold, I bring you good tidings of great joy, which shall be to all people." I hope that you will have a wonderful Christmas with Him this year.

10

THE NEXT HAPPENING
IN THE PROGRAM
OF GOD

1 Thessalonians 4:13–18

Today in southern California, as well as across the country, we're hearing some strange things in the area of prophecy coming from some men at whom I'm rather surprised. They are right on the border of setting a date. Some were saying Christ would come by 1980. Others say He will be here by the end of the century. Now they worry me because they seem to have a line into heaven that I don't have. That worries me a great deal because I'd like to have that line also, and I simply don't have it. And if you want to know the truth, they don't have it either.

WHAT'S NEXT?

The Word of God tells us what the next happening is. And the Word of God calls it the Rapture. There are three great passages of Scripture on the Rapture: John 14 is one; 1 Thessalonians 4, beginning with verse 13 is a second; and the third is 1 Corinthians 15. But now I'm turning to 1 Thessalonians 4, a very familiar passage for those that are acquainted with this field of prophecy.

But I would not have you to be ignorant, brethren, concerning them which are asleep, that ye sorrow not, even as others which have no hope. For if we believe that Jesus died and rose again,

135

even so them also which sleep in Jesus will God bring with him. For this we say unto you by the word of the Lord, that we which are alive and remain unto the coming of the Lord shall not prevent [shall not go before] them which are asleep. For the Lord himself shall descend from heaven with a shout, with the voice of the archangel, and with the trump of God: and the dead in Christ shall rise first: Then we which are alive and remain shall be caught up together with them in the clouds, to meet the Lord in the air: and so shall we ever be with the Lord. Wherefore comfort one another with these words (vv. 13–18).

This passage has been called one of the most important prophetic passages in Scripture, and certainly I would concur in that. Notice that it teaches the imminent and impending coming of Christ. And now hear me rather carefully. That does not mean the *immediate* or even the *soon coming* of Christ. Now we have used, and I have used, that expression for years—"The soon coming of Christ." But this is not the language of the Word of God. The word is the *approaching* coming. The next event on the agenda of God is when He takes His church out of the world. *When* that will take place, we are given no indication whatsoever. We're just told that's the next event. It may be tomorrow. It could be this year. It may not be. Don't quote me as saying He's coming this year—I didn't. I don't know. He may come this century—I don't know. He may not come this century.

Now let me illustrate this with a very homely illustration. Last winter Mrs. McGee and I made our annual trip to Florida. It seems strange for Californians to be going to Florida in the wintertime, but that's what we've been doing, and we've had a wonderful ministry down there. This time we got on one of the new DC-10s. We had never been on one of them before, and we were very much interested in this new plane. It took off, went out over the Pacific, circled to the left, and while we were still in sight of the airport, the captain came on the intercom and introduced himself. He told us what the weather was. He said, "The weather here in California is lovely, and the report we get from Florida is that the weather is lovely down there. But you know we go over Texas, and you can't tell about the weather there." We were listening to him very intently, of course. He told us the number of feet we'd be flying. He gave us a lot of other information about this new plane, and then he said, "Our next stop is Miami."

Well, we didn't grab up our bag that we'd carried on the plane and rush for the door, because it was five hours before we would get there. Yet it was the next event, provided we didn't go by Havana (which we didn't, by the way). But that was the thing he said, "The next stop will be Miami." Yet it was five hours away. Now it was imminent all the time, but it wasn't soon coming, not for a fellow like me who doesn't like to fly. Those to me are the longest five hours that I spend—when I fly across country. I wish I could get right on and right off, but it's not quite that quick. You have to stay there until you get to the place that you're going.

IMMINENT COMING

Now the thing that the Word of God teaches is the imminent coming of Christ, not necessarily the soon coming, although it's the thing we're to look for all the time. Now Paul put it just like that. Paul believed that Jesus could return in his lifetime. He never did say Jesus *would* return. He did not know. He just said He *could* return, and that means the imminent coming of Christ. For instance, he says here, "We which are alive and remain unto the coming of the Lord." Paul expected to be in that "we" group, but he wasn't. There have been many generations since then. Also he said something else to a young preacher: *"Looking for that blessed hope, and the glorious appearing of the great God and our Saviour, Jesus Christ"* (Titus 2:13).

This is something to look for. And, my friend, if some friends are not due for ten hours, you don't go out and start waiting for them. But if they might come any time within the ten hours, you can go out and wait for them. That was exactly the position of the apostle Paul. And that, I think, should be our position today.

Now Paul labelled this event, when the Lord Jesus would come and take His own out of the world, the Rapture. Today there is a group of the amillennial brethren who like to say that the Bible does not use the word *Rapture* at all, that it's not a Bible term and we ought not to use it. May I say to you that the Bible *does* use this term. Will you notice verse 17: *"Then we which are alive and remain shall be caught up together with them in the clouds, to meet the Lord in the air."*

Now *caught up* in the Greek is *harpazo,* and it has several meanings. It means "caught up," "to grasp hastily," "to snatch up," "to lift," "to transport." It means "to rapture"—that's one of the meanings of it. Therefore it is a Bible word. Now if they don't like the word *rapture,* then I suggest they call it *harpazo,* because they all mean the same. It's the Rapture of the church that he's talking about.

Now another rather startling thing here is that actually the primary consideration is not the Rapture. Really, it's not. The precise question is this: What about believers who die before the Rapture? That is the question which Paul is answering.

Now the background is simply this. Paul went to Thessalonica on his second missionary journey. Paul had covered the ground that he and Barnabas had been over on the first missionary journey. And we would gather from what Dr. Luke says in the book of Acts that all Paul and his party, with Silas and Timothy, intended to do was widen the circumference of that circle. Dr. Luke says he attempted to go down into Asia where Ephesus was the chief city and one of the greatest cities of the Roman Empire, but the Spirit of God put up a roadblock and would not let him go south. So Paul thought that if he couldn't go south, certainly he was to go north, since along the southern coast of the Black Sea there was a very large group of Jews and Gentiles that had settled in that area.

And Paul started out. Again the Spirit of God put up a roadblock. Therefore he's bottled in now. He has come from the east; he can't go south; he can't go north. He can go only one direction, west. You can see it was not Horace Greeley of the New York *Sun* who first said, "Go west, young man, go west." It was the Spirit of God speaking to the apostle Paul. He came to Troas and was given the vision of the man of Macedonia. He crossed over to Neapolis, went to Philippi, and founded a church there. Then he continued overland and came to the city of Thessalonica where he had a great ministry. We are told: *"And Paul, as his manner was, went in unto them, and three sabbath days reasoned with them out of the scriptures"* (Acts 17:2).

He was there three sabbath days, which means he was there less than one month. During that period he performed a herculean task. He did the work of a missionary. He opened up new territory and made new converts. Many were led to a saving knowledge of Christ. A local church was established, and he taught them the great truths of the Christian faith. He taught them, among other things, that the Rapture might occur at any moment. Paul then left Thessalonica. I say he left—he was run out of town. His enemies set the city in an uproar. He had to leave. Then he went down to Berea. I don't know how long he was in Berea, but there he formed a church. After that he went on to Athens, and he was there for quite a while. How long I do not know. He waited and waited for Silas and Timothy to come, but they didn't show, so he went on down to Corinth and waited there. And he had a ministry in Corinth also.

During that period Silas and Timothy joined him, bringing word from the Thessalonian church. It was a good word. It was news of how the Word of God was growing. But the Thessalonians, you see, only had Paul there for a month. They had been taught all the great truths, but there were many details that hadn't been told them. And in that interval, from the time that Paul left them until Silas and Timothy joined him, quite a few of the believers had died. And a question arose in the minds of the believers, "What about our beloved dead? Did they miss the Rapture?" And by the way, that means Paul had taught them it might occur at any moment, or they wouldn't have had the question in their minds. Their concern was, will the dead be included in the Rapture? Now at that time this was a pertinent question.

Of course, we've come a long way since then. Nineteen hundred years have gone by, and literally millions of believers have already gone down through the doorway of death; the spirits of multitudes of them have gone into the presence of Christ. Therefore, most of the church has already gone ahead, and today, comparatively speaking, a very small minority remains in the world.

THE RAPTURE AND THE DEAD

Now what about the Rapture and the dead? That is the question which Paul is going to answer. Now listen to him. He says: "But I would not have you to be ignorant, brethren." I love the way Paul says that. Paul was a very astute and a very diplomatic preacher. He would declare the truth, of course—he never compromised—but

Paul did use the very acme of politeness. He said, "I would not have you to be ignorant, brethren." And when Paul said that, you can put it down that the brethren were ignorant. That is a nice way of saying it, though, you see. He didn't come out flatfooted and say, "You're ignorant over there. You don't know." He didn't put it like that. He said, *"I would not have you to be ignorant, brethren, concerning them which are asleep, that ye sorrow not, even as others which have no hope"* (1 Thessalonians 4:13).

And death was pretty hopeless in the Roman world. The religions of paganism have never been able to offer much hope after death. Actually, today the modern thinking of philosophy and psychology, and the life style of most people, has left eternity out. They don't like to think about it. A man said to me, "Don't talk to me about that. I don't like to think about it. Keep that buried. I just don't want to hear about it at all."

In Thessalonica archeologists have found in their excavations an inscription on a stone that reads, "After death no reviving. After the grave no meeting again." Theocritus, a Greek philosopher and poet, wrote, "Hopes are among the living. The dead are without hope." So the pagan world had no hope at all. And today when I conduct a funeral (and I'm sure other pastors have the same experience), very frankly, I can always tell whether the one who has passed on and the loved ones of the deceased are Christians or not. You listen to an unsaved person weep at a funeral. My friend, it's the weeping of the hopeless and the helpless.

May I say to you, it's an awful thing to have no hope in this world today. It's a terrible thing when death comes and you have no hope, my friend. The motto of the Roman world was: "Eat, drink, and be merry; for tomorrow you die." And that's the way multitudes are living in this world today, by the way.

Now Paul says, "I don't want you to sorrow as those who have no hope. You *have* a hope concerning those who are sleeping." And that, may I say, is one of the loveliest things that Paul could have said.

Now *sleeping* is another word that I'd like to call attention to. In the Greek it's *koimaomai,* and it means "those that are lying asleep." I got down my classical Greek lexicon some time ago and found the word meant "to go to bed" back in classical times. And you know, you can't put a spirit to bed. You couldn't put your soul to bed to save your life. Which end would you stick in the bed if you put your soul to bed, my friend? It's utterly preposterous to use words like this in reference to the death of the soul. The soul never sleeps. The moment a person dies, if he's a child of God, Paul says he is "absent from the body; present with the Lord." But the body is put to sleep, and we'll see that in a few moments and talk about it. And I can't think of a lovelier word to use for death than *sleep*. Sleep never refers to the soul because the very language itself means to lie down, and only the body can lie down.

This is the same word, by the way, that's used of natural sleep. In Luke 22:45 we read that at the Garden of Gethsemane, *"when he rose up from prayer, and was come to his disciples, he found them sleeping for sorrow."* Peter, James, and John were asleep. In Acts 12:6 you have that word again. *"Peter was sleeping between two soldiers."* That fellow Simon Peter didn't seem to have much of a problem sleeping. He could sleep at the Garden of Gethsemane or go to sleep between two soldiers. We can say one thing about him. He did not suffer from insomnia; he was able to sleep at night. So this is the same word that's used of the body of a believer, and it's a very wonderful word.

Now why would that word be used to speak of the body? I have several suggestions to make. The first one is the similarity of sleep to death. A sleeping body and a dead body are similar. I'm sure that you've been to a funeral and you've heard someone say, "Oh, he looks just like he's asleep." And if you want to know the truth, if he is a child of God, that body is asleep. That's the picture. That's the way the Word of God says that we should look at it. And sleep is temporary. Death is also temporary. Sleep has its waking; death has its resurrection. Life is not just existence, and death therefore would not be just nonexistence.

Then there's another reason I'd like to suggest to you why this word is used. The very derivation of the word for sleep goes back to a word *keimai,* and *keimai* means "to lie down." It always refers to the body. And the interesting thing is that the word Paul always uses for resurrection is *anastasis,* which means "to stand up." *Histemi* means "to cause to stand." *Ana* means "up." And, my friend, may I say to you, resurrection only refers to the body, never to the soul or spirit. The spirit has gone to be with Christ. You remember the Word of

God makes it very clear. God said to man, "In the day that you eat of that tree you will die." Then when he disobeyed and ate of it, God told him: *"In the sweat of thy face shalt thou eat bread, till thou return unto the ground; for out of it wast thou taken: for dust thou art, and unto dust shalt thou return"* (Genesis 3:19).

In other words, you were taken out of the dust, as far as your body is concerned, and you're going to be put right back there. Solomon put it this way: *"Then shall the dust return to the earth as it was: and the spirit shall return unto God who gave it"* (Ecclesiastes 12:7). So it is the body that lies down in death. It is the body that's raised up in resurrection.

Many years ago in the city of New York (in fact, it was way back in the day when liberalism was called modernism, back in the 1920s), there was an argument about whether resurrection was spiritual. The liberal even today claims it's spiritual. He doesn't believe in bodily resurrection at all. A very famous Greek scholar from the University of Chicago read a paper on the passage from 1 Corinthians 15: *"It is sown a natural body; it is raised a spiritual body. There is a natural body, and there is a spiritual body"* (v. 44). His paper put the emphasis on the word *spiritual*. He concluded by saying, "Now, brethren, you can see that resurrection is spiritual because it says it's spiritual." The liberals all applauded, and somebody made a motion that they print that manuscript and circulate it.

Well, a very fine Greek scholar was there, and he stood up. And when he stood up all the liberals were a little uneasy. He could ask very embarrassing questions. He said, "I'd like to ask the author of the paper a question." Very reluctantly, the good doctor stood up. "Now, doctor, which is stronger, a noun or an adjective? A very simple question, but I'd like for you to answer it."

He could see the direction he was going and didn't want to answer it, but he had to. "Well," he said, "a noun is stronger, of course."

"Now, doctor, I'm amazed that you presented the paper that you did today. You put the emphasis upon an adjective, and the strong word is the noun. Now, let's look at that again, 'It is sown a natural body; it is raised a spiritual *body*'." He said, "The only thing that is carried over in resurrection is the body. It's one kind of body when it dies, a natural body. It's raised a body, but a spiritual body, dominated now by the spirit—but it's still a body."

And, you know, they never did publish that paper. They decided it would be better not to publish it. May I say to you, just a simple little exercise in grammar would have answered this great professor's whole manuscript and his entire argument which he presented at that time.

Now I want to turn to a passage of Scripture that's related here. It's 2 Corinthians 5. Paul begins: "For we know . . ." He's writing to believers now that know something. You notice he approaches it differently. He doesn't say, "I would not have you ignorant." He says, "We know"—we know something. *"For we know that if our earthly house of this tabernacle* [the word is "tent"] *were dissolved, we have a building of God, an house not made with hands, eternal in the heavens"* (v. 1).

THE TENT OF THE BODY

Paul calls this body that you and I live in a tent, just a flimsy little tent. That's all in the world it is. And our bodies are very flimsy, by the way. I found out that seven spots on your lungs could put you out of business. My, these little old tents that we live in are fragile. They can fall down most any time. And some of them are getting old now. I know that mine is beginning to wear out. But I'm thankful that He may give me a few more years. I want to stay in this tent in spite of the fact that it's got a lot of aches and pains.

Now you will notice, Paul says: *"For in this we groan, earnestly desiring to be clothed upon with our house which is from heaven"* (v. 2). Now let me just drop down to verse 4. *"For we that are in this tabernacle do groan."* Have you found that to be true? I sleep upstairs, and I used to come bounding down those steps. Twenty years ago I could do it easily. You ought to see me go down the steps now. I hold onto the side, take one step at a time, and groan at every step. My wife tells me, "You ought not to groan." And I say, "It's scriptural to groan." And I believe it is. I think that it's natural to groan in these bodies.

For we that are in this tabernacle do groan, being burdened: not for that we would be unclothed, but clothed upon, that mortality might be swallowed up of life. Now he that hath wrought us

143

for the self-same thing is God, who also hath given unto us the earnest of the Spirit. Therefore we are always confident, knowing that, whilst we are at home in the body, we are absent from the Lord (vv. 4–6).

Now we're home down here in the body, yet we're absent from the Lord today. But one of these days something is going to happen. *"(For we walk by faith, not by sight:) We are confident, I say, and willing rather to be absent from the body, and to be present* [at home] *with the Lord"* (vv. 7, 8). If you are a believer, the minute you leave this body, you're going home. And the body is put to sleep. That's the way the early Christians spoke of their own who died. In fact, they called the place of burial, the graveyard, the *koimeterion,* and that really means a rest house for strangers. It was the word for the inn that was closed to Mary and Joseph. Such places were all through the Roman Empire, and we get from it our word *cemetery* today. A cemetery is a resting place, a sleeping place. What do we call sleeping places today? We call them motels and hotels. You don't weep, do you, when your loved ones write, "We're going to spend a week at the Hilton Hotel in San Francisco"? We congratulate them and think it's wonderful. We miss them if they're close to us and are going to be away from us, but they're asleep up in the Hilton Hotel and will be for seven straight nights. Well, that was the feeling of the early church. They took their loved ones and put them out in the cemetery, in the ground, when they were asleep in death, and called it the *koimeterion.*

And let me just add this (although I know that I get in controversial places, but I have always done that) there's a great deal being said today about cremation, whether Christians ought to cremate. Now, very frankly, I don't think it makes very much difference as far as the individual is concerned, but I don't believe in it, and I don't think a Christian ought to practice it. I'll tell you why. An undertaker in Pasadena, who is also an aviator, told me that he made good money in taking the ashes of unsaved people and scattering them out over the Pacific.

Do you know why? The unsaved man says, "God, I dare you to bring me back. I don't want to be back." They want death to be the end of it. But, you see, the early church said, "This is not the end.

We're just putting them in the motel for the week, or for just a short time. The body is asleep. They've gone to be with the Lord." Even the book of Ecclesiastes, as pessimistic as it is, speaks of the fact that the dust shall return to the earth, but the spirit will return unto its Maker. So that today we reveal our faith when, instead of cremation, we bury our loved ones in a grave.

WE WILL AWAKEN

We believe the body is going to be awakened someday. And how will it be awakened? Will you listen to this in 1 Thessalonians, chapter 4: *"For the Lord himself shall descend from heaven."* And I love that. When the Lord comes to the earth to establish His kingdom at His second coming, He's going to send His angels to gather His elect, but He will not send any angels for His church.

Do you know why? Because angel ministry is not connected with the church. It's connected with Israel, never with the church. And there will be no angels connected with the Rapture. But notice here: "For the Lord himself shall descend from heaven." He's coming Himself. I love that. *He's* coming. Our Lord is coming. Will you notice this: He "shall descend from heaven with a shout." Now what is that shout? That is a word of command. That is the word which He gave in Bethany at the grave of Lazarus, "Lazarus, come forth." That is the shout of the Son of God. Then somebody says, "Oh, you slipped up because it says 'with the voice of the archangel.'" Well, whose voice is it? It's His voice. His voice is going to be like the voice of an archangel. It's the voice of majesty. It's the quality of His voice, the authority of His voice. It's the voice of the Son of God. No archangel is there.

Let me ask you a question, and I do not mean to be irreverent. Do you think the Lord Jesus will need an archangel to help Him raise His church from the dead? I don't think so. Can you imagine Him at the tomb of Lazarus saying, "Gabriel, will you come on over here and help me get this fellow out of here"? That is absolute blasphemy, if you ask me. He didn't do that. He didn't need to do that. My Lord was able to raise the dead. And He will be able to raise the dead at the Rapture. There will be no archangel there. His voice is like the voice of the archangel.

And then somebody says, "Wait a minute. 'And with the trump of God.' What is that?" It is the voice of the Son of God. It's still His voice. Well, somebody says, "It says that it's the trump of God." Yes, but His voice is like a trumpet. Somebody says, "Do you know that?" I know that from Scripture. Turn to Revelation 1:10 and you will find that John on the Isle of Patmos said: *"I was in the Spirit on the Lord's day, and heard behind me a great voice, as of a trumpet."*

And whose voice was it? He said, "I turned to see," and when he turned to see, it was the glorified Christ that he saw. His voice will be like the sound of a trumpet. It will be like an archangel's. It will be a shout, and I think it will roll over this earth, and those who are His own will rise up. Paul makes it clear here. "The dead in Christ shall rise first." And I think—beginning way back yonder with Stephen, the first martyr, and after him, the apostles—they will come.

After them, that great company of believers who were martyred during the first 200 years of the church; and then believers from century after century until it comes down to the time of those that are living. If we're living, we're just going to bring up the rear of the parade, that's all—that great parade of resurrection when He calls His own out of the grave with a shout. It will be His voice, not an archangel's, but His voice is like that of an archangel and the sound of a trumpet. Now that ought to get rid of the silly notion that Gabriel is going to blow a trumpet.

THE REAL HOPE

To begin with, I don't think Gabriel owns a trumpet. And even if he owns a trumpet, I don't think he can blow a trumpet. And I'm confident we're not talking about Gabriel here at all. It's the Son of God, and He alone is coming to claim His bride and call His church out of the world. And, my friend, that's the hope today. That's the next happening in the program of prophecy, when He calls His own out of this earth. That ought to be a blessed hope for us in these days in which we live.

Many years ago when I was a pastor in Pasadena, we were invited out to celebrate the fiftieth wedding anniversary of one of the loveliest couples I have ever met. There were congratulations and a great deal of conversation. During the time of the dinner he reached over and patted his wife on the hand and said the loveliest thing that any man can say who has been married to a woman for fifty years. He said, "We're still on our honeymoon."

Isn't that lovely? On the way home that night I said to my wife, "What happened to ours?" We hadn't been married twenty years at that time. They'd been married fifty years and were still on their honeymoon. It wasn't long after this that I conducted his funeral. After the service the friends and loved ones came by. He was greatly beloved; many were weeping. Then his widow came out leaning on the arm of a friend. She was sorrowing, but she had a hope. She came up to the casket. She leaned over and patted him on the hand; she reached down and gave him just a quick kiss, then said, "John, I'll see you in the morning." She was just putting him in the motel for the night. And the morning is coming, that bright morning someday when the Lord Jesus will come. That's the hope of a believer today, friend, and it's hopeless without Him.

When I was a very young fellow, I ran with a very fast crowd, and in that fast crowd there was a son from a very wealthy family. He was engaged to a girl who was a debutante. And they made great preparations for the home they were going to build. The father of the boy gave them the home. He built a lovely home, a two-story southern home with columns. Then this young couple searched everywhere for valuable antiques to furnish that home. And they had it furnished beautifully. The day came for the wedding, and it was lovely.

Then they started on their honeymoon, driving into the big Smokies. They went around a curve, and a truck that was coming crowded them off the road. In fact it knocked them off the road down a precipice several hundred feet. They both were instantly killed. I went out to that house and looked in the window. I couldn't help but weep—tragic. Later I came to the Lord, and when I came back from school one year, I said to a friend of mine, "Let's go out and see that home." We went out. The grounds were well taken care of. The father, when word came of their death, had put the key in the door, turned the lock, and never opened it. We looked in the window. Dust had covered everything. And again I couldn't help but weep, but this time for a little different reason. I wondered where they had gone.

Isn't it tragic to live down here and make every arrangement to live here and no arrangement for over there? Jesus says, *"I go to prepare a place for you . . . that where I am, there ye may be also"* (John 14:2, 3). Thomas said, *"We don't know where you're going. How can we know the way?"* And the Lord Jesus said, *"I am the way, the truth, and the life; no man cometh unto the Father, but by me"* (v. 6). My friend, are you on the way to that place today? A prepared place. Do you have a hope today? Or today are you living like that couple did, for the here and now? And you may not live to enjoy it. They never spent five minutes in that home as a married couple. But they went out yonder into eternity unprepared. That's enough to break your heart, my friend.

What about you? Do you have a hope? Are you on the way? Is Christ your Savior today? Right where you're sitting you can make that decision. If you're not a child of God, all He asks you to do is trust Him as Savior. He died for you. He rose again. He did that because He loves you. He couldn't save you by love, so He had to give Himself to pay the penalty of your sins. And when you accept Him, you have a place over there. You have a hope.

11

GRACE IN THREE
TIME ZONES

For the grace of God that bringeth salvation hath appeared to all men, teaching us, that denying ungodliness and worldly lusts, we should live soberly, righteously, and godly, in this present world; looking for that blessed hope, and the glorious appearing of the great God and our Saviour Jesus Christ (TITUS 2:11–13).

Some of us who have a horse and buggy mental chassis never cease to wonder at the speed of travel in this jet age in which we live. The acceleration of transportation is one of the characteristics and marvels of the twentieth century. One winter I left Love Field in Dallas, Texas, during a cold blustering norther, with the thermometer hovering down around zero, and in little more than one hour we dropped down here in the salubrious climate of southern California. The reason this distance could be covered in somewhat over an hour was due to the three time zones. You leave Texas in what is called the Central Standard Time zone, you cross over the Mountain Standard Time zone, and you land in California in the Pacific Standard Time zone, so that there is a two hour differential between there and here. We are told that when our new jets are introduced, which probably will travel at two or three times the speed of sound, you will be able to arrive in Los Angeles two hours before you leave Dallas! It looks as though that will bring to pass the far-out dream of the poet who said:

> *Backward, turn backward, O Time in your flight,*
> *Make me a child again just for tonight!*

If you could just keep on going west and could unwind yourself, eventually you could put yourself back to the time you were a child. That would be indeed the wonder of this age!

There is something else in this wonderful world of wonders that has never ceased to elicit the awe and amazement of men. That, of course, is the grace of God. And the grace of God also functions in three time zones. These three time zones are given in Titus 2:11–13.

The first time zone speaks of the past: *"For the grace of God that bringeth salvation hath appeared to all men"* (v. 11). The second time zone is for the present, the here and now: *"Teaching us that, denying ungodliness and worldly lusts, we should live soberly, righteously, and godly in this present world"* (v. 12). Then there is the third time zone, which reaches into the future: *"Looking for that blessed hope, and the glorious appearing of the great God and our Saviour Jesus Christ"* (v. 13).

THE FIRST TIME ZONE—THE PAST

The first time zone of grace refers to a past event: *"For the grace of God that bringeth salvation hath appeared to all men"* (v. 11).

The first word, the little conjunction *for,* ordinarily is passed over because it does not seem too important. But you will find that Paul employs these little conjunctions and connectives like cement used in holding building blocks together. This word *for* is an atomic word. It is a little word with a big idea behind it. God always swings the door on a little hinge, and that is what you have here. This word *for* goes back and gathers up everything that has preceded it.

What has preceded it? Well, when you read the first chapter of Titus and the second chapter up to this point, you find that all Paul has been doing is giving good advice to a young preacher by the name of Titus. He has been giving him instructions; he has been telling him how to live the Christian life. In fact he has been taking up all degrees of Christians, all classes, every strata of the society of the saints—the young, the old, the married, the single, the widows—and has told them how they are to live. All of this has been good advice up to the word *for.*

Actually the good advice is not the gospel. Dr. Dodd, formerly the great Baptist preacher in Shreveport, Louisiana, made the statement, "My pulpit is the place for good news, my study is the place for good advice." Unfortunately many preachers reverse this order and think that the pulpit is the place for good advice. It is not. The gospel is not good advice, it is good news. But wait just a minute. The gospel is more than good news. Paul says: *"For I am not ashamed of the gospel of Christ: for it is* [not good news; it is] *the power of God unto salvation"* (Romans 1:16).

The gospel is power. My friend, good advice is not worth the snap of the fingers unless there is power to see it through. Unless you are able to carry it out, unless there is dynamic to be furnished with the ethic, it is of no value whatsoever. So Paul here is enjoining this young man Titus, as he is ministering at this time to the Cretians, to demand of them that they live lives that adorn the gospel of God because it is the power of God. Now notice this amazing verse: *"One of themselves* [that is, one of the Cretians], *even a prophet of their own, said, The Cretians are always liars, evil beasts, slow bellies"* (Titus 1:12).

I do not know what a slow belly is (some have translated it lazy gluttons), but whatever it is, I would not want to be one! Paul says this is the natural bent of the Cretians, and he moves on to add this: *"Not purloining, but showing all good fidelity; that they may adorn the doctrine of God our Saviour in all things"* (Titus 2:10).

He is saying that these people who have such an unsavory background, who by nature are almost like animals, now since they have been redeemed by the grace of God and since the gospel has power in it, they are to adorn the gospel of grace. Let me insert this statement: There is no excuse for any Christian to live a life of defeat and failure, absolutely none. We have accepted failure and defeat as being the norm of Christian living. God never intended it to be that way. There is power in the gospel of grace.

Now after Paul has given instruction and advice to this young preacher, he comes to his subject: *"The grace of God that bringeth salvation to all men hath appeared"* (Titus 2:11).

Notice the language here (I have changed the translation a little to better conform to the original). It does not say grace hath appeared to all men; the modifier goes back to "salvation." It brings salvation to all men. The salvation is for all men, including Cretians, of every class and condition. It is a gospel that is global; it is a cosmic gospel; it is for every man, woman, and child, irrespective of class, irrespective of race, irrespective of nation, irrespective of circumstances. The gospel is for all. (By the way, this is the only global message the world ever had until Communism came along. And there are those who believe that if the gospel had not been discredited in Europe, Communism would never have gotten a toehold. But Europe, though grounded in the Bible even as Germany was in the past, came to the place of repudiating the Word of God, which threw open the door for another worldwide philosophy that has swept throughout the world.) Christianity offers a gospel that is for all men.

"The grace of God that bringeth salvation to all men, it hath appeared" (Titus 2:11). The word *appear* is, in the Greek, *epiphaino*. The coming of Christ into the world is called an epiphany, that is, a shining forth. Paul is saying that the grace of God that bringeth salvation to all men has appeared; it has shown forth into the world. For 1900 years it has been shining forth; and though there are still many dark corners, it is intended for every creature.

We are introduced here to another great word, it is the great word of the gospel—*grace*. *"The grace of God that bringeth salvation to all men hath appeared"* (2:11).

Someone says, "Oh, yes, grace means unmerited favor." Right. But I also want to add that you cannot fathom the meaning of this word *grace*. We are told that God saves us by grace—"By grace are ye saved through faith." I want you to follow me very carefully now. We are not saved by the *love* of God, we are not saved by the *mercy* of God, we are saved by the *grace* of God.

Notice how Paul brought together all three of these great words in the Ephesian epistle:

> **But God, who is rich in mercy, for his great love wherewith he loved us, even when we were dead in sins, hath quickened us together with Christ, (by grace ye are saved)** (Ephesians 2:4, 5).

Notice that he does not say that we are saved by the love of God; he does not say that we are saved by the mercy of God. Mercy is the compassion of God that prompted Him to send the Savior to men, but mercy, even with God, is handcuffed. You can go into a hospital and see a loved one lying there sick. Your heart goes out in compassion and mercy to that loved one, but you cannot help him. Someone may come to you with a tragic story, and you can shed tears for him but still not be able to help him. You see, mercy must be able to act;

it has to be more than compassion if it is to be of any value whatsoever. If today God, by being big-hearted and merciful, could save one sinner, He could save all men. If He could save men by mercy, it was unnecessary for Christ to die. We would circumvent the cross, and all we would have in the sky would be a big-hearted old man. I do not mean to be irreverent, because He is not that kind of God. God is merciful, but He is more than that.

Then, my friend, love is the divine motive for God—"God so loved the world"—but He cannot save by love. He saves by grace: "By grace are ye saved." God, you see, is not only love. When you say that God is love, you have not said all you can say about God. God is righteous, God is holy, God is just. There are holy demands of a righteous God that must be met; there are just claims; there are righteous standards, and all of these must be satisfied. God cannot move in love without at the same time being righteous and just. Christ, by dying on the cross, met the demands and satisfied the claims of justice of a holy God. Love may long to save, but the immutable law of justice makes love powerless to do anything until the claims of justice have been satisfied. The reason Christ left heaven's glory was to come down to this earth to meet the just claims of God so that God might become unshackled. Christ paid our penalty so that all the debris might be moved out of the channel and His love might be free to flow. God who so loved the world may now shower that love on sinners because Christ died, and salvation is by grace.

You will recall several years ago that there was a Communist riot in South Korea when many thousands were killed. One young Communist boldly shot down two young men who stood up and declared themselves Christians (they were brothers). The Communists were defeated, and the murderer of these two boys was brought up for trial and sentenced to death. He would have been executed had it not been for the father of the two boys he had killed. The father was a pastor in Korea. He pleaded on behalf of the murderer, saying, "My two sons are dead and are now safe in heaven. But if this young man dies, he will go to hell." The judge was moved, and the young man was acquitted. The pastor soon after adopted him as his own son. This young Communist was marvelously and wonderfully saved, and at this time of writing is training in a Bible institute in Korea.

This is mercy extended without justice being satisfied. However, in this country, to be legal, the law must exact a penalty. Either the guilty man pays it, or someone else must pay it for him. There is a case on record in the South which involved a prominent judge and his delinquent son. The judge's only son had committed a serious crime and was to appear in his father's court. His father did a strange thing. Ordinarily a judge in that circumstance would disqualify himself; he did not. The boy was brought up, the evidence was presented, he was found guilty, and the judge said to him, "Though you are my own son, I shall have to sentence you." He sentenced him to ten years of hard labor in the penitentiary and assessed him a fine. The court was startled, and those who had come in as spectators were absolutely shocked to see the judge do this to his own boy. The boy was dismayed because he had thought he would get off. But after handing down the sentence, this judge left the bench and came around to the prisoner in the box. He said to his son, "Move over. You are going free because I am going to pay the penalty."

This is what God did for you. That is the reason God does not save by some sentimental gesture. When God saves, He does not open the back door of heaven and slip you in under cover of darkness. You come in the front door through the One who is the way, the truth, and the life. Because Christ took your penalty, the demands of justice have been met; and now the love of God, that was restrained because of His righteousness, is expressed. He is now able to save you by *grace*. When we were guilty, Christ paid the penalty.

Grace, furthermore, is not complicated by nor implicated with human effort. When God saves you by His grace, He gets no cooperation from you. He does not ask for any conduct or character on your part. God only asks men to believe Him, to trust Him, to receive Christ, to take His way. I sometimes hear the song, "God's Way Is the Best Way." I like that number. But may I say to you that it is not only the best way, it is the only way. There is no other way to save sinners. God actually is not receiving from man even faith. Have you noticed that? *"For by grace are ye saved through faith; and that not of yourselves: it is the gift of God: not of works, lest any man should boast"* (Ephesians 2:8, 9).

The whole package deal is the gift of God, faith included. There is no merit in faith; you can believe in the wrong thing. And faith is not some sort of leap in the dark, as I have heard a theologian in a seminary say. And it is not, my friend, that Indian rope trick. An Indian fakir comes out with a coiled up rope. He can do his trick in two ways, I am told. He can let the rope go up gradually until it is extended, or he can say, "Presto, hocus-pocus," and the rope jumps up and hangs suspended in the air. I have heard of fakirs who say to their helpers, "Saboo, climb up the rope." And the interesting thing is that he climbs up, then when he comes to the end of the rope, he just keeps climbing out of sight. I saw this Indian rope trick on the stage one time—not the man climbing, but the rope going up. A friend of mine who was working backstage told me that what I did not see was the black thread that was tied to the rope by which it was pulled up. As far as we know, the feat has never actually been done; it is just in the imagination of men. But I want to tell you that there are a great many people in our churches today who are trying to do it. My friend, the rope of faith does not hang in mid-air. Faith has to be anchored up yonder, and that anchor is none other than the Lord Jesus Christ himself. You remember that He said to Nathanael, whom he chose to be a disciple:

> *Because I said unto thee, I saw thee under the fig tree, believest thou? thou shalt see greater things than these. . . . Hereafter ye shall see heaven open, and the angels of God ascending and descending upon the Son of man* (John 1:50, 51).

He is the way, He is the rope; and faith must be placed in Him to have any value whatsoever, for He alone saves. God saves you by His grace. Oh, to believe that He is that good! I talked to a man in the hospital, and he received Christ. He kept repeating, "I can't believe God is that good!" But He is. God is that good. And yet multitudes of people have placed their faith in their own good works, thinking that somehow they are climbing the rope that leads to heaven. My friend, you are saved by grace, not by holding on to some little rope that you have made!

It is reported that some of the Eskimos up in the frozen North, in order to get rid of the wolves, take razor-sharp knives and bury them in the ice, then smear seal's blood over the surface. The wolves come along, smell that blood, and begin to lap it up. As they do so, those sharp knives cut their tongues. But they are intent upon lapping up

155

that blood. As fresh blood pours out, they think they have struck it rich. They will keep lapping it until they drop in their tracks, feeding on their own blood. There are multitudes of people right here who are feeding on their own goodness, their own righteousness, as if that could save them.

My beloved, "by grace are ye saved through faith" and "the grace of God that bringeth salvation hath appeared." It *hath* appeared. John Newton, who was a sinner if ever there was one, said, "I am not what I ought to be; I am not what I want to be; I am not what I hope to be in another world; but still I am not what I once used to be, and by the grace of God I am what I am." At this moment the grace of God alone can do this for you.

THE SECOND TIME ZONE—THE PRESENT

We come now to that which is all important for us today and that is the second time zone, the present.

Teaching us that, denying ungodliness and worldly lusts, we should live soberly, righteously, and godly, in this present world (Titus 2:12).

Two words here are important: *teaching* and *live*. The grace of God teaches us, and the grace of God teaches us how to live. In this verse God is not speaking to all men. He is speaking only to those who have come through the first time zone. He is speaking to those who have been saved by His grace. Now as we come into the present where we are today, God says, "I have something more for you. The grace of God will not only save you, the grace of God will teach you—teach you how to live." And it is the only thing that will. If you have been saved by the grace of God through the merit of Christ, then God has some demands to make upon you. But remember, He is not talking to the world now. Will you hear me carefully? I want to be kind but I want to be very firm. God is not trying to reform the world; He is redeeming men who will accept Christ. God has no good advice to offer unsaved men; the gospel is not an appeal to Christ-rejecting men to do better. I asked a man who came to me if he wanted to accept Christ. He said, "Well, I-I'll talk to you later about that. You know, I'm going to try to do better." I think I shocked him by saying, "You are a liar. You are not going to try to do better because if you are honest you know you have tried before, haven't you?"

"Yes," he admitted.

"How did you come out?"

"Well, I didn't do it."

"Neither will you do it this time. And I have news for you—God is not asking you to do better!" No, He is not. God has not asked the unsaved man to reform. I want to say this: If you have rejected Jesus Christ, if you have never accepted Him as your Savior, and you are trying to work this thing out yourself, you should try to get all you can out of life. The government at this moment is attempting a health education program and is asking you to give up cigarettes. But *God* is not asking this of you. No, He is not. Eat, drink, smoke cigarettes, for tomorrow you'll die of lung cancer, and they will put you in a flip-top box. Just to reform will not save you, so go ahead, get all you can out of this life, because you are lost. However, God is calling those who are His own, whom He has redeemed by the blood of Christ, to live for Him. He is teaching them to live. The word *teach* means to train a child, to educate. It is a process. The reason He saved you and left you in this life is that He might train you, that He might develop you.

There are two specifics concerning the teaching of grace that I want to mention.

The first specific is that the standards of grace are immeasurably higher than the standards of the law in the Old Testament. Someone asks, "How could David get by with sin?" My friend, if you read the record aright, you will find that he did not get by with it. And if you have been saved by the grace of God, you won't get by with sin. You have been called to a higher plane than were the men of the Old Testament. The Mosaic law said, "Love thy neighbor as thyself." Now listen to the law of Jesus: *"A new commandment I give unto you, That ye love one another; as I have loved you, that ye also love one another"* (John 13:34). He has called you to a much higher plane. Love your neighbor, not as yourself, but as Christ loves him! He repeats this standard: *"This is my commandment, That ye love one another, as I have loved you"* (15:12).

Paul was confronted by this new standard. Paul was a Pharisee, proud as a peacock. He kept the Mosaic law, and he said that he could stand blameless before God. But he was filled with pride—pride of place, pride of race, pride of face, pride of grace. That is the quartet that moves in upon all of us. Pride of place—he said, "I am a man of Tarsus, a citizen of no mean city." Pride of race—"I am a Hebrew of the Hebrews." Pride of face—"I am a Pharisee," a religious ruler, probably the most brilliant man of his day. Pride of grace—a cultured gentleman, a Roman citizen, and educated in all of the Greek philosophies. With all of this, he was lost. And when he came to Jesus Christ he found that there was a new standard altogether. He mentions it: *"In lowliness of mind let each esteem others better than themselves"* (Philippians 2:3). These commandments are on a higher plane than was ever presented under the law. It is so high that you may say, "That is a superhuman standard, and I cannot measure up to it." You are right. It is superhuman. God knows you cannot live up to it, and that brings me to this second specific of teaching us to live today.

Not only is the standard superhuman, but He has given supernatural enablement to live for Him. Listen to His provision:

> *Now we have received, not the spirit of the world, but the spirit which is of God; that we might know the things that are freely given to us of God* (1 Corinthians 2:12).

And to those who were carnal believers:

> *What? know ye not that your body is the temple of the Holy Ghost which is in you, which ye have of God, and ye are not your own? For ye are bought with a price: therefore glorify God in your body, and in your spirit, which are God's* (1 Corinthians 6:19, 20).

Also he points out this to the Galatian Christians:

> *This only would I learn of you, Received ye the Spirit by the works of the law, or by the hearing of faith? Are ye so foolish? having begun in the Spirit, are ye now made perfect by the flesh?* (Galatians 3:2, 3).

And through the beloved apostle John He writes:

> *And he that keepeth his commandments dwelleth in him, and he in him. And hereby we know that he abideth in us, by the Spirit which he hath given us* (1 John 3:24).

God, you see, has provided a supernatural enablement so that His child is not left to his own devices. God has given to him the Holy Spirit whereby he can live for God. He not only has delivered us from the penalty of sin, but He has delivered us from the *power* of sin. No wonder John Newton could say, "I am what I am by the grace of God." God by His grace provides the power to live for Him in the here and now.

THE THIRD TIME ZONE—THE FUTURE

"Looking for that blessed hope, and the glorious appearing of the great God and our Saviour Jesus Christ" (Titus 2:13). The "blessed hope" is the greatest beatitude for the believer today. Blessed are you if you have this hope, the object of which is the coming of the Lord Jesus Christ.

I wonder if you are aware of the pessimism felt by men in high places in our contemporary society. In an issue of the *Wall Street Journal*, James Reston, a very brilliant writer, discloses that there is a greater difference today between what public men say in public and what they say in private than at any time since the war:

> But the private conversations of thoughtful men here in Washington are quite different. For the first time since the war, one begins to hear doubts that mortal men are capable of solving or even controlling the political, social and economic problems life has placed before them.

Also George Bernard Shaw in *Too True to Be Good* penned this pathetic confession:

> The science to which I pinned my faith is bankrupt. . . . Its counsels which should have established the millennium have led directly to the suicide of Europe. I believed them once. . . . In their name I helped to destroy the faith of millions of worshipers in the temples of a thousand creeds. And now they look at me and witness the great tragedy of an atheist who has lost *his* faith.

159

These men are very pessimistic, are they not? And it was Bertrand Russell who predicted calamity before the end of this century:

Unless something unforeseeable occurs, one of three possibilities will have been realized . . . 1. The end of human life, perhaps of all life on our planet. 2. A reversion to barbarism after a catastrophic diminution of the population of the globe. 3. A unification of the world under a single government. . . .

What to Bertrand Russell is something unforeseeable, is to the child of God the blessed hope. *"Looking for that blessed hope and the glorious appearing of our great God and Saviour Jesus Christ"* (Titus 2:13). Our hope is anchored in our great God. There are those who say that Paul did not claim the deity of Christ. How much stronger can he make it than to say, "our great God and Saviour Jesus Christ"? My beloved, our hope of the future is in Him.

I remember the night I looked out my window at the moon, and thought, *Man in the moon, you may have a visitor before morning.* To me it is marvelous that man has made a little gadget that can put him on the moon. But infinitely more marvelous is the certainty of our rendezvous in space with Christ.

For the Lord himself shall descend from heaven with a shout, with the voice of the archangel, and with the trump of God: and the dead in Christ shall rise first: then we which are alive and remain shall be caught up together with them in the clouds, to meet the Lord in the air; and so shall we ever be with the Lord (1 Thessalonians 4:16, 17).

And if man can plot a course and determine the time he is going to arrive on the moon, certainly we should not doubt that God can take us off this earth to be with Himself.

And He will do it by grace—saved by grace, living in grace; and our hope is one that comes by grace.

Grace is Love blessing the ill-deserving,
Mercy helping the needy,
Power lifting the downtrodden,
Fullness filling the empty,

Compassion loving the hopeless,
Beauty clothing the naked, cleansing the defiled,
Tenderness melting the hardened,
And Joy gladdening the miserable.

Grace meets the sin of the sinner and removes it.
Grace answers for the sinner by dying for him.
Grace lives to empower the saint and live in him.
Grace equips the soldier and conquers through him.
Grace leads the child of God and cheers him.
Grace employs the servant and for service fits him.
Grace undertakes for the believer and supplies all his need.

What have you done with the marvelous, infinite, amazing grace of God, my friend? What have you done with it?

12

THE SHEPHERD AND
THE SHEEP—ASSURANCE

John 10

Had the important relationships between Christ and His church because of the cross been kept in mind, the disease of denominationalism and the curse of sectarianism might have been prevented. Thus would the church have been delivered through the years from much of its sorrow and heartbreak which have resulted from its divisions.

We understand that there are about three hundred sects in America today. My, how the church is divided! "Like a mighty army moves the church of God" may be on blueprint in a song, but it has not progressed beyond that stage. In fact, someone has written a parody of "Onward, Christian Soldiers," and it runs like this:

> *Like a halting caravan*
> *   Moves the church of Christ;*
> *We are feebly faltering*
> *   Toward our timid tryst.*
>
> *We are all divided,*
> *   Many bodies we,*
> *Kept apart by doctrine*
> *   And lack of charity.*
>
> *Careful, Christian pilgrims!*
> *   Walk in doubt and fear,*
> *With the cross of Jesus*
> *   Bringing up the rear.*

163

My friend, that is the picture at the present moment. Were the scriptural relationships observed and obeyed, the narrow and limited conception of the church would not prevail as it does in this hour. These relationships, as we find them in God's Word, enable believers to see beyond the limited borders or confines of the church or little group to which they belong. The church needs a full-orbed view today. It desperately needs 20-20 vision to see what the real church of the living Christ is and always has been. Certainly its vision must be cleared of the myopic, jaundice-blurred view of some group that wears a certain label.

Right now, loyalty to a sect is the test under the present system. A man may be rank in doctrine, but if loyal to some certain organization, he will pass muster. The *organization* is the sacred cow of the present day. Beloved, the total body of Christ, the family of God, is lost sight of at the present moment, and, as a result, there has been a movement—a superorganization—forged and forced down upon the church, operating under the title of the World Council of Churches. That organization is not the solution to the problem of the hour. This relationship between Christ and His church is not maintained by an organization functioning from the outside but must rise from the grassroots as the individual believer keeps the unity of the Spirit. That is the thing that will cure today's sectarian sickness. It is the one remedy.

To see this we must note the seven figures used in Scripture to clearly delineate the relationship that exists between Christ and His church. We list them here: the Shepherd and the sheep; the Vine and the branches; the Cornerstone and the stones of the building; the Head and the body; the High Priest and the priesthood of believers; the Bridegroom and the bride; and the Last Adam and the new creation. All of these wonderful figures set forth the blessed relationship between Christ and His church—because of His cross.

Did you note as you read this list that each figure is drawn from life? All are familiar figures; they are commonplace and are to be found in the everyday experiences of most people. We find that they are drawn from the animal, vegetable, and mineral kingdoms: from the animal kingdom, the sheep; the vegetable kingdom, the vine; the mineral kingdom, the stone. The Lord Jesus just reached out and drew from those things that were around Him.

Again we would like to pass on to you a bit of verse that expresses the fact in a wonderful way.

> He talked of grass and wind and rain,
> And fig trees and fair weather,
> And made it His delight to bring
> Heaven and earth together.
> He spoke of lilies, vines, and corn,
> The sparrow and the raven;
> And words so natural, yet so wise,
> Were on men's hearts engraven.
>
> Author Unknown

So the Lord just reached out and from life drew these figures of speech which carry a wealth of spiritual meaning to us today.

THERE ARE SHEEP OF KINDS

Let us break into this study of relationships at the figure of the Shepherd and the sheep. The figure of the sheep is, no doubt, the broadest term He ever used. It is the broadest term set down in Scripture. Actually we find all humanity spoken of as sheep. Every person is a sheep. This term fits every man who ever lived upon this earth. Read this: "All we like sheep have gone astray." That applies to everyone. Now someone is going to say, "Yes, but the Bible says that there are sheep and goats." If you go back to the twenty-fifth chapter of Matthew and read it carefully, you will find that He is not talking of individuals, but of nations. He never did call an individual a goat. It is recorded that when He saw the multitudes, He was moved with compassion for them for "they were as sheep without a shepherd." That is His figure for every man on earth—a sheep. Pin that down in your thinking; it is important. Note that the Gentile nations are called "goat nations" in the twenty-fifth chapter of Matthew.

Also we must recall that He made a distinction in sheep. He said to the religious rulers, "Ye are not of *my* sheep," and then He said, "*My* sheep hear my voice." So then, there are two kinds of sheep—those who are His and those who are not His. But let us understand one thing: They are sheep and not goats; all are sheep in His eyes.

Now it is true that the nation Israel was spoken of in just that fashion back in the Old Testament. Turn to Psalm 74, for instance, and read this reference to the nation Israel: *"O God, why hast thou cast us off forever? Why doth thine anger smoke against the sheep of thy pasture?"* This is the nation Israel. Then in Jeremiah 23:1: *"Woe be unto the pastors that destroy and scatter the sheep of my pasture! saith the LORD."* He speaks there of the nation Israel.

Now in Christ's day, when He was here upon the earth, it was true that the nation Israel was considered in Scripture as being in a particular way God's sheep. The religious rulers, however, assumed that those of Israel were the only sheep that God ever had or could have. That is where they made their blunder! Therefore, the statement made by the Lord Jesus Christ in the tenth chapter of John, which seems so natural and normal to us because we have heard it ever since we were children, was without the shadow of a doubt the most revolutionary, the most radical statement the religious rulers had ever heard.

Notice that it all went back to the incident of the opening of the eyes of the blind man who was sent down to the pool of Siloam. When he returned from the pool, his sight restored, he sought the Lord but could not find Him. However, the religious rulers quickly seized him who had been blind, for he had been healed on the Sabbath day. They questioned him, but he could tell them very little. He as much as said, "To begin with, I did not see the Man with my eyes because He anointed them and sent me to the pool of Siloam. It was not until I reached there that my eyes were opened, and then He was gone. I do not know a great deal about Him, but I do know one thing: Once I was blind, now I can see—that is my testimony."

The statement of the blind man so enraged the Pharisees that in their mad effort to condemn the Lord, they called in the man's parents. But the parents were afraid to testify, for they knew that they were in danger of being excommunicated. Therefore, they quietly compromised and moved out of the picture.

But this man whose sight had been restored still came at the Pharisees with his argument which virtually was as follows: "It is a funny thing that you are saying that this man is not one who works miracles of God. My eyes are opened. I know that He did it, and I know that it is a miracle!" It is a wonderful thing, beloved, when you come to know that much! When you can say, "Once I was blind, but now I see. Once I was lost, but now I am found." It is a gift of His grace in your life. This poor blind man knew it.

The positive nature of his testimony so heightened the anger of the religious rulers that they called a meeting of the Sanhedrin and put the man out of the synagogue. He was excommunicated. It was then that he found himself in a precarious position, for he was ruined socially and economically. They wrecked him. Scripture records that "they cast him out" (John 9:34). Then the Lord Jesus came to his defense and told the religious rulers that they really did not understand.

CHRIST—THE SHEPHERD

Thus He began to set forth the truth. John records His words in chapter ten, verse one: *"Verily, verily, I say unto you, He that entereth not by the door into the fold of the sheep, but climbeth up some other way, the same is a thief and a robber"* (ASV).

We must first understand that the sheepfold was Israel, and then we are ready to follow our Lord as He patiently opened the truth to these men of the synagogue.

He explained to them that He had not crawled over the fence as a robber but had come to the sheepfold in a regular way, though He could have come in many ways. He could have come as an angel of glory or have been born in Caesar's palace. This He did not do. He was born of the line of David, followed the Mosaic law all the way through, and had thus come in at the *door* of the sheepfold. He had not climbed over the fence as a thief or robber.

As we follow His telling of this great truth, we are startled with a tremendous statement He makes in verse three when He says that the porter opened the door for Him. Did you notice that? And have you read carefully enough to ask yourself who this porter might be? The writer believes that the porter is none other than the Holy Spirit.

Then He said a most radical thing to them: *"But he that entereth in by the door is the shepherd of the sheep. To him the porter openeth, and the sheep hear his voice; and he calleth his own sheep by name."* Now listen, *"and [he] leadeth them out"* (John 10:2-3). Remember, the sheepfold is Israel, and the Lord Jesus said, "I am the Shepherd who has come in a regular way into the sheepfold, and I

167

have called my sheep. My sheep hear my voice and they follow me, and this man who was blind has come out because he is my sheep. Other sheep came out also, but there were those which stayed inside." He said, "I am the shepherd, and Israel is the sheepfold." Now read this: *"When he hath put forth all his own, he goeth before them, and the sheep follow him: for they know his voice"* (John 10:4, ASV). Thus the Lord defends the blind man by the simple explanation: "I have come in the regular way into the nation Israel. I am not a thief or robber but have come into the sheepfold and am calling My sheep by name and leading them out of the sheepfold, Israel." This is tremendous!

THE SHEPHERD FORMS HIS FLOCK

To these bewildered men He further says in verse sixteen: *"And other sheep I have, which are not of this fold."* Unfortunately this has been translated "fold," and it really ought to be "flock." Let us read it again. "And other sheep I have, which are not of this flock." This body which He is forming by a calling out could not be a fold or sheepfold, because Israel is the sheepfold. Christ says that He is forming a new flock and that He has called out this man who was blind and was in the sheepfold to be a member of His new flock. Then He added that He has sheep other than those whom He has called out of this sheepfold: *"them also I must bring, and they shall hear my voice; and there shall be one fold* [flock]*, and one shepherd."*

As far as His flock is concerned, it is one flock today. How tragic it is, and has been, to have the Baptist sheep over here and the Presbyterian sheep over there and the Methodist sheep in still another area. After all, sheep are sheep, and those who are in His flock are one. There is one flock and one Shepherd—that is the picture of His church today.

He said, "There are other sheep I have who are not in this flock here. I must bring them. I have called the blind man, but I have some red, some yellow, some black, and some white; and even in Los Angeles, New York, London, and other points down yonder two thousand years from now, there will be more sheep that are to be members of My flock." He has one flock, and there is one Shepherd today.

We find that the Lord Jesus Christ has a threefold relationship to this flock which is known as His church. First of all, He is the *Good Shepherd,* and He defines the Good Shepherd in verse 11: *"I am the good shepherd: the good shepherd giveth his life for the sheep."* Then He is the *Great Shepherd,* for we read in the magnificent benediction given in Hebrews 13:21: *"Now the God of peace, who brought again from the dead the great shepherd of the sheep with the blood of an eternal covenant, even our Lord Jesus, make you perfect in every good thing to do his will"* (ASV). He is also the Great Shepherd of the sheep in Psalm twenty-three. But wait, that does not tell the total picture. He is also the *Chief Shepherd.* That speaks of the future. Peter says in his first epistle, chapter five, verse four: *"And when the chief Shepherd shall appear, ye shall receive a crown of glory that fadeth not away."*

THE GOOD SHEPHERD

We have already seen verse 11 of John 10, but drop down to verse 15 and read: *"Even as the Father knoweth me, and I know the Father; and I lay down my life for the sheep"* (ASV).

He is not through with this thought for it is very important to Him, as we see in verse 17: *"Therefore doth the Father love me, because I lay down my life, that I may take it again"* (ASV).

Again and again He repeats the fact that He is the Good Shepherd and that the Good Shepherd will lay down His life for the sheep. That was an amazing figure of speech to those people, for in the Old Testament we learn that while the shepherd cared for his flock, at times he reached down into the flock and took a sheep to be slaughtered for food when he was hungry. If he was cold he would slaughter a sheep for his clothing. If he needed a sacrifice he would use a sheep for the sacrifice. In other words, the little sheep had to die for the shepherd.

But it is passing strange that here is a Shepherd who will die for His sheep. Stranger still, He identifies Himself with His sheep. *"He was oppressed, and he was afflicted, yet he opened not his mouth: he is brought as a lamb to the slaughter, and as a sheep before her shearers is dumb, so he openeth not his mouth"* (Isaiah 53:7). He not only is the Shepherd, but He came down here into the flock and became a sheep that He might die on the cross. *"But we see Jesus, who was*

169

*made a little lower than the angels for the suffering of death,
crowned with glory and honour; that he by the grace of God should
taste death for every man"* (Hebrews 2:9).

But that is not all. We must read in verses 14–16 of that same
chapter:

*Forasmuch then as the children are partakers of flesh and
blood, he also himself likewise took part of the same; that
through death he might destroy him that had the power of
death, that is, the devil; and deliver them who through fear of
death were all their lifetime subject to bondage. For verily he
took not on him the nature of angels; but he took on him the
seed of Abraham.*

My beloved, this is wonderfully strange. Here is a Shepherd who not
only dies for His sheep, but He comes down into the flock and becomes one of the sheep! May I say, ever so reverently, Mary had a
little Lamb.

When Abel brought the offering to God of a little lamb, he knew
that there was coming a day when a forerunner would step out, put
an X mark on a sheep, and say, "Behold the Lamb of God that taketh
away the sin of the world." Jesus Christ was the Good Shepherd giving His life for the sheep.

You may recall having read David's account of his purpose to go
out and meet Goliath. It is given in 1 Samuel 17:33–36.

*And Saul said to David, Thou art not able to go against this
Philistine to fight with him; for thou art but a youth, and he a
man of war from his youth. And David said unto Saul, Thy
servant was keeping his father's sheep; and when there came a
lion, or a bear, and took a lamb out of the flock, I went out after
him, and smote him, and delivered it out of his mouth; and
when he arose against me, I caught him by his beard, and smote
him and slew him. Thy servant smote both the lion and the
bear: and this uncircumcised Philistine shall be as one of them,
seeing he hath defied the armies of the living God* (ASV).

The strong Son of God, the Good Shepherd, came down to this
earth and went out and met the devil. The other sheep could not!

170

Certainly we could not meet him—we are no match for him. But Christ met and conquered him and wrought salvation on the cross. Today He gives this invitation out of His great heart of love, "I am the door"—the door to the flock—"by me if any man enter in, he shall be saved."

THE GREAT SHEPHERD

"I am the good shepherd, and know my sheep, and am known of mine. As the Father knoweth me, even so know I the Father: and I lay down my life for the sheep. And other sheep I have, which are not of this fold: them also I must bring, and they shall hear my voice; and there shall be one fold [flock], *and one shepherd"* (John 10:14–16).

The emphasis here is upon the word *my.* They are *my* sheep. Now that is where the twenty-third Psalm comes in. Listen to Him as He says, "They are *my* sheep." And His sheep can say, "The Lord is *my* shepherd." Oh, how wonderful is the little possessive pronoun there! My sheep—my Shepherd. It makes all of the difference in the world whether you say "Christ is *a* Shepherd," or whether you say, "Christ is *my* Shepherd."

There was a group of believers who got together and started a Christian day school in Pasadena, California. How thrilled we were that first year to see all of the little ones who came. I went almost every day to watch them come, and then back again to watch them as they left for home when school was out. Little lambs, they were. Then one day I took *my* little lamb over. I never shall forget. She did not want me to go in but asked that I leave her at the sidewalk. I did and then watched her walk up to the door. I did not know it was so far from the walk to the door; nor did I know that she was so small compared to that small building. Then I was right back over there when the hour came for school to be dismissed, and they came out— those precious little lambs. But all of a sudden, I saw *my* little lamb! There is a lot of difference between sheep and *my* sheep.

YOUR SECURITY AS HIS SHEEP

Listen to the Lord Jesus now. My friend, you can be included here. "My sheep hear my voice. I know them. I give unto them eternal life, and they shall never perish, neither shall any man pluck them out of my hand. My Father which gave them me is greater than all, and no created thing can pluck them out of my Father's hand. I have the hand of deity; He has the hand of deity. And I and my Father—we are one. When we put a sheep between our hands, the little fellow never gets out! We do not lose sheep. We are not in the business of losing sheep!" One may get out of the flock—yes, they do—but this Shepherd went out on the mountainside and got that one that everyone else had given up. He was not satisfied with ninety-nine; He had to have one hundred.

"I give unto them eternal life and they shall never perish." Now we can well imagine that someone might say, "I do not like that. After all, I might get saved today and lost tomorrow." It is true, my friend—you might, and so might I. For if it depended upon me, I might be lost within the next five minutes.

Let us imagine one of these little sheep trotting up and saying, "Say, I am a clever little sheep, and I am smart. I know my way around. Do you want to know how I remain safe, how I have missed the wolf? Well, now, look here, do you see these claws of mine, how sharp they are—lions are afraid of them. I am a mean little sheep. And look at these fangs—I can bite wild animals with them. Say! if I get in a tight place these legs of mine can run." You say that is utterly ridiculous because no sheep has sharp claws and fangs and neither can a sheep run fast. You are right. Do you know why our Lord said that His sheep are safe? It is because of the keeping power of the Shepherd and certainly not because of any ability that lies in the sheep. *"My sheep hear my voice, and I know them, and they follow me. And I give unto them eternal life; and they shall never perish."* Why? Because no man is going to pluck them out of His hand!

We must return to His invitation: *"I am the door: for by me if any man enter in, he shall be saved."* I do not know who you are as you read this message, but if you are His sheep, you will hear His voice. If the Spirit of God speaks to you—and I say this very kindly and carefully—for God's sake listen to the Shepherd; He is calling you. "I am the door." If you will not step through this door, it is because you *will* stay out. His invitation is to you.

13

THE VINE AND THE
BRANCHES—ABIDING

John 15

To gain a new truth for a new day we must go to the Upper Room and there hear our blessed Lord as He gives the famous discourse of John, chapters thirteen through seventeen. Many new things were given to His disciples in these chapters, and they were given in full view of the cross of Christ. He constantly repeated the fact, "I am leaving you. I am going away. I am now facing the crisis through which I shall pass." Actually, at the time He gave this discourse, He was less than twenty-four hours from death. In other words, twenty-four hours after He gave this message, He was lying in death in the tomb of Joseph of Arimathaea. So then, this at which we are looking is tremendous!

This fifteenth chapter of John doubtless was not given in the Upper Room—at least this is the belief of many, and we judge that to be true because the last verse, in fact, the very last statement of the fourteenth chapter of John is, "Arise, let us go hence." He left the Upper Room, and chapters fifteen through seventeen were spoken somewhere else.

There has always been a question as to just where He gave the metaphoric teaching of the vine and branches found in the fifteenth chapter of John. There are two ideas relative to this, both of which have merit in them.

In the first place, there are those who believe that after Christ and

His disciples left the Upper Room they stepped out into a beautiful eastern night, made brilliantly clear by a full moon which commonly shone at the time of the Passover. And wending their way along Jerusalem's deserted streets, through the gate, down the valley to the Brook Kidron, they crossed over. At this point, no doubt, the Lord paused and directed the attention of the little company to a well-kept vineyard on the hill slope just beyond and above them. As they looked, the soft glowing silver of the moonlight brushed each leaf and fruit cluster, making the vineyard seem to nestle against the hillside as a beautiful mosaic—a perfect illustration for our Lord to use in sealing a great truth to their souls as He gave them John 15. If you accept that view you will find yourself in very good company in the world of scholarship.

And again a large body of thinkers, primarily British scholars of the past, held that Christ did not give His discourse at Kidron, but that in going to the Garden of Gethsemane that night, He passed by the temple. And it was there that He gave the discourse. Personally, I rather follow this position.

The temple of Herod had great gates. They were massive works of art, and at that time—though the temple was not actually completed—the gates were open all night long, for this was the custom on Passover night. Thus He must have stopped before the gates.

Those gates were one of the sights to be seen in Jerusalem, and it is doubtful if any tourist would have gone to Jerusalem without being taken to the temple and shown them. They were wrought of bronze by expert craftsmen in Greece and had been floated across the Hellespont, then brought down to Jerusalem and with great difficulty swung in place on mighty hinges.

Those massive gates of bronze had cast into them a grapevine of solid gold, and that vine symbolized the nation Israel—a sort of coat of arms of Israel. Go back into the Old Testament, and again and again that figure is used. In Psalm 80:8 we find that Asaph said, *"Thou broughtest a vine out of Egypt: thou didst drive out the nations, and plantedst it"* (ASV). That meant Israel, for the minute God called them out of the land of Egypt, He called them a vine, the vine of His planting.

And the prophets picked up that theme. Isaiah, Hosea, Jeremiah, and Ezekiel all spoke of the vine, the vine that was the nation Israel;

but it was Isaiah who so richly developed the theme. In the fifth chapter of Isaiah, verse one, we find, *"Let me sing for my well-beloved a song of my beloved touching his vineyard"* (ASV), and the remainder of that chapter is a song about the name of Israel and the fact that they were God's vine.

In Christ's day that vine stood for Israel in the profoundest sense of the term. It stood for the nation Israel as probably nothing else did, and that night it was to have its greatest significance burned into the thinking of God's children throughout all time.

REVOLUTIONARY TEACHING

When the Lord Jesus Christ left the Upper Room with His company, He walked with them down the deserted streets of Jerusalem to the temple. Standing before the great gates that gave to Israel her "coat of arms," the gates which by their presence had told the world that the nation Israel was God's vine, the Son of God said, "I am the true vine."

Now when He said, "I am the true vine," He said something that was plainly amazing for the very reason that the word used here for *true* (and a thing can be true, of course, in two different ways) was *alethinos*. This can mean truth as over against error, or it can mean that which is genuine as over against that which is spurious or counterfeit. Here it is used in the latter sense. He was saying to them, "I am the *genuine* vine, and the nation Israel from now on is a spurious vine—it is counterfeit. I am the genuine vine."

Just how revolutionary that was would be hard to state. Nothing more startling or sensational could have been said to those standing there with Him, for they had been schooled in the Mosaic system; they had been brought up under Judaism—a God-given religion. And here He said to them, "Now it is no longer a religion, no longer a system to which you belong, no longer identification with Judaism, no longer important that you be of the seed of Abraham. No longer can you reach God through ritual, nor will ceremony bring you into right relationship with God." He swept it all away from them when He said, "I am the genuine vine."

This was all revolutionary; it was unheard of, upsetting and unbelievable to these men. Then He added a great new truth, "My

Father is the husbandman." You can go directly to God; no longer must you go through a priest. There was no longer a ritual and system between you and God. You are to go directly to a Person, directly to God!

Now that teaching is so familiar to Bible students today that the writing of it seems redundant, but for those men it was just out of their world; it was hard for them to grasp at the time. If this is familiar to you, remember that you and I need to lay hold of it in a new way.

Before we look at the teaching, we want to find what He meant when He used the metaphor, "the vine and the branches." Why did He use the term "the vine" at all? What objective had He in mind?

The primary function of a vine is to produce fruit. Actually, a grapevine is a plant, the wood of which has no value. You cannot make furniture of it. You would not go to a furniture mart and ask to be shown the latest models in "grapevine wood." You would be shown maple, cherry, or walnut, but not grapevine wood. The only value that a grapevine has is to produce fruit. This is the primary thought about which He is going to talk, for He says that He is the Vine and we are the branches. And the whole purpose of the relationship is that He might increase the yield of our lives.

Note that there are three degrees of fruit-bearing of which He speaks: *"Every branch in me that beareth not fruit he taketh it away; and every branch that beareth fruit, he purgeth* [cleanseth] *it, that it may bear more fruit"* (John 15:2). First He says there shall be *fruit*. Second, there shall be *more* fruit. But He is not satisfied with that. Third, *"he that abideth in me and I in him, the same beareth much fruit."* So we find that the three degrees of fruitbearing are fruit, *more* fruit, *much* fruit.

We must emphasize something here, for there are those who have come to this passage and have tried to say that this proves you can be joined to the Vine today and removed tomorrow; thus you lose your salvation. Let us understand one thing clearly: He is not talking about salvation here at all; He is talking about fruit. If you want salvation discussed, go back to the figure of the sheep and the Shepherd—you have salvation and the assurance of salvation there. Here the figure is used to reveal the fact that He wants to produce fruit, and He gives the method that He uses to produce fruit in the lives of those who are His own.

In talking about cutting off a branch, He is not conveying the meaning of the loss of salvation—definitely not! He means that the branch is removed from the place of fruit-bearing. Sometimes that means for the unproductive Christian that He removes him from this world through death.

It was said of Joseph in Jacob's prophecy concerning him: He shall be *"a fruitful bough, he will be even a fruitful bough by a well,"* and then he went on to say, his *"branches run over the wall"* (Genesis 49:22). In other words, there is to be fruit which can be picked by those going by.

My friend, it is His desire that there shall be fruit in the life of believers so that the world can see the fruit and know what the fruit is. Follow then His teaching as you read it in verse 2: "Every branch in me that beareth not fruit, he taketh away." The believer who bears no fruit is taken away from this place of exhibition of fruit-bearing.

Verse six of this fifteenth chapter holds a tremendous teaching: *"If a man abide not in me, he is cast forth as a branch, and is withered; and men gather them, and cast them into the fire, and they are burned."* What is burned? The fruit is burned! You ask me, "Are you sure of that?" My friend, I am not only sure of that; I know it!

If you will turn to the third chapter of 1 Corinthians, you will find that Paul the Apostle used the same figure of speech in referring to the works of believers. He says in effect, "For other foundation can no man lay than that which is laid, which is Jesus Christ. You cannot lay that foundation; all you can do is to build upon it. If any man build on this foundation, wood, hay, stubble, precious stones, silver . . . every man's work shall be tested by fire." What is tested by fire— his salvation? No! His *works*.

Paul says that if a man is on the foundation, every work that he builds thereon will be tested by fire, and if it is nothing but wood, hay, and stubble, it will be burned. But the Apostle hastens to say, "but he himself shall be saved; yet so as by fire" (v. 15).

If a man's life brings forth thorns and thistles year in and year out, there is only one conclusion at which we can arrive—he is not "in Christ." Now if he accidentally stumbles and falls into sin and does not bring forth fruit, the Lord Jesus will prune him and trim him. And if he continues, then the Lord will remove him—"every branch in me that beareth not fruit he taketh away." This is God's Word; it means that he is taken from the place of fruit-bearing by death. God will not let one of His branches continue to go on and on without bearing fruit.

WHAT IS THIS FRUIT?

Now can we identify this fruit? I think we can determine the kind of fruit about which He is talking.

There are those who say that this means soul winning. If you believe that, there is Scripture for your position. In Romans 1:13 Paul tells the Romans, *"I would not have you ignorant, brethren, that oftentimes I purposed to come unto you, (but was let,) that I might have some fruit among you also, even as among other Gentiles."* Beloved, that refers to souls that are saved, and Paul calls that fruit-bearing.

But in John 15, I think he means something else. He means that the logic of the work of the Holy Spirit in the life of the believer is that the fruit *results* in soul winning. Let us look at it. In Galatians 5:22 we find what is the fruit of the Spirit in the life of God's child: *"But the fruit of the Spirit is love, joy, peace, longsuffering, kindness, goodness, faithfulness, meekness, self-control; against such there is no law"* (ASV). That is the kind of fruit of which Jesus is speaking. When that fruit is in the life of a believer, you may be sure he has an influence on someone, and that someone will come to Christ.

In this day and hour in which we are living, it seems that more people are influenced by the life lived by the individual believer than by any sermon that is given. The frustrated person looks at the child of God who moves with a calm, steady tread regardless of difficulties—the product of his unswerving faith—and the unbeliever is moved by such display of the fruit of the Spirit.

This present moment is as good as any for making an honest search of our lives to find what fruit there is for the hungry world about us.

With the search ended, did you find fruit, or to the great joy of your heart, did you find *more* fruit, or by having given the Holy Spirit free rein in your life, did you find *much* fruit?

Can it be that the search leaves you discouraged—you feel that you cannot honestly say that there is fruit to be found? Then I have good news for you. With the child of God there should not be the blight of discouragement, for God has made every arrangement for you and me to have fruit in our lives, and of the kind that He wants grown there.

My friend, look carefully with me at these conditions of fruit-bearing. They are simple. There are just three of them.

IN CHRIST

The first is found in the little expression that the Lord Jesus used here in the very first statement that He made, "Every branch *in me*." Immediately we learn that we must be "in Christ." I suppose the greatest expression in the New Testament is the expression "in Christ." I shall call your attention to it as we read—it occurs again and again.

"In Christ" is *justification*. "He was delivered for our offences; He was raised for our justification." "Christ in us" is *sanctification*. If we are to bear fruit, we must be "in Christ." Then by what means is it possible for us to meet this condition? That is simple. Simply trust Him! When you and I come to the place where we realize that there is nothing within ourselves, "nothing in my hand I bring; simply to thy cross I cling," then the Spirit of God puts us "in Christ."

He tells us in direct terms that we cannot do anything to produce fruit. "As the branch cannot bear fruit of itself, except it abide in the vine, so neither can ye, except ye abide in me." What He is saying is that when you and I come to Him and trust Him as our Savior, the Spirit of God, in a very vital way, joins us to Christ as the branch is joined to the vine. In examining a grapevine, it is difficult to tell where the branch begins and the vine leaves off!

Among the folk who come to my office from time to time, many will ask, "Why do you keep that little piece of wood on your desk?" Well, I took this from a vineyard up in San Joaquin Valley. It is a section of vine out of which grows a branch. The owner of the vineyard told me that if two folk would have a tug of war with this section, it would break, but never where the vine and branch are joined together for that is the strongest point. Now if you pull on a branch that goes into a tree it will always break at the trunk of the tree—in a tree that is the weakest place. But in a grapevine that is the strongest point. Where I split that grapevine wide open you could see that the life of that vine went down through the branch—a living, vital relationship. Before we can produce any fruit at all we must be sure of one thing: that we are joined to Christ.

It is not until we get to verse 5 that He mentions the fact that we are branches: *"I am the vine, ye are the branches."* And we become one in Christ when we trust Him as our Savior and are identified with Him.

I think that the greatest term that expresses salvation, according to the Bible, is this one word *identification.* To be saved does not mean to be joined to a church, to go through this, or to do that; it means to be identified with Christ, vitally joined to Him through a living faith in Him as Savior.

PURGED

He mentions the second condition of fruit-bearing immediately by saying, *"Every branch in me that beareth not fruit he taketh away, and every branch that beareth fruit* [even a little] *he purgeth it."* That is, He prunes it. Actually the word there for "prune" is the word *kathairo.* It means that He actually cleanses it. Many times in our lives we are not producing much fruit—there is not much love, not much joy, not much peace in our lives (perhaps some, but not much). The Heavenly Father, the husbandman, steps in close with His pruning shears and He trims. And it hurts when He trims. Years ago a Puritan divine observed, "The husbandman is never so close to the branch as when he is trimming it." He is never so close to you as when He is trimming you, my friend. And when He is trimming you, it is wonderful to get in close to Him.

There is a story, though personal, that is worth the telling. When I was a boy, I used to play hooky from school. Today, they call such boys juvenile delinquents, but back in those days they did not call us that. I recall that I went to school one April morning with good intentions. I did not intend to play hooky, but I got under the influence of some "bad boys," and they suggested that I go fishing with them. I went fishing with them, and we fished all day. We didn't catch a thing! And in the afternoon our consciences bothered us; personally I was afraid to go home without my books, and they were at school. The other fellows felt the same way, and we decided that when school was out, we would get our books and go home, acting as though we had been to school. It did not work.

Apparently the professor anticipated that, and the minute we stepped into the schoolroom, he stepped into the room also and invited us into his office for a conference. So we went in. One of the boys had been in there before, and he knew the nature of the "conference." He said to us, "Now he uses a long, thin hickory switch, and when he begins to strike you, don't back away from him. It will kill you if you do. The thing to do every time he hits you is to take a step toward him. The closer you get to him the less it will hurt you." So I tried it—it worked! It was wonderful! By the time I took two or three steps I was so close to him that I could not even feel it.

I have thought about that a great deal since then. In the case of many of God's children, He has stepped in and pruned. He has done surgery and, oh, it has been terrible! They have said, "It hurts so much!" My friend, why do you not move close to Him where it does not hurt? The closer you get to Him, the less it will hurt.

But the Father always prunes His branches that they might not just bring forth fruit, but that they might bring forth *much* fruit. He is not even satisfied with *more* fruit. He wants a bountiful crop. You recall what He said in another parable, "Some bring forth thirtyfold, and some sixty, and some an hundredfold." Here they are: fruit, more fruit, much fruit. He wants a hundredfold from those who are His, and so He steps in to prune them. But how does the Husbandman prune us? What does He use? Will you listen to this: *"Now ye are clean through the Word which I have spoken unto you"* (John 15:3). The Word of God is the pruning knife. *"The Word of God is quick* [living] *and powerful and sharper than any two-edged sword"* (Hebrews 4:12).

Beloved, I state this with all the force I can muster: I believe that the Bible is God's Word. I believe that this Book is more than just a book. I believe that this Book has a cleansing power. If you will read it, "you are clean through the Word which I have spoken unto you." The Bible will clean up your life. As someone has said, "The Bible will keep you from sin or sin will keep you from the Bible."

ABIDING IN CHRIST

Let us examine the third condition for fruit-bearing. First of all, we must be identified with Christ, just as the branch is identified with the vine. Then comes the pruning of those who are His, and then the third thing is—abiding! That is mentioned again and again here. Will you listen to this? *"Abide in me, and I in you. As the branch cannot bear fruit of itself, except it abide in the vine; no more can ye, except ye abide in me"* (John 15:4). Three times in one verse He talks about abiding. "I am the vine, ye are the branches: he that abideth in me, and I in him, the same bringeth forth much fruit: for without me ye can do nothing." Now listen to verse six: *"If a man abide not in me, he is cast forth as a branch."* Abiding in Christ.

Listen to Him: *"Without me ye can do nothing"* (v. 4). I want to make this startling statement: You *cannot* live the Christian life. And I have something more sensational than that to say: God never asked you to live the Christian life! Beloved, listen to Him: "Without me ye can do nothing." Oh, how important it is—"Without me ye can do nothing." You and I may produce fruit that is imitation, but the only way we can produce fruit today that is acceptable to Him, fruit that is genuine fruit, is to abide in Christ.

He says that *He* wants to live the Christian life *through* you—as from that vine there comes life flowing into the branch, and the branch produces fruit. But that branch can never say, "I produced this fruit on my own. I did it of myself. What a smart branch I am." Friend, that branch knows that the fruit it produced came out of the vine to which it is joined. You and I need to abide in Christ. You can move away to a place out of His will and try to produce fruit, but there will not be any there. "Without me ye can do nothing."

Someone says, "How do you abide in Christ?" I think it is very simple myself. He says, "If ye keep my commandments, ye shall abide in my love." Obedience to Christ is abiding in Christ. *"If ye keep my commandments ye shall abide in my love, even as I have kept my Father's commandments and abide in His love." "Ye are my friends if ye do whatsoever I command you."* He is talking here about obedience to Him. Now listen: "If ye abide in me and my words abide in you, ye shall ask what ye will, and it shall be done unto you." Oh, my friend, that means He will answer your prayer, and in your life there will be the fruit—the joy and the love that He talks about. It comes by abiding in Him. It comes by obeying Him.

Dr. Ironside told over and over again the story of a time when he was holding a meeting in a certain church, and, as he sat on the platform, the pastor said, "Did you notice that young lady who came in and sat about midway back?" When the doctor answered that he did, the pastor said, "That girl has a very sad and strange story. She is very bitter. The fact of the matter is she is very bitter against God. At one time she was the most active young person we had in this church. But she started slipping into the ways of the world with a group she had chosen, and before long she gave up her Sunday school class and gave up the choir and all else. She is as bitter as anyone could possibly be."

That night Dr. Ironside took as his text, "If ye shall ask anything in my name, I will do it." And he noticed that this girl grew red in the face and angry. When the service was over, she came down to him and started berating him, "Look here, you have a lot of nerve telling those people that God will answer their prayer." Dr. Ironside said, "Why do you say that?" "Well," she said, "I know from experience that that verse is not true. I *know* it is not." Dr. Ironside asked that she sit down and tell him about it. "Well," she said, "several months ago, my father, whom I loved dearly, being all that I had following my mother's death, became ill, desperately ill." She said that when the doctor reported him to be very low, she slipped upstairs to her room, got down on her knees, opened her Bible, and turned to that passage in John and said to the Lord: "Look here, this is what You have promised, 'If ye abide in me and my words abide in you, ye shall ask what ye will, and it shall be done unto you.'" She continued, "I asked God to spare the life of my father, and I really believed He would do it. I had faith He would do it. I got up off my knees and went down the steps. When I reached the bottom step, the doctor came out of my father's room and said to me, 'Your father has just slipped away, he's gone.'"

Then she said, "Now don't you tell me God answers prayer, that God makes good that verse; He did not make it good to me!" Dr. Ironside said to her, "Young lady, suppose you were walking down the street and you found a check, a very large check made out to somebody else, and you took that check down to the bank and signed your name to it and tried to cash it. What would you be?" She blushed and replied, "A forger, but I would not do that." Dr. Ironside replied, "No, not down here, but that is what you were doing. You went to the Bible and you found a promise made to somebody else. It was not to you, and you tried to cash it. And you are angry because God would not hear your prayer. Listen, my dear, He said, 'If ye abide in me and my words abide in you, ye shall ask.'" Knowing what the pastor had said, Dr. Ironside asked her, "Were you abiding in Christ?" She bowed her head and began to sob and said, "No, I was not."

My friend, it is His will that we bear fruit, not just little fruit, not just more fruit, but much fruit. That is His will, and He has made every arrangement. Identified with Christ, as the branch is identified with the vine, drawing His life, His power. And then He comes in and prunes that He might get a better yield. Beloved, He says, "Abide in me. Obey me."

14

THE GREAT HIGH PRIEST
AND THE PRIESTS—ACCESS

Hebrews 5:1–10; 7:23–28; 8:1–6

Customarily we choose only one text as the basis for a discussion, but in this instance we shall employ two texts. We invite you first to a reading of the third chapter of the epistle to the Hebrews, verse one: *"Wherefore, holy brethren, partakers of the heavenly calling, consider the Apostle and High Priest of our profession, Christ Jesus."* And then our second text is found in 1 Peter 2:9: *"But ye are a chosen generation, a royal priesthood, an holy nation, a peculiar people; that ye should shew forth the praises of him who hath called you out of darkness into his marvellous light."*

I am a priest. I am a catholic priest, but I am not a Roman Catholic priest. As we look at the term Roman Catholic, we find a contradiction lying there, for Roman means *particular* and catholic means *general*. And it is very difficult to have a "particular general" anything. However, I can truly say that I am a catholic priest. Every believer is a priest. You do not have to turn your collar around in order to be a priest—the important thing is to turn your life around.

In Great Britain the clergy, for the most part, wear their collars buttoned in the back. The story is told of a curate who was making his rounds on a motorcycle one cold, slippery morning. As he attempted to make a turn, the motorcycle skidded and went into a telephone pole. It was a very serious accident. One of the first to arrive on the scene was a simple-minded boy who made efforts to give aid. When the police finally arrived, the man was dead, and they

185

asked the boy in what condition he found the man. "Well," he said, "when I got here he was still alive but in a very bad fix. He had hit the telephone pole so hard that it had knocked his head all the way around and the back of his collar was in the front. By the time I got his head turned around he was dead."

My friend, there is danger in just turning the collar around in order to be a priest and not turning your life around. You are a priest if your life has been turned around and you have turned to Jesus Christ.

One of the greatest difficulties, which is a source of confusion in the church today, is the fact that men are not making a distinction between Israel in the Old Testament and the church in the New Testament.

In the Old Testament Israel *had* a priesthood, but in the New Testament the church *is* a priesthood. Every believer is a priest under God. "Ye are a royal priesthood," and you must remember that it was Simon Peter who said that.

New Testament ministers are never called priests in the Bible; they are called teachers, evangelists, ministers, shepherds, and they are called elders. They are never called priests because every believer is a priest.

Priesthood is the very basis of religion, of all religion. Every pagan religion, regardless of how corrupt and degenerate it might be, has a priesthood. Judaism has a priesthood. Roman Catholicism has a priesthood. The human heart cries out for a priest.

That was the heart cry of Job. You will recall in the ninth chapter, verses 32–33, he said concerning God: *"For he is not a man, as I am, that I should answer him, and we should come together in judgment. Neither is there any daysman betwixt us, that might lay his hand upon us both."*

Job is saying here that he needs someone to represent him before God, someone who will take his side. My friend, is the heart cry of the human family and the heart cry of the Christian to be denied? Scripture answers that: *"We have such an high priest, who is set on the right hand of the throne of the Majesty in the heavens"* (Hebrews 8:1).

Every Protestant has a priest—a Great High Priest; and every believer is a priest under God today. We feel that there is a reason why

Protestantism has neglected this great truth. In rebounding from the great error of Romanism at the time of the great Reformation, unconsciously the reformers turned from this subject altogether. John Knox made the statement that "priestism and demonism are synonymous," and when this great Scottish reformer so spoke, it is easy to understand why they turned from this subject.

I can recall what a tremendous impression was made upon my heart when, as a young minister, I got hold of this great truth.

PRIEST DEFINED

We began with the figure of the shepherd and the sheep—the animal world; then followed with that of the vine and the branches—the vegetable kingdom; and now we are in the realm of religion in dealing with the High Priest and the priests.

First of all we must define the term *priest*. Who or what is a priest? The Scripture is very explicit in its answer on this subject. Notice what the writer to the Hebrews says in chapter five, verse one: *"For every high priest taken from among men is ordained for men in things pertaining to God, that he may offer both gifts and sacrifices for sins."*

In this passage we see that the priest is one who moves from man to God. He is the godward aspect of service. He represents men before Almighty God. He goes to God on man's behalf. Actually, he is the opposite of the prophet. Let us turn back to the sixth chapter of Exodus, the last clause through verse one of the seventh chapter in which Moses said before the Lord: *"And how shall Pharaoh hearken unto me? And the LORD said unto Moses, See, I have made thee a god to Pharaoh: and Aaron thy brother shall be thy prophet."* That is, he will speak for you. So a prophet is manward—he speaks for God to man. A priest goes from man to God, and they pass each other on the way. That is something to keep in mind. The Lord Jesus Christ came from God to this earth with a message from God. He was a prophet. He went back to God from man as a priest.

Every priest must have his credentials, and certainly the Lord Jesus has His. He is our Great High Priest. First of all, He must have fellowship with man. He must be taken from among men. Obviously He must be a man; obviously the Lord Jesus was a man. No one

187

denies that today; everyone accepts the fact that He was a man. That is important. A priest must be a man to represent man. Only a man can understand a man. You will remember that Paul said in 1 Corinthians 2:11: *"For what man knoweth the things of a man, save the spirit of man which is in him?"* He became a man that He might enter into our infirmities and sympathize with us. He became a man that He might enter into our family and know us, and thus He might be a faithful High Priest and represent us before Almighty God. The Lord Jesus Christ became a man.

The second essential: He must be divinely appointed. *"And no man taketh this honour unto himself, but he that is called of God, as was Aaron"* (Hebrews 5:4).

Certainly our Lord Jesus Christ has His credentials here, for He was divinely appointed. That point would always be the question in my mind in going through any human priest down here in any religion. I would want to know that he was acceptable to Almighty God. This credential is most important.

CHRIST AS PRIEST

The Lord Jesus Christ was acceptable to God not only because He was a man, but because He was also God. He is called the Son of God. In reading the fifth chapter of Hebrews, verse five, we find that statement of fact: *"So also Christ glorified not himself to be made an high priest; but he that said unto him, Thou art my Son, today have I begotten thee."*

That refers to His resurrection because He became a priest by His resurrection from the dead. The Lord Jesus was not a priest before His resurrection. This you must note. We are not being tedious when we ask that you turn to another passage of Scripture, for we follow along in the reading to our proof in Hebrews 8:4: *"For if he were on earth, he should not be a priest, seeing that there are priests that offer gifts according to the law."*

He was of the tribe of Judah; He could not be a priest on this earth. It is interesting that you do not see Him performing that function at all down here. He was the sacrifice here. When John marked Him out, he did not say, "Behold the High Priest that taketh away the sin of the world." No, he said, "Behold the Lamb of God." He is the sacrifice on the cross. He becomes the offering and the offerer, for He offered Himself. But it is not until after His resurrection that He became the High Priest—our High Priest!

A beautiful picture of Christ becoming our High Priest after His resurrection is given us in the case of Aaron, the high priest of Israel.

You will recall that there were those of Korah and his band who were calling his priesthood into question. They rose up and said, in effect, "We do not like the idea of Aaron going in for us before God. We do not want him to represent us. We shall do it ourselves." God said, in effect, "No man takes this upon himself, for he must be appointed by Me, and I put My badge on Aaron. Let all the heads of the tribes bring a rod into My presence." Twelve rods were brought, and Aaron's rod was one of them. All twelve of those rods were completely dead—not one spark of life in them. When the men returned to the place in the morning, eleven of them were still as dead as before, but one of the rods was in blossom. It bloomed and had fruit upon it; this rod was an almond bough and life had come into it. God commanded that that rod be put in the ark for that was the badge of the priesthood of Aaron—life out of death! In Romans 1:4 it is said of Jesus: *"And declared to be the Son of God, [not made to be the Son of God] with power, according to the spirit of holiness, by the resurrection from the dead."*

Christ became our Great High Priest by His resurrection from the dead, and that is His present ministry. We read further of Him in Hebrews 9:11, 12:

> *But Christ being come an high priest of good things to come, by a greater and more perfect tabernacle, not made with hands, that is to say, not of this building; neither by the blood of goats and calves, but by his own blood he entered in once into the holy place, having obtained eternal redemption for us.*

Back in the Old Testament we find the great Day of Atonement when the high priest went into the holy of holies, tarried a moment to sprinkle the blood on the mercy seat, and returned as quickly as he entered. This he did once a year. Now that has passed away—it was a shadow. There is no longer a priesthood, for our Great High Priest, by His own blood, entered into heaven itself. He has not hurried to come back out. Some of us think He is taking a long time. Well, He sat down at God's right hand, and today we have a Great High Priest who has entered there. *"For Christ is not entered into the holy places made with hands, which are the figures of the true; but into heaven itself, now to appear in the presence of God for us"* (Hebrews 9:24). Thus we have a Great High Priest, the living Almighty Christ, seated in power at God's right hand. The only way known in which you can go to God is through Him, but you *can* go through Him. Everyone is bidden to go through Him.

Again we want to turn to the Old Testament and look at the garments Aaron wore which were called garments of beauty and glory. On them were precious stones. One of these garments was an *ephod* on which were two stones, one on each shoulder. On one stone were the names of six of the tribes of Israel, and on the other the names of the other six tribes. When Aaron went into the holy of holies, he carried the nation Israel on his shoulders, and he carried them there by name.

What a lovely picture that is of our Almighty Christ who carries us on His mighty shoulders into the very presence of God. Scripture says, "He is mighty to save." "He is able to save to the uttermost those that come unto God through Him."

We are told of the shepherd who went out on the hillside and found the little sheep that was lost. He put it on his shoulder. There never was any question that he could carry the little sheep on his shoulder, and today our Shepherd carries you and me on His shoulder. If you are His today, your name is on the shoulder of the Almighty Son of God!

Then there was another garment called the *breastplate*. On it were twelve stones. On these twelve stones were the names of the twelve tribes of Israel. He wore this over his heart. Let us look from Aaron to our Great High Priest who is entered into heaven and not only has us on His shoulders but also has us on His heart.

We can well understand that in Old Testament times when some folk might come to the high priest and he might say to them, "I do not know you, I do not have any special interest in you—I do not love you," that is, if he told the truth he would have to say that. But you and I have a compassionate Great High Priest, and you have no notion how much He loves you.

Can you, with Paul, stand beneath the cross with the fixed confidence that He loves you, that He gave Himself for you, and that you are engraved upon His heart? My friend, if you are His child you are engraved upon His heart—He could never forget you, nor could He ever cease loving you. We have a Great High Priest who is entered into the heavens. We are on His shoulder; we are on His heart. Could we ask God to do any more for us?

ACCESS

With this knowledge, the writer to the Hebrews sends out an invitation:

Having therefore, brethren, boldness to enter into the holiest by the blood of Jesus, by a new and living way, which he hath consecrated for us, through the veil, that is to say, his flesh; and having an high priest over the house of God, let us draw near (Hebrews 10:19–22).

So today we have an invitation that has been sent out to us, "Let us come with boldness to his throne of grace that we might obtain mercy and find grace to help in time of need."

Somehow I have the feeling that in our conservative churches we are too flippant with God—there is a great danger of that. Some use the name of Christ as if it were commonplace, but we must remember that it is a high and holy privilege to come to God.

If we were to ask for the privilege of a talk with the president of the United States, do you feel it would be granted us? It doubtless would not. Though God is infinitely higher than the president, yet in the next five seconds we can be in His presence and have an audience with Him! That high privilege comes through our Great High Priest, and we ought to be very reverent in our approach to Him.

Then there is something else we must watch. There is the grave danger we will not come, that we might be timid and reluctant. But the invitation is pressed upon us: *"Let us therefore come boldly unto the throne of grace, that we may obtain mercy and find grace to help in time of need"* (Hebrews 4:16).

Do you need him? Do you wish that you might go to the throne?

Well, go there. He bids you come, and to come with boldness—not in yourself, but in Christ. I rejoice today that we do not need someone to go to God for us. We do not have to go through some human instrumentality, but we can go immediately and directly to God through Christ. That is a privilege that you and I should value above everything else.

PRIESTHOOD OF BELIEVERS

We have had this study of the theme of our Great High Priest, and now we want to look at the other aspect of this great subject of priesthood, that of the priesthood of believers. We must enquire about that which we can do down here as priests with such a Great High Priest. Since we have access through Him to God, then there is something that we can do; we can be intercessors on behalf of others. Do you realize what a glorious, holy privilege it is to be an intercessor for others? We, as priests, are enjoined to be that. In 1 Timothy 2:1, Paul admonishes the young preacher: *"I exhort therefore, that, first of all, supplications, prayers, intercessions, and giving of thanks, be made for all men."*

Have you as a believer interceded on behalf of someone who is not praying for himself, who is not even interested in his salvation? You as a priest have the privilege of taking that one right to the throne of grace and talking to God about that individual. What a privilege that is!

Dr. George Gill frequently said that one of the reasons in our day we are not seeing more people born again is because when anyone is born in the physical realm, some woman must travail, and if anyone is to be born again, someone must travail spiritually. But it is difficult in this day to get someone to travail on behalf of others.

In the fourth chapter of Colossians, verse twelve, we are told something else that should set our hearts on fire: *"Epaphras, who is one of you, a servant of Christ, saluteth you, always labouring fervently for you in prayers, that ye may stand perfect and complete in all the will of God."*

Epaphras was a great Christian in the early church. We do not know how much he gave to missions. Neither do we know whether he was chairman of some committee or not. Further, we do not know if he ever preached a sermon, but the record says that this man was a great intercessor on behalf of other believers. He entered into their ministry because he interceded to God for them.

It would be interesting to know how many of you reading this ever mention your missionaries before the throne in prayer. You can be an intercessor for them and help in their ministry. Then how many pray for the ministry of the man who stands behind the pulpit of the church in which you worship?

When I was a senior in seminary, a terrible trouble broke in a church, dividing that body. However, they called a man to the pastorate who was later to become nationally known and beloved; that man was Peter Marshall. He was to come in the summer. It was deemed advisable to secure a seminary student as supply until he arrived, for the student could not hurt the congregation either way. So they asked me to supply. On the first Sunday the atmosphere was frigid. Each member glared at the other and hoped to twist anything the preacher said to their advantage. The evening service was the most difficult service I have ever had, and I cried out to God about it. I told the professor who sent me that I did not want to return, but he insisted that I return since it was only for a few Sundays.

The next Sunday I did return. It was a different congregation, but I did not know what had happened. I was to make a discovery later on. The evening service was Youth Night, and many of the State Tech students were there. Though this was a very dignified church, I felt led to give an invitation at the close of the sermon, and five young people came forward. Then I knew something had happened.

After the service a dear little lady in her eighties—she was so tiny and frail—came to me and said, "Mr. McGee, I sensed the difficulty that you have been having, so I arose at five o'clock this morning and stayed on my knees in prayer until church time, praying that God would move in a mighty way here." Thus a little intercessor had realized her privilege and had gone to God through Christ and had laid hold of God in a mighty way.

The world has heard much of Peter Marshall, who went there, but I have a notion that no one has ever heard of that little lady until I have mentioned her here in these pages. I cannot tell you her name for I have forgotten it, but I am confident that she shared heavily in the ministry of the man who became great there! Hers was intercessory prayer in action.

WHAT CAN THE PRIEST OFFER?

Every priest (believer) must offer a sacrifice. We are conscious of the fact that we are moving into a delicate field on this point, for this is a day when we do not hear much about folk making sacrifices. At earlier times we used to have periods of "self-denial" in the church, but we hear nothing of that now. Some folk suggest that they do not come to church because it is difficult. Of course it is difficult. If you are going to worship God, it is going to cost you something. What must the unsaved world think of the price tag we have put upon our position as priests? Some of us have certainly brought it down to a position of little value. A priest must offer a sacrifice to God.

A priest can offer his possessions. The Philippians, who were so close to Paul, sent him a gift for which he thanked them, but in thanking them he also called their attention to the fact that they were not just giving an offering to him, but that it went beyond him to God as a sacrifice acceptable and pleasing: *"But I have all, and abound. I am full, having received of Epaphroditus the things which were sent from you, an odour of a sweet smell, a sacrifice acceptable, well-pleasing to God"* (Philippians 4:18).

When you bring your possessions to God, you are a priest offering a sacrifice that is acceptable to Him. Actually, we have fallen so low in our privilege of making an offering to the Lord, that all too often either an amusing or a sad story must be told just before the ushers take the offering. We have come to the place where we must be moved by our emotions! Oh, my friend, we are *priests* making an offering before God, and that offering should have on it the mark of blood—the mark of sacrifice that it might be acceptable to God!

As priests we can offer praise unto God. Every Christian can do this today. In Hebrews 13:15 we learn: *"By him therefore let us offer the sacrifice of praise to God continually, that is, the fruit of our lips giving thanks to his name."* That does not mean just to sing the doxology on Sunday morning and then follow it with the "blues" on

Monday morning. It means that for seven days a week we should have a paean of praise unto God upon our lips continually and in every circumstance of life. God says that is acceptable to Him.

Not only can we offer our possessions and our praise, but *we can offer our person*. That is what Paul is talking about in Romans 12:1 when he says: *"I beseech you therefore, brethren, by the mercies of God,* [by His glorious salvation] *that ye present your bodies a living sacrifice . . . unto God, which is your reasonable service* [spiritual worship]."

That is something which you and I can do as priests. If you have never done this, you have left undone the basic function of a priest. If you are a Christian, it is your privilege as a priest to go into His presence through the Great High Priest and lay yourself upon the altar. First of all, lay there your possessions, then your praise and adoration—then yourself!

WHAT OF THE UNBELIEVER?

If you are not a Christian, we trust that you will understand that what is written here has no application to you. Christ is not asking for your possessions, your praise, or your person. He does not want anything from you, but He does long to *give* you something.

My friend, He wants you to know that the way to God is open and that all may come directly and immediately to Him. The only thing that can possibly hold you back is your will.

Many people give an intellectual assent to the great historical facts of our faith—even church people. They will say, "Yes, I believe that Jesus died and that He rose again. I believe the Bible is the Word of God." Those persons are not saved, for they have not come the way He has made back to God, a way of access. He says that by our will we are to come to God.

Perhaps a simple illustration will make clear this point. The highway to San Diego is wide open, and a few Sundays ago I went down there. Hundreds of cars were going that way. I did not worry because hundreds of cars were coming back this way. The highway was open. That Sunday I pulled up in front of the hotel at five o'clock in San Diego, but I shall not be there next Sunday afternoon. Do you know why? The way is still open, but I do not have the will to go. So I say to those out of Christ, the way to God is open. All you have to do is come—just have the will to come. Christ has made the way, and it is open to God through Him. You can come. Anybody can come.

15

THE BRIDEGROOM AND THE BRIDE—ANTICIPATION

Genesis 24:50–67; Matthew 25:1–6

As the central theme of *relationship* strikes the area of proof, it fans out into these various figures that we are studying.

The figure of the Bridegroom and the bride moves us into the social sphere, and in these days of marital failure it may not seem a very likely or apt symbol for our Lord to use.

Recent issues of our papers carried headlines telling us of a playboy who had married thirteen times, and his thirteenth wife was suing for divorce. Another playboy forgot about the marriage ceremony altogether and, as it were, wiped his feet upon it. Our present age carries much cynicism about marriage. A lovely Christian girl, in talking with me on this subject, was plainly cynical about marriage in this hour. Later on, a toastmaster at a banquet gave this little story to the group assembled. He said, "You know marriage is an institution and love is blind. Therefore, marriage is an institution for the blind."

These are days when folk speak freely in that vein. Nevertheless, there is no symbol of our relationship with Christ which is more colorful, more extravagant, or more beautiful than the one which we are considering here. It is engaging, expressive, and exhilarating to consider marriage—the bridegroom and the bride—as we look to Christ the Bridegroom and the Church as His bride.

A number of years ago, E. W. Bullinger attempted to distort this truth. We have been advised that before he died he retracted the heresy which he had started. But the heresy is still abroad, and you will find it in many places. The teaching is that the Church is the *body* of Christ and that the nation Israel is the *bride* of Christ. And the reason Dr. Bullinger gave for this unusual interpretation was that it is inconsistent for the church to be at one time both a body and a bride. We have already looked at symbols which are contrary and conflicting. Could anything be further apart than branches of a vine and sheep? Actually there is a total of seven symbols to add to the strange confusion of a mind such as that of Dr. Bullinger.

In the epistle to the Ephesians we find this remarkable symbolism: the Church is called a "new man," and then immediately it is called "the bride." This does seem conflicting. But, my friend, it takes many figures of speech to present as many facets of this vital and personal relationship which exists between Christ and His church today. If we are to have the picture in its entirety we must see all of them.

Back in the Old Testament, Israel is called the wife of Jehovah. *"For thy Maker is thine husband; the LORD of hosts is his name"* (Isaiah 54:5). But there is something which you should add to that when it is used, for in Jeremiah 3:20 we read: *"Surely as a wife treacherously departeth from her husband, so have ye dealt treacherously with me, O house of Israel, saith the LORD."* So, in the Old Testament Israel is called an unfaithful wife. It is needful to recall that the prophet Hosea was commanded to marry a harlot who proved unfaithful and returned to her slimy business. And yet this tragedy was to be used as the burden of Hosea's prophecy in illustration of the fact that God still loved Israel, and Israel had been unfaithful to God.

When you come to the New Testament you will find a most remarkable thing in John 3:29. Here John the Baptist is making it very clear that he is not a member of the bride of Christ. *"He that hath the bride is the bridegroom: but the friend of the bridegroom, which standeth and heareth him, rejoiceth greatly because of the bridegroom's voice: this my joy therefore is fulfilled."*

Now as John the Baptist, an Old Testament prophet, walks out of the Old Testament and delivers the last message of the Old Testament, he says in effect, "I am not the bridegroom. Not only that, I am not part of the bride; I am just a friend." That is the best summary that this man, who was a forerunner of the Lord Jesus Christ, could give concerning himself. Certainly he never thought of himself as part of the bride at all.

Let me make this very clear: The Church is spoken of as that which is to become the *bride* of Christ some day. *"For I am jealous over you with godly jealousy: for I have espoused you to one husband, that I may present you as a chaste virgin to Christ"* (2 Corinthians 11:2).

Certainly everyone is aware that there is a difference between an unfaithful wife and an engaged virgin! Israel in the Old Testament was an unfaithful wife, while in the New Testament the Church is yet to become the bride of the Lord Jesus Christ. So then, the bride symbolism speaks of the future, not of a present reality.

THE FUTURE PICTURE

Note this most familiar passage of Scripture, Ephesians 5:25–27:

Husbands, love your wives, even as Christ also loved the church, and gave himself for it; that he might sanctify and cleanse it with the washing of water by the word, that he might [future] *present it to himself a glorious church, not having spot, or wrinkle, or any such thing; but that it should be holy and without blemish.*

This speaks of a future day when the Church is to be presented to the Lord Jesus Christ, and at that time the Church is to be presented to Him as a bride. He is the Bridegroom.

When we come to the last picture of the Church presented in the Bible, we find that we are taken to the wedding—the marriage supper of the Lamb. *"Let us be glad and rejoice, and give honour to him: for the marriage of the Lamb is come, and his wife hath made herself ready"* (Revelation 19:7). How does the Church make herself ready? There are definite things she must accomplish to be ready for her marriage. They are soul winning and missionary work. These she must do in order that she may be complete and ready to be presented to Him some day as a bride. Note two pictures.

The first—

And I John saw the holy city, new Jerusalem, coming down from God out of heaven, prepared as a bride adorned for her husband. And I heard a great voice out of heaven saying, Behold, the tabernacle of God is with men, and he will dwell with them, and they shall be his people, and God himself shall be with them, and be their God (Revelation 21:2, 3).

Then the second—

And there came unto me one of the seven angels which had the seven vials full of the seven last plagues, and talked with me, saying, Come hither, I will shew thee the bride, the Lamb's wife (Revelation 21:9).

My friend, the picture presented here is a glorious one that is yet future when the Church is to be caught up and presented to Christ as a bride.

That is the explanation of the twenty-fifth chapter of the gospel of Matthew. There are those who have attempted to make these ten virgins symbolic of the Church. Let me state that nowhere do we find the Church mentioned as several virgins; it is called *the* virgin bride of Christ. It is always singular, never plural.

The second thing is that Matthew 25 is on Jewish ground. The Lord Jesus was answering certain questions that pertained to Jerusalem: "When shall these things be, that there shall not be left here one stone upon another?" That was Jerusalem. "What shall be the sign of thy coming, and the end of the age?" The age pertains to the nation Israel.

Now the Church just does not happen to be in the Olivet discourse. I do not know why people will not let the Lord Jesus take the disciples aside and talk to them about things which pertain to the nation Israel. The ten virgins mentioned here are symbolic of the nation of Israel, and the language of Matthew 25:1 is interesting as you read it: *"Then shall the kingdom of heaven be likened unto ten virgins, which took their lamps, and went forth to meet the bridegroom."*

The Peshitto manuscript, which is the Syriac, is not the best manuscript, but it is more interpretative of the customs of that day, and you will find that it is used in the Vulgate. It reads like this: "They took their lamps and went forth to meet the bridegroom *and the bride*" (italics mine). This is after the marriage supper of the Lamb when Christ comes to this earth to establish His kingdom, and His bride comes with Him.

The ten virgins are Israel. They cannot be the Church for the simple reason that the basis of acceptance is not the question of whether or not they are looking for Him to come the second time. We always emphasize prophecy in our teaching, and we want to be very careful now in what we are going to state. It is not what you think about the *second coming* of Christ that saves you, it is what you think about His *first coming* and your relationship to His coming about two thousand years ago. In contrast the ten virgins are tested on His coming again. Five were wise; they were looking for Him and had oil in their lamps. Five were not wise; there was no oil in their lamps. No one in this church age is saved on that kind of basis.

Here we have a tremendous picture. The real triumphal entry did not take place nineteen hundred years ago when just a few gathered around to shout hosannas while some lay palm branches along His path. No, here is the great triumphal entry in Matthew 25 when the shout goes forth, *"Behold, the bridegroom cometh!"* The bride is with Him, for He has called her out, has been united to her in marriage, and they are returning from the marriage supper of the Lamb. He is coming to this earth in triumph to establish His kingdom here! What a beautiful picture that is.

THIS BLESSED HOPE

We know, of course, that someone is going to ask immediately, "But, Preacher, what is the value of this relationship for today? You state that it is something to be realized in the future, but we have the urgent need of something practical for our living now." Can this truth be brought down to earth and be translated in value to our various walks of life? Yes, it can, and there are two aspects which we need to consider: It is *help* for today; it is *hope* for tomorrow. Here is something that is a present help in time of trouble. We realize that in this day we need something that will bring encouragement to our hearts and proof to our minds that the Lord Jesus Christ loves us. When we were in the nursery we were taught to sing:

Jesus loves me, this I know,
For the Bible tells me so.
Little ones to Him belong,
They are weak but He is strong.

Then follows the chorus, "Yes, Jesus loves me." Does Jesus love us? Is that song going to rise up and mock us as we grow up and go out into a cruel, cold world? After a while, through incident after incident, we come to the conclusion that maybe no one does love us.

A young man who was graduated from college rushed out and said, "World, here I am. I have my A.B. degree!" The world said, "Sit down, young man, and I shall teach you the rest of the alphabet." And you may count upon it, the world can teach you the rest of the alphabet. You can get an A.B. in college, but the world outside has the remainder of the alphabet for you. And when we meet life with all of its problems, its difficulties, its doubts and disasters, we find that this world has rugged, rough edges. When we have been up against it, we become bruised and beaten. Through it all we fail to find a ray of love. Then comes the question, "Does anyone love me?"

A very splendid woman asked for an interview a few days ago; and when she began to tell her tragic story, she cried out in the gall of bitterness, "As a child, I was taught about the love of God, but today I wonder. Does He really care?"

In these present storms we need to be assured that Jesus still loves us. We need a very positive answer to that question. The great truth which we are considering in this chapter assures my heart that Jesus loves us.

THE LOVE OF CHRIST

For years I have wondered why people go to weddings. As a minister I always try to analyze human nature, and in this instance I have had ample opportunity with the many couples that have stood before me to be united in marriage.

But why is it that people go to weddings? I believe that in this world in which we live people like to draw aside for a few moments and view a scene of loveliness where two young hearts have been brought together and have come to audibly express their love each for the other. It is a scene of beauty where two young folk stand before a minister; one, a fine stalwart man, the other, a radiant and beautiful young woman.

And here it is safe to comment that all brides are beautiful. Of all those who have stood before me, there has never been an ugly one. I have seen them before they were married, and then ten years after, and some of them would never win a beauty contest. But never have I seen a young lady who was not beautiful on her wedding day. I do not know how, but God seems to do something for them on that day that the beauty parlor cannot do.

I have seen the young folk stand there, madly in love with each other, their very souls exposed as they pledged their love. If they do not love each other, then that service does not make sense. A wedding of two Christians is a picture of Christ and the Church. The Lord Jesus Christ loves the Church more than that young man loves that girl. Frankly, their love is a very poor figure, for you cannot know how much Christ loves you. It is impossible for you to understand.

That Christ may dwell in your hearts by faith; that ye, being rooted and grounded in love, may be able to comprehend with all saints what is the breadth, and length, and depth, and height; and to know the love of Christ, which passeth knowledge, that ye might be filled with all the fulness of God (Ephesians 3:17–19).

What is Paul talking about when he says that you might be "rooted and grounded in love"? He is not speaking of some little human sentiment that we may have for Christ, but he is talking about our Lord's love for us, a love that passes human knowledge.

Paul prayed that the Spirit of God might somehow make clear to you and me the height of that love, something of the depth of it, of the length of it, and some impression of the width of that love. There is no yardstick down here that can measure it, no human illustration to be had of it. Do you want just a little measuring rod of His love? Here are two verses given us: *"And walk in love, as Christ also hath loved us, and hath given himself for us an offering and a sacrifice to God for a sweetsmelling savor"* (Ephesians 5:2).

Then he says to husbands, *"Husbands, love your wives, even as*

Christ also loved the church, and gave himself for it" (Ephesians 5:25). The measure of that love is that He left heaven's glory. He came down to this earth and willingly died upon a cross. The motive behind it was that He loved you and me. And we, with our cold hearts in this materialistic age, have become hardened to this love of His. Our hearts do not always respond to His love. Nevertheless, Christ loves *you* at this very moment with a love that you cannot understand.

Let us see Jesus at the tomb of Lazarus. Scripture records that "Jesus wept." A lovely thing was said by those who were standing by when they said simply, "Behold, how he loved him." And that is exactly the way He feels about you today. You are the object of the love of Christ. He died for you individually, He died for me individually—we are beloved of Him. John tells us that "God so loved the world," and again he tells us, "Beloved, now are we the sons of God"—not for just a moment. It is not just some little passing sentiment, for after the episode in the Upper Room (recorded in John 13) it says of Jesus, "having loved his own . . . he loved them unto the *end*." And Paul says that he is fully persuaded that there is nothing in life, nothing in death, nothing in heaven, nor in hell that can separate us from the love of God which is in Christ Jesus our Lord. Human love can be destroyed, but nothing can touch His love for us.

Years ago in Georgia, during antebellum days, there was a prominent planter with large holdings near a little town. The tragedy of his home was a son who was an alcoholic. One of the touching scenes of the small town was the aging father going to some saloon to find his son and take him home. The lad was treated with kindness. Many of the townsfolk grew rather impatient with the father, feeling that he should be sterner.

One afternoon when the boy came home drunk, his mother approached him from her chair on the great front porch of that southern mansion, and he struck her so that she fell. The father jumped up and said, "Son, you can't do that," and the son felled him with his fist. Rising up on his elbow, badly injured from the blow on his mouth, the father said, "Son, get out of here. I never want to see you again. I want you to go through that gate and never return."

The servants were instructed never to admit him should he come.

The boy asked friends to mediate for him, but the father was firm, "I shall never see him again." The boy drifted away from the little town, and a few years later the father came to his last illness. When asked if he wanted to send for the son, he refused. He replied, "The day he struck his mother I said I would never see him again and I meant it."

We can reach the place sometimes when the one who loved us will no longer do so, but we can never reach the place where God will not love us. That is one of the great truths in Scripture: *"When my father and my mother forsake me, then the LORD will take me up."* (Psalm 27:10). Those who have entered into that love have no frustration in their lives. Instead, there is satisfaction and rejoicing. It is help for today and hope for the future.

There is a glorious petition which the Lord Jesus mentioned in His prayer. You will find it again and again as you go through Scripture. *"Father, I will that they also, whom thou hast given me, be with me where I am; that they may behold my glory, which thou hast given me: for thou lovedst me before the foundation of the world"* (John 17:24).

Here He prayed that those who come to Him, those whom we call the church, should behold His glory. In fact, He prayed that they might partake of that glory, that they might share in that glory in a very wonderful way. And we are told that *"When Christ, who is our life, shall appear, then shall ye also appear with him in glory"* (Colossians 3:4). That is the glorious hope of the church today. Someday we are going to be brought into His presence, and His glory will be our glory. He will receive us as a bridegroom receives his bride. His wonderful love will cause Him to one day share His glory with His church!

A PICTURE IN SCRIPTURE

There is a wonderful picture in Scripture which is given for the purpose of making clear a blessed truth to our hearts; it is the story of Isaac and Rebekah. You will recall how Abraham wanted a bride for his son, Isaac, and he sent the servant back to his own country to get a bride. The servant, whose name is not recorded, I believe to be a picture of the Holy Spirit who is in the world today wooing and calling men and women to turn to Christ.

So the servant went forth and found Rebekah, for he said, "Jehovah hath led me in the way." He was led very definitely to the home of Bethuel, the father of Rebekah, and, following a very sumptuous meal that evening, the servant brought out for display some of the beautiful jewels which were a part of the wealth of Abraham's house. He told of Abraham, the great man that he was, and then of Isaac, his son, who was miraculously born when Sarah had passed the age of childbearing. He told of the young man grown up, the only begotten of his father, and how at thirty-three years of age he was placed on an altar on Mount Moriah to be offered as a sacrifice, and how God delivered him alive. "And," he added, "I am here to get a bride for my master's son, and I think Rebekah is the one."

The family looked at each other in amazement and in summary said, "Evidently the Lord is in this. We knew Abraham when he lived here in our country, but he went out years ago. He was a great man then and we are glad to hear how the Lord has blessed him. Now he has a son whom we have never seen; but from the story you tell and the wealth you display, we believe you; our sister may go. But wait just a minute, you will have to talk with her and get her permission."

Rebekah was called, and as that lovely, brown-eyed girl stood there in the shadows, the servant told her the story of Isaac. When she was faced with the question, she said, "I will go." There was none of the coy I-will-have-to-think-it-over attitude. She said that she had made up her mind and would go.

THE FAITH OF REBEKAH

We constantly hear of the faith of Abraham, but how often is thought given to the faith of Rebekah? She did exactly as Abraham had done. She left her own land and country and went into a country she knew not of. She went by faith. We can see the servant as he starts back across the burning sands of the desert with Rebekah and her maidens. The journey is indeed long and the heat very great.

Perhaps we might give vent to our imagination as we follow them through those days of hard travel to find them by a welcome oasis one night, very worn and weary. The servant advises that all get a good rest that they might be ready for the coming day of similar travel. But the sweet young woman, Rebekah, might say, "Please wait a minute. I do wish you would tell me again the story of Isaac—how he was born, the climb up Mount Moriah, and the sacrifice on the altar. I should like to hear again how Isaac was received back, as it were, from the dead." The servant, weary with the responsibility of travel, could but argue, "It is late, we are tired, and I have already told you the story many times." But in her eagerness she could not help but ask, "Tell me the old, old story of Isaac and his love."

The next morning the camels are saddled and the threads of the journey are picked up again across the desert. Later we can hear the servant say to Rebekah, "I am sorry that the desert is so hot and the journey so long." But she would reply, "Yes, it is, but the desert is not so hot for me as you think, nor the journey so hard, for I am traveling in the anticipation of seeing Isaac." Peter meant that when he wrote, "Whom not having seen, ye love," speaking of Christ.

Then we find them as the journey is drawing to the end, and the servant tells her that they will arrive at the home of Abraham in the evening of that day. Quite late in the afternoon, as she looks across the desert, she sees a fine young man approaching and inquires of the servant who he might be. The servant tells her he is Isaac, his master's son. It is then she puts on her veil—picturing the future when the church is clothed in the righteousness of Christ—and she goes out to meet him.

Beloved, what a meeting that was! Scripture says, *"And Isaac brought her into his mother Sarah's tent, and took Rebekah, and she became his wife; and he loved her"* (Genesis 24:67). I do not know how to express it better than does the Word of God.

Christ loves you today, and some day we will go into the presence of the One whom we have not seen on this wilderness journey down here. Is the way getting long for you? Is the journey getting hard for you? Are the pressures of life great upon you? Friend, there is good news: We will be there before long. We will be in His presence, and we love Him because He first loved us.

16

THE LAST ADAM AND THE NEW CREATION

For as in Adam all die, so also in Christ shall all be made alive
(1 CORINTHIANS 15:22 ASV).

Many great men were given to the world in the first half of the twentieth century. There were inventors, tycoons, soldiers, statesmen, and scientists whose names will be recorded in history. One of them was Winston Churchill, the late prime minister of England, who was said to have resigned with the sad but significant statement, "I am now nearing the end of my journey." He surrendered, as the press expressed it, "to the weight of years." Time did what no dictator could do—removed him from his high office. Death, the greatest dictator of all, was standing in the shadows, preparing to knock at the door at the appointed hour.

It is highly significant and suggestive that we remember the death of another man who was more than a man, for the shadow of death did not lead to His resignation but to His resurrection. The shadow of death did not force Him to step down but to step up. We meet at Easter to celebrate the resurrection of the Lord Jesus Christ from the dead. He said that death was not the end of the journey, but rather the entrance into real life: *"I am the resurrection, and the life: he that believeth in me, though he were dead, yet shall he live"* (John 11:25).

There is certain to be a difference of opinion relative to such an important issue, but every Christian is bound to agree that the resurrection of Jesus Christ is the most important event in the history of the world. It is of greater resident value to mankind than all else. It has a practical application to each one of us. Someone has said, "The hope of half a world was in that empty tomb." Let it be said also that the other half had an equally vital stake in the great demonstration of power within the confines of Joseph's tomb.

Every device has been used by the enemy to discredit the fact of the resurrection of Jesus Christ. All these explanations have the hollow ring of insincerity and counterfeit, from the very first excuse concocted by the chief priests and elders in bribing the soldiers into saying, *"His disciples came by night, and stole him away while we slept"* (Matthew 28:13). It is difficult to conceive of a Roman soldier reporting to his superior officer that he had slept on guard duty!

FACT

The resurrection of Jesus Christ is an established fact which has historical evidence to sustain it. The evidence is available to any person who will examine and evaluate it. It can be taken into a scientific laboratory. It would be admissible in a court of law as evidence. There are creditable witnesses who have taken the witness stand. Christ showed Himself alive by "many infallible proofs."

There are two lines of evidence which are important. There is, first of all, the testimony of Christ Himself to the resurrection. This is often neglected and passed over. Very seldom is the Lord Jesus called to the witness stand, but He has a right to be heard in His own behalf. In a criminal case many men have gone to the witness stand in desperation as a last resort to save their lives. If they are guilty, a clever lawyer will keep them off the witness stand. The Lord Jesus Christ wants to be heard. He gives His testimony eagerly, and He is a creditable witness. His enemies say that no man taught as He did. The Pharisees agreed that He was a teacher come from God. His enemies stated, "We know that thou art true." He deserves to be heard.

Many times the Lord Jesus predicted His death and resurrection.

Then certain of the scribes and Pharisees answered him, saying, Teacher, we would see a sign from thee. But he answered and said unto them, An evil and adulterous generation seeketh after a sign; and there shall no sign be given to it but the sign of Jonah the prophet: for as Jonah was three days and three nights in the belly of the whale; so shall the Son of man be three days and three nights in the heart of the earth (Matthew 12:38–40 ASV).

And again:

> *From that time began Jesus to show unto his disciples, that he must go unto Jerusalem, and suffer many things of the elders and chief priests and scribes, and be killed, and the third day be raised up* (Matthew 16:21 ASV).

Death was not the end of the journey; it was only one side of the door, but the other side of the door was resurrection.

He showed Himself alive after His resurrection. He is the faithful and true witness who says, *"I am he that liveth, and was dead; and, behold, I am alive for evermore"* (Revelation 1:18).

The second line of evidence for the resurrection of Christ is the testimony of Scripture. The statements here are abundant, but the following will suffice to show this type of evidence and the conclusive nature of it. There were many predictions concerning the resurrection in the Old Testament.

> *And certain of them that were with us went to the tomb, and found it even so as the women had said: but him they saw not. And he said unto them, O foolish men, and slow of heart to believe in all that the prophets have spoken! Behooved it not the Christ to suffer these things, and to enter into his glory? And beginning from Moses and from all the prophets, he interpreted to them in all the scriptures the things concerning himself* (Luke 24:24–27 ASV).

Peter states it in another way: *"Searching what time or what manner of time the Spirit of Christ which was in them did point unto, when it testified beforehand the sufferings of Christ and the glories that should follow them"* (1 Peter 1:11 ASV). Compare Psalm 16:9–10 with Acts 2:31.

In the New Testament the resurrection becomes the heart and hope of the gospel. All four gospels record the resurrection of Christ, although not all record the Sermon on the Mount or the Transfiguration or other great incidents. The resurrection was the center of the New Testament preaching. There is not a recorded sermon in the book of Acts that does not mention the resurrection. All writers of the New Testament make this central in all they present.

However, our point of emphasis is not the fact of the resurrection but the manner of it; not the statement about it but the significance of it; not the account of it but the accuracy of detail; not the history but the current value; not the record but the reality; not the proofs but the power. How can the resurrection be geared and meshed into our contemporary society?

THE BODILY RESURRECTION

There are three cogent considerations which make the resurrection of Jesus Christ meaningful for our time. These three give us a true perspective of the resurrection in our day when certain perversions of the resurrection are put forth.

The resurrection of Jesus Christ was a bodily resurrection. This is both primary and vital in a day when an attempt is made to spiritualize the resurrection. This sophistry reduces the resurrection to a meaningless platitude.

One group of doubters applies the word *resurrection* to the soul. Another group of scoffers waters it down to no more than the influence of Jesus, tying it up in the same area of thought as the influence of Shakespeare upon contemporary literature. Naturally this destroys even the thought of the personality of Christ being carried beyond death. This is unbelief in its boldest form.

While there are those who express doubt, the Scriptures are clear on this great truth. The word in Scripture which is translated as resurrection is the Greek word *anastasis,* which simply means to "stand up." It refers to the body and cannot refer to the soul. It is the body that dies and it is the body that is raised up. The soul does not die; therefore it is never raised up. Those who scoff have never successfully explained how a spirit stands up and in what respect it is different when it lies down.

The entire consensus of thinking outside of conservative Christian circles spiritualizes the resurrection.

Life magazine carried a lead article on the resurrection, and the

212

content was a repetition of the ancient heresy of spiritualizing the resurrection of Jesus Christ. A Unitarian preacher in Chicago announced for his Easter subject this amazing title, "Spring Is Here." In Chicago spring is quite an event, but it is not quite appropriate as a subject in dealing with the resurrection of Jesus Christ!

In California, where spring does not make such an impact, a liberal preacher came up with this engaging subject for Easter, "Easter Is a Time for Flowers." For several years now I have watched the announcements of subjects by liberal preachers, and it would be amusing if it were not so tragic. This might well be labeled Operation Evasion, an attempt to evade the hard fact and crucial truth of the bodily resurrection of Christ.

Even today many of our illustrations of resurrection fall short. An egg, a bulb, or a dormant plant do not represent a resurrection, for there is a germ of life resident in all of these.

Christ's body was a dead body—there was no life in it. The body was raised up. "He was buried" is the clear and succinct statement of Scripture. This means a body was buried, and no body was more dead than His. It was a crucified body, and when the enemies had done with it, Scripture says, He was marred more than any man. That body had been scourged, punished, and crucified; a spear had been thrust into it. There was no life in it.

Kind friends took the body down from the cross and embalmed it. When He did appear to His disciples, He said, "A spirit does not have flesh and bones such as ye see me have." The resurrection of Jesus Christ was a bodily resurrection. This is an important consideration today.

NOT RESTORATION

The second consideration which should come to your attention is one that is most important and likewise neglected. *His resurrection was not a restoration to this life;* it is unique and unparalleled in the history of the world. The Bible records only one resurrection. Someone will say, "But what about Lazarus? What about the son of the widow of Nain? What about the little girl who was raised from the dead?" My friend, none of these were resurrections; all were restorations to this life. They were resuscitations.

Medical science has on record the case of a man whose heart stopped beating for five minutes, and I understand there are cases of even a longer cessation, after which the patients have been restored to life. I noticed an article recently that wanted to call that resurrection, but it is not in the biblical sense. May I impress upon you the fact that Christ did not return to *this* life; He was not wakening out of sleep; He did not come back from the dead; He did not put back on His old garments. Rather, He went through to the other side of death. He came out of the grave in a new, glorified body. That is something that is completely unique. He knocked both ends out of the grave. Christ made a thoroughfare of death; He went straight through and came out on the other side. That is exactly what Paul is talking about in 1 Timothy 6:16: *"Who only* [speaking now of Christ] *hath immortality, dwelling in the light which no man can approach unto; whom no man hath seen, nor can see: to whom be honour and power everlasting. Amen."*

A NEW CREATION

When Christ came forth from the dead, He came forth in a body, but a glorified body. Thus He introduced a new order. *He began a new creation;* He entered a new realm which had never been entered before. It was a new creation; it was the beginning of the church, if you please.

The resurrection of Jesus Christ is the most important event ever to take place on the earth. It is more stupendous than the creation of Adam in the Garden of Eden. When Christ came back from the dead, He began a new creation. And now we read: *"For as in Adam all die, even so in Christ shall all be made alive"* (1 Corinthians 15:22). It is amazing how little has been made of this creation born in His resurrection.

The scarcity of writing on this subject is appalling. We can pick up any good book dealing with theology and find that virtually the whole volume is given to the death of Christ, but rarely ever more than fifteen pages are given to His resurrection. There are very few hymns that are written on the resurrection compared to the large number written about the cross.

Why has there been this neglect of dealing with the resurrection of

Christ? The answer is obvious: it is because there has not been an emphasis on the fact that He came back into a new order, to begin a new creation. And that creation, beloved, is the church. In Colossians Paul makes one of the most important statements in the Word of God; I am of the opinion that there is nothing to compare with it anywhere. *"Who hath delivered us from the power of darkness, and hath translated us into the kingdom of his dear Son"* (Colossians 1:13).

That is tremendous! You and I are born into the family of Adam, and because of the entrance of sin in the family, drudgery, doubts, darkness, defeat, and death have come to us. These all came through Adam—"In Adam all die."

As you look around you, all the folk whom you see, as well as yourself, are dying, for all are in Adam, and "in Adam all die." But thank God that the Lord Jesus Christ came down to this earth and entered into the human family, went to the cross and died for our sins, was put in the grave, and on the third day came out in a glorified body in the newness of life. Thus He is able to take you and me out of the kingdom of darkness and sin where we are lost and lead us into His kingdom. He is the last Adam and is forming a new creation by His resurrection from the dead.

NEWNESS OF LIFE

When you come to Jesus Christ, it is as if you come from behind the iron curtain of death, for that is what it is. We were dead in trespasses and sin, and when we come to Him, He brings life. Oh, we know that if the Lord tarries, our bodies will have to go down into the grave. But, thank God, just as His body was raised, so shall ours be raised!

In Galatians 6:15 we read this startling language: *"For in Christ Jesus neither circumcision availeth any thing, nor uncircumcision, but a new creature* [creation]." Paul is saying that religion is not something that you rub on the outside; it is something that produces a new creation on the inside because of the resurrection of Jesus Christ from the dead.

We have another verse that is very important, found in 2 Corinthians 5:17: *"Therefore if any man be in Christ, he is a new creature*

215

[creation]: *old things are passed away; behold, all things are become new.*" Now that does not mean that a few little habits have been dropped off and we have acquired new habits. What he is saying here in the phrase "old things have passed away" is that the old relationship to Adam, the old relationship to the flesh, has passed away, and now we have become new. All things are new. Now we are joined to Christ, and the language is, "if any man be in Christ [the living Christ, the resurrected Christ, the One whom we can trust today as Savior], he is [made] a new creation."

Therefore, Paul could say to the Colossians: *"If ye then be risen with Christ, seek those things which are above, where Christ sitteth on the right hand of God"* (Colossians 3:1).

Then he could say further: *"Lie not one to another, seeing that ye have put off the old man with his deeds; and have put on the new man, which is renewed in knowledge after the image of him that created him"* (Colossians 3:9, 10).

My friend, Easter is not a time for a new spring outfit; it is the time for a new life. It is not just new clothes; it is a new creation. It is not for putting something on the outside; it is having something real on the inside.

Beloved, do not become religious! Get through to Jesus Christ, the living Savior. That is the thing that is essential today. Do not just join a church, go through a ceremony, and adopt a few pious platitudes —that is but to rub religion on the surface. Get through to the living Christ! It is very important to get through to Him. The New Testament opens on that note. Notice the opening words: *"The book of the generation of Jesus Christ"* (Matthew 1:1). As you read that, you will naturally note that it is an unusual expression for the New Testament: "The book of the generation of Jesus Christ." You will not find it again even though you read through the whole of the New Testament.

Then in going back as far into the Old Testament as the Pentateuch, you will not find it in Deuteronomy or Numbers or Leviticus or Exodus. But in Genesis, the fifth chapter, we find the opening words, "This is the book of the generations of Adam." Therefore, we have two books: the book of the generations of Adam and the book of the generation of Jesus Christ.

Every person is in the line of Adam, and "in Adam all die." Sin has come into the human family. But, my friend, there is another book, the Lamb's Book of Life. The New Testament opens with the book of the generation of Jesus and closes with the Lamb's Book of Life.

The important thing is that you got into the book of Adam by birth; you get into the Lamb's Book of Life by new birth, by trusting the resurrected Christ as your Savior. Is your name in the Lamb's Book of Life?

17

LISTEN TO
A PICTURE

In Atlanta, Georgia, I was walking down a street a few years ago and noticed that one of the art galleries was having an exhibit with the theme, "Listen to a Picture." They are trying in the South to recover some of the rich culture that has been lost in the past few decades. There has been a decline there in the love and appreciation for some of the finer things in this life. Since I felt that my culture had worn a bit thin in places, I went by to listen to the pictures.

I discovered that there are two extreme schools of artists and art critics. There is the old-fashioned and there is the modern school. The old-fashioned school is mild; the modern is wild. The old-fashioned school believes in art being photographic. The modern one believes in its being realistic, and they include the impressionist and expressionist schools. Or, if you want to put it like this: There is the old-fashioned, the concrete; and there is the modern, the abstract.

Honestly, I found out that I have no real appreciation of modern art. They can print a picture of Whistler's mother, and it can look like a dish of wilted artichokes. In fact, that's the way it did look. She wasn't even sitting in the chair; she was off her rocker—and so was the artist, from my point of view. But if you appreciate that kind of art, fine.

THE LORD'S ART

May I say to you that our Lord drew pictures. Some think that the pictures He drew belong to the old-fashioned school—photographic. There are others who think that the pictures He drew belong to the modern school—the abstract. I do not know which side you want to take. The only thing I'm concerned about is to look at one of His pictures. He didn't paint with a brush. He painted with words. The only record we have of His writing, you will recall, was when He wrote on the sand, and careless feet passing over it rubbed it out shortly afterward. But His word pictures have survived the years and are still colorful and alive.

Dr. Luke is the one who majors in the pictures our Lord painted, for Dr. Luke, a medical doctor and a scientist, was also an artist. He himself had an appreciation for the finer things. He records all the songs of Christmas, and he's the one who gives us some of our Lord's glorious parables which the other gospel writers omit.

A CLOSER LOOK

Look now at one of His pictures. This picture is the one that has been called by men "The Prodigal Son." Actually, it's not a single picture, but it's really one of three pictures. Dr. Luke says, "He spake this parable unto them," and He didn't stop with one, He gave three. There is the picture of the lost sheep, the picture of the lost coin, and the picture of the lost son. And they're all in one frame because they are one parable. This is what is known as a triptych. Many of you folk who can go back quite a few years will remember that you used to have in the parlor three pictures in one frame called the triptych. When I used to visit my aunt, I remember seeing a picture like that which she kept in the attic (that's where she used to make me sleep when the house filled up with relatives). I always looked at that picture because it was very interesting. It was really three scenes depicting the prodigal son in one frame.

Now in this picture which our Lord gives us, we have the lost sheep, the lost coin, and the lost son. And they all belong together. They really constitute one picture. However, we are going to look at just one third of it. This is actually a talking picture and a moving picture; and it is a triptych, if you please.

And he said, "A certain man had two sons" (Luke 15:11).

Immediately, our Lord begins to put the background on the canvas. I see a lovely home (because this will represent the home of the Father, the Heavenly Father), and it's a glorious home. It's a home that has all of the comforts, all of the joys, and all of the love that ever went into a home, for it is the heavenly home. In that home there is the "certain man," who is God the Father. This Father had two sons. He has more sons than that, but these are representatives, you see. One of these boys is called the elder and the other is called the younger. We see that palatial home, and out in front there stands the Father and the two sons.

Now let's watch our Lord add some more to the picture for us.

And the younger of them said to his father, Father, give me the portion of goods that falleth to me. And he divided unto them his living. And not many days after the younger son gathered all together, and took his journey into a far country, and there wasted his substance with riotous living (Luke 15:12–13).

Here in this lovely home, a home in which there was everything in the world that the heart of man could want—love, joy, fellowship, comforts—this younger boy did a very strange thing. He had grown tired of the discipline. He wanted to stretch his wings. He wanted the excitement and glamor of another country, a new world. I do not know why that is true, but to you and me the grass in the next pasture always looks greener. The boy looked out from home and said, "If I could only get away off yonder on my own, it'd be wonderful." He didn't like it at home. He fell out with his father, lost fellowship with him, and said, "Father, give me the portion of goods that falleth to me." So the father divided his estate between them, and the boy left with his pockets full of money—money that he had not worked for. He had done nothing to earn it. Every bit that came to him was what his father had given to him. He had not gotten it by his ability nor by his labor. He had money in his pocket because he had a very generous father. And so the boy started out for the far country.

Now our scene shifts, and we must put in another picture here, the picture of the far country. You can paint it any way you want to. May

I say to you that you can paint it in lurid colors, as many have attempted to do. And I do not think it's overexaggerated to paint it that way. This boy knew what it was to have what the world calls a good time. He made all of the nightclubs; he knew café society. He had money, and when you've got money, fair-weather friends flock to you. And believe me, he had fair-weather friends. For a time he lived it up. He enjoyed the pleasures of sin for a season, there in the far country. Our Lord did not put in any detail of what the son did, but we can well imagine some of the things.

IN TROUBLE

However, there did come a day after he had lived it up, that he reached into his pocket and there was not anything left. Not only was he in a very bad way financially, but the whole country was in a bad way. You see, that land in which he thought the grass was greener was now experiencing famine. The grass had now dried up. And this boy didn't know what to do. If you want to know the truth, he was afraid to go home. He should not be afraid, but he was afraid to go home. Now he was desperate. He was so desperate that he was going to do something that no Jewish man would ever have done unless he had hit the bottom. This boy hit the bottom.

He couldn't get a job. He went around to see some of his fair-weather friends and said, "Bill, do you remember how you used to come to the banquets I gave and the dinners, and that I always picked up the check? I paid for the liquor, and I paid for the girls. Do you remember that? Now I'm in a bad way. I wonder if you couldn't tide me over, or maybe you could give me a job." The fair-weather friend said, "I'm sorry. You say you've lost all your money? Well, that's too bad. I'm not interested in you anymore. My secretary will show you the door." And the boy found, after going from place to place, that he didn't have any real friends in the far country.

Finally he ended up by going out to the edge of town. Out there was a man who was raising pigs, and you could tell it a mile away. The boy went over to him and said, "I'd like to have a job." The man said, "Well, I can't pay you. You know we're having a lot of difficulty, but if you can beat the pigs to it, you can eat here at least." That's exactly the point to which he had sunk.

When our Lord said that this man "would fain have filled his belly with the pods [swill] that the swine did eat," every Israelite—both Pharisees and publicans who were listening to Him that day—winced, because a Hebrew couldn't go any lower than that. The Mosaic law had shut him off from having anything to do with swine, and to stoop to the level of going down and living with them was horrifying. That is the picture. And it's a black picture. You see that this boy had hit the very bottom.

Somebody is immediately going to say, "Well, this was the fellow who was a sinner and he is going to get saved." No, I'm sorry to tell you that such is not the picture that is given to us here. This is not the picture of a sinner who gets saved. May I say to you, and say it very carefully, that when this boy was living at home with the father and was in fellowship with him, he was a son—there was never any question about that. When this boy got to the far country and was out there throwing his money around, he was still a son. That is never questioned. And when this boy hit the bottom and was out there with the pigs—if you had been a half-mile away looking over there, I don't think you could have distinguished him from a pig—he was not a pig. He was a son. In this story that our Lord told, there is never any question as to whether the boy was a son or not. He was a son all the time.

THE GOSPEL

Somebody says, "Then this is not the gospel." Yes, it is the gospel also. And I will hang on to that application for the very simple reason that an evangelist in southern Oklahoma many years ago used this parable to present the gospel. People said he imitated Billy Sunday, but since I had never heard of Billy Sunday, it didn't make any difference to me. He was a little short fellow, holding services under a brush arbor. The thing that interested us boys was the fact he could jump as high as the pulpit. He'd just stand flat right there and up he'd go—a little short fellow. We'd sit out there and watch him, and the next day we'd practice to see if we could jump that high. May I say to you that one night he preached on the prodigal son, and that was the night I went forward, acknowledging my sins. Don't tell me the gospel is not here. It *is* here.

However, let's understand what the parable is primarily about. It reveals the heart of a Father who will not only save a sinner but take back a son, and our Lord painted the son into the picture right down in the pigpen. Now, friend, you can't get any farther down than this young man was. Back in the first century in Jerusalem, speaking to both Pharisees and publicans, there was no use trying to describe somebody lower than this boy. In their eyes nobody could be lower. From where he was, any direction was up. He was on the bottom. Now will you notice:

And he went and joined himself to a citizen of that country; and he sent him into his fields to feed swine. And he would fain have filled his belly with the husks that the swine did eat: and no man gave unto him (Luke 15:15–16).

Maybe you thought a moment ago I was exaggerating when I said his fair-weather friends wouldn't help him. Our Lord made it very clear when He said, "No man gave unto him." Why is it today that Christians sometimes get the impression that the man of the world is really his friend when he's trying to lead him into sin and lead him away from God? Well, believers do get that impression. This boy got that impression also. He was being led away from home and from his father, farther and farther away. And he thought these folks were his friends.

Now we don't have any letters that he wrote back to some of his friends at home. But if we had one, I think that it would have said, "Hey, you ought to come over here! There are some real people over here where I am. They know how to really live. I'm having a fantastic time. You ought to come over." But, may I say to you, the day came when he found out these were not his friends. "No man gave unto him."

Now that's the black part of the picture, and I think it's about time for us to see some of the bright colors our Lord painted into the picture. Our Lord always put down a black background, and then He added the bright colors in the foreground of the picture. Have you ever noted that God paints that way? I don't know whether it is abstract or concrete art, but that is His technique all the way through the Bible. He has put the blood of Christ over the blackness of man's sin. In the epistle to the Romans He puts down a background that is as black as ink on which he writes in glowing colors the story of justification by faith. You can always tell when it's God painting because He paints like that. And men are beginning to learn that.

Out on my freeway, which is the oldest one in this area (I do feel as if it's *my* freeway after paying taxes—I know *part* of it belongs to me), they originally put up signs having a white background and black letters, and there are a few of the old signs left out there at certain places. But that's not the best way to do it. They're now using a dark background and white letters. It took man a long time to learn that, but that's the way to paint. That's the way God paints.

And so on the dark background of this boy's sin—down in the pigpen, out of fellowship with his father, having left home in a huff, mad at his father—our Lord begins to brush on the bright colors.

And when he came to himself, he said, How many hired servants of my father's have bread enough and to spare, and I perish with hunger (Luke 15:17).

REPENTANCE

He came to himself. Sin does an awful thing to us. It makes us see the world wrong. It makes us see ourselves in the wrong light, and it makes us see the pleasures of this world in the wrong perspective. We just don't see right when we are in sin. This boy, when he was at home, looked out yonder at the far country—it all looked so good. The grass was green and the fun was keen, but now he came to himself.

And the first thing he did was to reason a little. He began to use his intelligence. He said, "You know, I'm a son of my father, and here I am in a far country. I'm down here in a pigpen with pigs, and back in my father's home the *servants* are better off than I am, and I'm his son." When he began to think like that, he began to make sense. And this fellow now acts like he's intelligent:

And when he came to himself, he said, How many hired servants of my father's have bread enough and to spare, and I perish with hunger! I will arise and go to my father, and will say

225

unto him, Father, I have sinned against heaven, and before thee, and am no more worthy to be called thy son: make me as one of thy hired servants (Luke 15:17–19).

This is the decision of the man. After he did a little intelligent thinking about it, he said to himself, *The thing I'm going to do is get out of here and go to my father. And when I get to my father, I'm going to tell him I've been wrong. I know my father has not been wrong. I have been wrong. I'm going to say that I have sinned against heaven and before him. I'm no more worthy to be called his son. If he'd just let me come back home and be a servant, I'd be lots better off than here in the pigpen.* So he arose and came to his father.

Now we get to a really bright picture, the brightest one of all. It is the picture of that lovely home we were telling you about. Oh, it's a beautiful home. It's the father's house. The Lord Jesus said, "In my Father's house there are many abiding places." This is the house that it pictures. The house is there in the background, and I see a father looking out the window. He has been looking out the window every day since his boy left. And do you know why he's been looking out the window? He knew that one day that boy would be trudging down the road coming home.

Somebody asks, "Do you believe that if you're once saved you're always saved?" Yes. Somebody asks, "Do you believe that a Christian can get into sin?" Yes. "Can a Christian stay in sin?" No. Because in the Father's house the Father is watching, and He says, "All my sons are coming home. My sons don't like pigpens because they do not have the nature of a pig. They have the nature of a son. They have *My* nature, and they won't be happy except in the Father's house. The only place in the world they'll love is the Father's house. And every one of *My* sons who goes out to the far country and gets into a pigpen—regardless of how dirty he gets or how low he sinks—if he's *My* son, one day he'll say, 'I'll arise, and I'll go to my Father.'" And the reason he will say this is because the Man who lives in the big house is his Father. Up until now, after at least 6,000 years of recorded human history, there never yet has been a human "pig" who has said, "I will arise and go to my Father's house." Never, never. Pigs love it down there in the pigpen. They don't want to go to the Father's house. The only one who wants to go to the Father's house is a son. And one day the son will say, "I will arise and I will go to my Father."

Now the son in our story started home.

And he arose, and came to his father. But when he was yet a great way off, his father saw him (Luke 15:20).

Maybe you thought a moment ago that I was exaggerating when I said that this father had been looking out the window every day, but he had. And now as he saw his hungering and hurting son coming, he ran and said to his servant, "Go down to the tree and cut me about a half dozen hickory limbs. I'm going to switch this boy within an inch of his life." Is that the way your Bible reads? Well, mine doesn't either. It ought to read that way. Under the Mosaic law a father had a perfect right to bring a disobedient son before the elders and have him stoned to death. This father had a perfect right to say, "This boy took my name and my money, and he squandered it. He disgraced my name. I'll whip him within an inch of his life." He had a right to do this. But instead, his father did something amazing.

GRACE

When our Lord got to this part of the parable, and when He brushed this bright color on the canvas, it caused all of those who were present to blink their eyes. They said, "We can't believe that. It's bad enough to see that boy hit the bottom and go down yonder with the pigs, but it's worse for the father to take him back home without punishing him. That's the thing that we don't like. He ought to be severely punished." Will you notice what the father did. Let me read it accurately now:

But when he was yet a great way off, his father saw him, and had compassion, and ran, and fell on his neck, and kissed him (Luke 15:20).

I have tried for years to get a satisfactory picture of this scene. Although I have collected several, there is only one that I really like. In most of the pictures the boy looks pretty decent, but the one I like shows him in rags, and you can almost smell him—oh, that pig smell! There stands the boy, and the father goes and puts his arms around him and kisses him. And will you notice what happened: *"And the son said unto him, Father."* Isn't that wonderful? *"Father!"* Regardless if he is a boy who is dirty and smells like a pig—though he ought not to—that one is his *father.*

And the son said unto him, Father, I have sinned against heaven, and in thy sight, and am no more worthy to be called thy son (Luke 15:21).

He had memorized this little speech, you see. He had been repeating the thing he had planned in the far country. I think he repeated that little speech over and over all the way home. I think every step of the way he said to himself, *When I get home, I'm going to say to him, Father, I have sinned against heaven, and before thee, and am no more worthy to be called thy son: make me as one of thy hired servants.*

He started to say it all to his father, but got only as far as, "I am no more worthy to be called thy son," when he was interrupted.

But the father said to his servants, Bring forth the best robe, and put it on him; and put a ring on his hand, and shoes on his feet: and bring hither the fatted calf, and kill it; and let us eat, and be merry: for this my son was dead, and is alive again; he was lost, and is found. And they began to be merry (Luke 15:22–24).

And, as Dr. George Gill used to say, "It says that they *began* to be merry, and it doesn't say they ever stopped." They just kept right on. This boy found that the place where he could really have a good time was in his father's house.

My friend, if you really want to have a ball, you can't do it in the far country. If you're God's child, you can't sin and find happiness. You may even go to the pigpen, but, my friend, you can never enjoy it. If you're a child of the Father, there will come a day when you are going to say, "I will arise and go to my Father," and you will go. And when you go, you will confess to Him.

If we confess our sins, He is faithful and just to forgive us our sins, and to cleanse us from all unrighteousness (1 John 1:9).

That's the way a sinning child gets back into the fellowship of the Father's house. In fact, the only way back is by confession.

Have you ever noted the things the father says he's going to do for his son? He says, "Get a robe." Now a robe was clean clothing that went over him after he'd been washed. "If we confess our sins, He is faithful and just to forgive us our sins, and to cleanse us from all unrighteousness." Our Lord washes us. The One who girded Himself with a towel is the One who will wash one of His sons who comes back to Him. We have to be cleansed when we have been to the far country. And that robe is the robe of the righteousness of Christ that covers the believer after he is cleansed.

The ring is the insignia of the full-grown son, with all rights pertaining thereto. He is brought back into his original position. Nothing is taken from him. He is restored to his place in His Father's house. The older brother—if you'll follow the parable on through— complained about that very thing. He felt his brother ought not to be brought back, but the Father brought him right back where he belonged.

And then he says, "We're going to kill the fatted calf." There has to be a sacrifice. All of this is made possible because Jesus Christ about two thousand years ago died to save us from sin. And, my friend, today He lives to keep us saved.

Right now, Christ is at God's right hand, still girded with the towel of service for one of His own who gets soiled feet or soiled hands by being in the far country.

However, let me repeat, don't think you can rush back into the Father's house and have fellowship with Him without first getting clean. There are a lot of Christians who think they can do this, but they are doing nothing in the world but presuming. They have this grand assumption, and they're saying things that are not true. They're not having fellowship with God until they confess their sins. When we confess to Him, He is faithful and just to forgive us our sins and to cleanse us from all unrighteousness. We have to come as the prodigal son came. "Father, I have sinned, and I'm no longer worthy to be called your son. Make me a hired servant." And the Father will say, "I'd never make you a hired servant. You're my son. I'll cleanse you, I'll forgive you, I'll bring you back into the place of fellowship and usefulness."

A son is a son forever.

18
DEATH OF A LITTLE CHILD

At the death of my firstborn, God gave me some words of comfort which I desire to pass on to parents and to loved ones of little ones who die. There is no sorrow quite so heart-rending as the death of a little child. The image of the little one is written so indelibly upon the mind and heart that during the long watches of the night it appears on memory's screen to haunt us.

If the child lives long enough to walk and to talk, the faltering steps and childish prattle are like a lingering fragrance in the home that seems so strangely silent. The arms are empty, the eyes are filled with tears, and the heart is like a vacant house. Yet there is no affliction for which God has provided such tender comfort and such sweet solace. He is *"the God of all comfort"* (2 Corinthians 1:3).

The following comforts are mentioned with the prayer that the Comforter, the Holy Spirit, will apply them to broken hearts and to wounded spirits as strong splints and sweet ointment.

A BRIEF LIFE IS NOT AN INCOMPLETE LIFE

We sometimes feel that a life which was so brief was in vain, and that God has mocked us by giving us the little one and then by taking it away immediately. The child had no opportunity to perform a work, nor was there any time given to develop character. Let us remember, first of all, that the little one had an eternal spirit, and that

231

it has gone into the presence of God where there will be an eternity to perform works and develop character.

With eternity as a measuring rod, the long life of Methuselah was merely a pinpoint on the calendar of time. Although the span of life of your little one was brief, it completed a mission, served a purpose, and performed a God-appointed task in this world. Its presence turned your thoughts to the best, its helplessness brought out your strength and protection, and its loveliness roused your tenderness and love. Its influence will linger in your heart as long as you live. If anything can bring a man to God, it is a child. "A little child shall lead them" is not idle rhetoric. We think of Methuselah in connection with old age, but did you ever consider him as an infant? Well, he was once a baby, and a most arresting thing is recorded about his birth. He was the son of Enoch, and it is written:

And Enoch lived sixty and five years, and begat Methuselah: and Enoch walked with God after he begat Methuselah three hundred years, and begat sons and daughters: and all the days of Enoch were three hundred sixty and five years: and Enoch walked with God: and he was not; for God took him (Genesis 5:21–24).

We do not know what the life of Enoch was for the first sixty-five years, but when the day came that he looked down into a crib at a little boy named Methuselah, he began to walk with God. If Methuselah had died in his crib, he would have accomplished about as much as evidently he did in his long life.

Your little one served its purpose. A brief life is not an incomplete life.

YOU CAN BE ASSURED THAT ALL IS WELL WITH THE CHILD

David lost two sons for whom he grieved deeply. One was Bathsheba's child, who died shortly after birth. David was greatly exercised about the life of this child. The record reveals the magnitude of his grief.

David therefore besought God for the child; and David fasted, and went in, and lay all night upon the earth. And the elders of his house arose, and went to him, to raise him up from the earth: but he would not, neither did he eat bread with them. And it came to pass on the seventh day, that the child died. And the servants of David feared to tell him that the child was dead: for they said, Behold, while the child was yet alive, we spake unto him, and he would not hearken unto our voice: how will he then vex himself, if we tell him that the child is dead? But when David saw that his servants whispered, David perceived that the child was dead: therefore David said unto his servants, Is the child dead? And they said, He is dead. Then David arose from the earth, and washed, and anointed himself, and changed his apparel, and came into the house of the LORD, and worshipped: then he came to his own house; and when he required, they set bread before him, and he did eat. Then said his servants unto him, What thing is this that thou hast done? thou didst fast and weep for the child, while it was alive; but when the child was dead, thou didst rise and eat bread. And he said, While the child was yet alive, I fasted and wept: for I said, Who can tell whether God will be gracious to me, that the child may live? But now he is dead, wherefore should I fast? can I bring him back again? I shall go to him, but he shall not return to me (2 Samuel 12:16–23).

David knew that the child was with the redeemed, and that he would join him some day by death and would be with him forever.

David had another son, Absalom, who in manhood became rebellious and sinned grievously. While ruthlessly attempting to seize the kingdom from his father, he was killed in battle. Upon learning of his death, King David, a strong, rugged old soldier, wept as a woman. The Bible records his appalling grief.

And the king was much moved, and went up to the chamber over the gate, and wept: and as he went, thus he said, O my son Absalom, my son, my son Absalom! Would God I had died for thee, O Absalom, my son, my son! (2 Samuel 18:33).

David did not know the destiny of the soul of Absalom, or at least he doubted his salvation. David wished it had been possible to have died in his stead so that Absalom might have another chance. David could be sure of the first child, but he was not sure of Absalom.

You, likewise, may have the assurance of the salvation of your child; it is "safe in the arms of Jesus." You would be willing to turn over your child to the care of a faithful nurse in this life, and you can rejoice that your little one is in the arms of the Good Shepherd who is more tender than any human nurse. In fact the little one is better off than if it were asleep in its crib in your home. It is beyond this veil of tears. There is no danger or evil to beset its pathway. We may rest in the confidence that our children are safe with Christ. Remember that when He was here on earth, He took up little ones into His arms, saying, *"Suffer little children to come unto me, and forbid them not: for of such is the kingdom of God"* (Luke 18:16). On another occasion He said, *"Take heed that ye despise not one of these little ones; for I say unto you, That in heaven their angels do always behold the face of my Father which is in heaven"* (Matthew 18:10).

If you could but know the blessedness of your little one at this very moment, it would reconcile you to the loss of the darling of your heart.

HEAVEN SHOULD BE MORE REAL TO YOU

The Lord Jesus has gone to prepare a place for those who are His own. Part of this preparation is the taking of your child. Heaven will mean more to you now—your dearest treasure is there. And where your treasure is there will your heart be also. He takes from the family here to form the family there. Baby hands are beckoning to you, and a baby voice is calling you home.

I did not realize how many parents there were who had lost children until our first baby was taken. One after another in the congregation came with tears in their eyes to tell of their secret sorrow. One dear lady and her husband always sat down in the front pew. They were elderly and they had a son who was a great sorrow. In spite of this, they were always smiling and seemed never to be defeated by life. I shall never forget my surprise when I discovered the reason for this as they told me of the loss of their firstborn and of their happy anticipation of seeing the little one in heaven some day.

THERE ARE NO MISTAKES IN GOD'S PLANS

God has permitted this to happen to you. It was no accident, nor was it something over which He had no control. He knows the way you take; your times are in His hands, and He numbers the hairs of your head. Somehow and some way God will make this work out for His glory and your good. *"All things work together for good to them that love God, to them who are the called according to his purpose"* (Romans 8:28). Perhaps you do not see this now, and I am sure that I cannot explain it in detail, but here is where you can trust God. He permits us to suffer here, and in this world of sin it is part of His discipline for a higher place. *"For whom the Lord loveth he chasteneth, and scourgeth every son whom he receiveth. If ye endure chastening, God dealeth with you as with sons; for what son is he whom the father chasteneth not?"* (Hebrews 12:6, 7).

YOU DID THE BEST YOU COULD UNDER THE CIRCUMSTANCES

Perhaps you are rebuking yourself for not having done something more in behalf of the child. You may be harassed by a haunting fear that you did something wrong. Martha and Mary felt that the death of their brother could have been averted. They both said to Him, *"Lord, if thou hadst been here, my brother had not died"* (John 11:21, 32). Yet in the providence of God it was best for Lazarus to die, though it could have been averted—but only with divine help. Humanly speaking, you did the best you could. You are not as wise nor as strong as God. You did what you could, and you must leave the results to Him. Do not reproach yourself for negligence or ignorance. Regardless of what you had done, you are still a fallible and feeble creature. You did the best you could.

SUPPOSE YOUR CHILD HAD LIVED

Multitudes of children today growing up to maturation are entering upon a life of crime or shame. Think of the children who bring disgrace and suffering to their parents. A father in Atlanta, Georgia, a man of wealth who was known for his gentleness and graciousness, said to me that he wished he had buried his son the day that he sent him away to college. Think of the sad parents who have nothing but bitter memories of a debauched and godless son or daughter. Think of the anxiety of parents as their children are swept along in today's changing world. Think of the millions of starving children in Europe and Asia, of the multitudes of boys and girls being brainwashed behind the Iron Curtain. Think of the pinched faces and swollen tummies of children who are the victims of war. You will never know a haunting dread for the future of your child, nor will there ever be a sting in your memory.

God knew what was in the future for your child. Perhaps there would have been a life of illness, a disfiguring accident, or brain damage, or a lingering, incurable disease. God knew all of this, and I am confident that He has given you the better part. You can be certain about your child's future now; you could not be certain if he were alive.

YOU WILL SEE YOUR LITTLE ONE SOMEDAY

If you have faith in a living Savior who was victorious over death and the grave, then you will someday see your little one. We are told through Paul, *"I would not have you to be ignorant, brethren, concerning them which are asleep, that ye sorrow not, even as others which have no hope"* (1 Thessalonians 4:13). Notice that he did not say we are not to sorrow, he said that we are not to sorrow as those who have no hope. Death is yet to be defeated. Some day the dead in Christ are to be raised from the grave.

For the Lord himself shall descend from heaven with a shout, with the voice of the archangel, and with the trump of God: and the dead in Christ shall rise first: then we which are alive and remain shall be caught up together with them in the clouds, to meet the Lord in the air: and so shall we ever be with the Lord (1 Thessalonians 4:16, 17).

236

The little form of your child will be raised from the grave and the spirit joined to the glorified body. If you are in Christ, you at that time will be reunited, and together you will be at home with Christ forever.

Will our children be as we last saw them? I do not know nor can I prove it from Scripture (for Scripture is silent at this point), but I believe with all my heart that God will raise the little ones as such, and that the mother's arms that have ached for them will have the opportunity of holding them. The father's hand that never held the little hand will be given that privilege. I believe that the little ones will grow up in heaven in the care of their earthly parents—if they are saved. One of the worst things of which I, as a father, can conceive, is of parents being in hell knowing that they cannot have their child—there are no children in hell. What an added joy this lends to heaven in looking forward to having your little one again! Though the Scriptures do not teach this explicitly, this does seem to be the sense. Remember that David expected to go to his *child*. And referring to children Christ said, "Of such is the kingdom of heaven."

YOU CAN PROVE THE REALITY OF GOD'S COMFORT

His comfort is real; His presence is vital; His words are life. He can become a mighty reality to you now. He wants to enter into your sorrow and sympathize with you. When Jesus went to a funeral, these amazing words are recorded, *"Jesus wept"* (John 11:35). Because He had our humanity and was touched with the feeling of our infirmity, when He went to the cemetery, He wept—in spite of the fact that He intended to restore life.

> *In every pang that rends the human heart*
> *The Man of Sorrows had a part."*

There is a story of sweetness and beauty which enlightens the heart of every parent who has lost a child. It concerns a custom among the shepherd folk of the Alps. In the summertime when the grass in the lower valleys withers and dries up, the shepherds seek to lead their sheep up a winding, thorny, and stony pathway to the high grazing lands. The sheep, reluctant to take the difficult pathway infested with dangers and hardships, turn back and will not follow. The shepherds make repeated attempts, but the timid sheep will not follow. Finally a shepherd reaches into the flock and takes a little lamb and places it under his arm, then reaches in again and takes another lamb, placing it under the other arm. Then he starts up the precipitous pathway. Soon the mother sheep start to follow and afterward the entire flock. At last they ascend the tortuous trail to green pastures.

The Great Shepherd of the sheep, the Lord Jesus Christ, our Savior, has reached into the flock, and He has picked up your lamb. He did not do it to rob you, but to lead you out and upward. He has richer and greener pastures for you, and He wants you to follow.

Will you follow Him?

You will, if you catch a glimpse—

> *Of the good Shepherd on the height*
> *Or climbing up the starry way,*
> *Holding your little lamb asleep,*
> *While like the murmur of the sea*
> *Soundeth that voice along the deep,*
> *Saying, "Arise, and follow Me."*

There is a new lamb cradled on Thy breast tonight,
A sweet small lamb, so lately mine
I scarce can keep my arms from reaching out
As though to snatch her back from Thine.

These arms of mine are wonted so to her, dear Lord,
They curved about her little form
So sweetly, and from dawn of time my breast was
meant
To be her pillow, soft and warm.

What does one do with aching arms and empty hours,
With silent rooms, and dragging days?
The things I knew before will not avail me now—
Teach me new lessons and new ways.

Take Thou, I pray, these idle folded hands of mine
Which can no longer busied be
With dear, familiar tasks for her . . . . In mercy, Lord,
Fill hands and heart with tasks for Thee!

MARTHA SNELL NICHOLSON